Southern Women

Also by the Editors of
Garden & Gun

....

The Southerner's Handbook

....

Good Dog

....

The Southerner's Cookbook

....

S Is for Southern

Southern Women

More than 100 Stories of
Innovators, Artists, and Icons

AMANDA HECKERT

and the editors of
GARDEN&GUN

Foreword by **ALLISON GLOCK**

HARPER WAVE
An Imprint of HarperCollins*Publishers*

HarperCollins books may be purchased for educational, business, or sales promotional use. For information, please email the Special Markets Department at SPsales@harpercollins.com.

Interviews have been condensed and lightly edited for clarity.

FIRST EDITION

Designed by Leah Carlson-Stanisic
Photo direction by Maggie Brett Kennedy

Library of Congress Cataloging-in-Publication Data has been applied for.

ISBN 978-0-06-285936-5

19 20 21 22 23 LSC 10 9 8 7 6 5 4 3 2

CONTENTS

Grit & Grace

W hen we named *Garden & Gun* back in 2007, we wanted to evoke a love of the land, a sensibility that adds depth to the stories we tell about the South and the way we live here. But when I think about those two words, I also can't help but recall my grandmothers.

I wrote once, in an early issue, about how those two women represented the essence of not only the garden and the gun, but also grit and grace. My maternal grandmother—we called her Mama—lived on a tobacco farm in North Carolina, where she raised my mother and five other children. Summer days spent with Mama were magical—gathering eggs, riding tractors, eating fresh-picked watermelon on the front porch. My paternal grandmother lived in the little town of Warrenton, North Carolina, and her social graces were impeccable. Our visits were announced in the local paper, and while she and my grandfather were not well-off, she set a beautiful table—sparkling goblets, lovely linens, and plates full of perfect biscuits and bacon.

Like many Southern women, Grandmother and Mama, different though they may have seemed, each possessed both grit and grace, and I like to think I inherited those traits from them. Growing up in Columbia, South Carolina, I did nothing by half measures. Instead of giving an ordinary book report on *Pippi Longstocking,* I dressed up as the fun, irrepressible redhead and bounded into the classroom in character to tell my tale. I

graduated at the top of my class in high school. And I fully attribute this drive to do just a little bit *more* than everyone else, and to try to do it *better,* to my mother and father. He was a college professor, and she was a former English teacher, and they encouraged me at every turn to spread my wings—to do anything I set my mind to.

In retrospect, that work ethic—that grit—and the grace I learned as a woman growing up in the South were both key to my success in the magazine world. I moved to New York after college and quickly made my mark selling retail advertising for *GQ* magazine—creating a new, nationwide business of in-store promotions for guys, a first in the men's magazine world. When I was named the first female publisher of the *New Yorker,* the announcement made a splash, but I was focused on the gargantuan task of turning around what was at the time a money-losing magazine.

Invariably, I would be asked throughout those years in New York, "Isn't it difficult to be a Southern woman in business in the Big Apple?" I always balked at the question—it wasn't until I returned to the South in 2004, following stints at *Mirabella* and *Fortune,* that it occurred to me that perhaps I *did* approach business differently because of my Southern roots. When I first went over to the *New Yorker* as associate publisher, an interviewer asked me why the publisher wanted me, and I answered, "I think he knows I'll bust my ass." But looking back, that willingness to work hard was also aided by a little bit of Southern savvy—that ability to know how to sweeten your asks, to get people to see your side, to be fair and gracious to those you meet and manage.

It certainly took that same pluck to get *Garden & Gun* off the ground. When we first proposed the idea of a national magazine and brand about the South, no doubt we were looked at askance, and we experienced our bumps in the road along the way. But we knew that by celebrating the best of the Southern lifestyle, with spirit and soul, and by sharing captivating stories, we could appeal to an audience that was underserved—one that craved compelling writing about the land they loved.

One of the great privileges of this job has been meeting and spending time with our readers over the years—many who remind me of the fearless, funny, smart, driven, dynamic women from across the region whom you'll meet in the following pages. Musicians, writers, chefs, actors, designers, entrepreneurs, artists, public servants, and more—from the MacArthur "genius" singer-songwriter-instrumentalist Rhiannon Giddens, to the Oscar-winning legend Sissy Spacek, to the late Queen of Creole Cuisine Leah Chase, to Pulitzer-winning poet Natasha Trethewey, to the Wall Street powerhouse (and another South Carolinian who turned New York on its head) Darla Moore.

Through interviews, odes, essays, and more, these world changers paint a portrait of the Southern woman today. Strong, richly diverse barrier breakers who have thrived because of—and in some cases, despite—the South. Women whose stories for too long have been overlooked or underestimated.

My teenage daughters, Lily and SaSa, are my highest accomplishments. My hope is that I've been able to pass down the grit and grace that run through my family and so many others in the South. And that they see themselves reflected in these portraits of risk-taking, big-dreaming Southern women. I think they will.

Rebecca Wesson Darwin
Cofounder & CEO, *Garden & Gun*
Charleston, South Carolina

Soul of the South

I n 2011, I wrote an essay for *Garden & Gun* on why Southern women are inherently different. That essay generated more response than anything I've published before or since in a nearly thirty-year writing career. Most of the feedback was positive. Some was less so. But the passion behind both the writing and the reading of that initial exploration into Southern womanhood could not be denied, and led the editors of *Garden & Gun* and me to start discussing the possibility of a book. We Southern women may not agree on all things, but we certainly have *opinions*, and that very willingness to hold and share our convictions is a kind of cultural glue.

It is an admittedly tricky thing to summarize a subset of people, to generalize, to group. Inevitably there will be those who argue, rightly, that they don't fit into the mold. And yet, over my years of interviewing dozens upon dozens of Southern women (never mind being raised by many), I've found those women to be the first to assert their own social distinctiveness, often with pride, always with ownership.

Southern women identify as Southern women, and whether that means drinking sweet tea or lassoing bucks or walking barefoot in sun-dappled hollers or graduating summa cum laude from Spelman or galloping Thoroughbreds across a carpet of bluegrass or dancing at cotillion or sweating over a Lowcountry boil or singing soul-swelling gospel in church, the imprint of *Southernness* remains. Despite the reflexive stereotyping that happens around all things Southern (and all things female), Holly Hunter is not Sandra Bullock, who is not Jesmyn Ward, who is not Octavia Spencer, who is not Nina Simone, who is not Beyoncé, who is not Dolly Parton (just as Shelby is not M'Lynn, who's not Truvy nor Ouiser nor Annelle nor Clairee). But Southern is as Southern does, and when it comes down to it, the granular particulars fade in the beam of our uncommon commonalities.

Southern women recognize themselves in each other. We suss it out and we smile at the detection. We draw together like magnets, especially when we're no longer in the South and finding a kindred spirit feels like nothing so much as quenching a thirst. It is a relief to feel at home in the company of another. To not have to explain your peculiarities. To jettison shame. To laugh as loud as you please.

Southern women, regardless of where we hail from in the region, share a consciousness of certain truths, a lean toward humor and humility and hard work, a tether (whether we like it or not) to the landscape, an impulse to give, a yearning for glory. We take the ingredients we're handed and make delicious gumbo. We leave nothing out. We prefer it that way. We also carry in our cells a brutal, burdensome history, an awareness of wrongs that can never be made right. We plant flowers anyway.

The first Southern woman who shaped me was my grandmother. She spent most of her years in a no-stoplight West Virginia factory town where she knew everyone and everyone she knew worked long shifts in dank, dusty halls making fancy dishware for restaurants in cities they'd never visit. This did not stop her from curling her hair and painting her face every day. A habit less about vanity than self-respect, a refusal to let anyone look down his or her nose at her simply because she lived along the tar-stripped roads of Appalachia. She taught her three daughters the same. To stand up straight, to carry themselves with dignity and class, to have manners. To be unimpeachable in the larger world, should they have the good fortune to find themselves amid it one day.

My aunt Jill was a tomboy, the type of Southern girl who raised tadpoles and spent as many hours as possible among animals of all sorts. Her sister Jody was a firecracker. Mouthy and funny with no appetite for bullshit unless it was her own. My mother was the eldest, a local beauty queen who worked her way through college at West Virginia University even though her father assured her she could "meet a husband" at home. Instead, she met her spouse, my birth father, the first day of freshman year. He asked her out for an ice cream sundae. ("If he'd asked me to go for a drink, I'd have said no.")

They married, she got pregnant, he left. Still, she stayed in school, raising an infant with the help of neighbors who took pity on the pretty young coed and her baby girl, leaving boxes of canned goods and homemade pound cake at the rental apartment doorstep.

My mother was a different sort of Southern woman than her mother and her sisters, but they shared a collective spine, a familiar hunger. West Virginia was in their bloodstream, and all had hillbilly pride, even as they knew the folly of such. I inherited said pride, the chippiness of a child reared in an overlooked class on donated beans and cake, and I carry it with me now, that same spine, the same hunger that my female ancestors had.

So it is for all Southern women, this inescapable infusion of the past, the ghosts of what came before us as distracting and fated as a moth batting a porch light with its wings. Southern girls come of age in a land riven with contradiction and cruelty. The South is not simple or unsullied, and we see no reason to believe otherwise. Say what you will about the saccharine ethos of the Southern belle: On matters that matter, Southern women do not pretend. We see it all, in all of it. Ugliness knotted with beauty, glorious blankets of kudzu that strangle the trees, frogs that serenade like jazz ensembles, longhorn skulls bleached to ivory in the Texas sun. We understand life is gravy. That there is no true separation between one thing and another, that mercy can be found in the foulest well, wisdom in pockets of madness. As such, we crave vinegar as much as we crave sugar. We welcome excess and flavor and drama and music and being moved by the spirit. We know life is one giant drag show, and we dress accordingly.

Over my lifetime, I've met so many Southern women who have taught me how to behave, how to misbehave, how to love, how to leave, how to be a mother, how to be a child. My sisters, warm but tough Southern mamas, who will spit needles as easily as they set a welcoming table if you cross them or their kith and kin. Miss Elaine, a surrogate mother of absolute grace and graciousness, who inspires me to stand taller, to be better than I believe I am. Friend and poet Nikky Finney, who brings me to tears nearly every time we speak, so brimming is she with fire and hope, her talent a rebuke to the world's brutality. My cherished girlfriends: Melissa, who left Texas but carries its bigheartedness with her everywhere; Misty, whose fizzy eccentricities make me feel drunk with happiness; and Peggy, who can do everything from bake a perfect chocolate cake to play fiddle to paint portraits of her daddy, a gal for whom nothing seems too challenging—a quality I've found more often than not among Southern women, who can always be counted on to get the job (any job) done.

I recently visited Tennessee to call on Peggy and my other female confidants there. We all made supper together, swirling around the small kitchen as if dancing, touching each other's shoulders and hips as we inched past, pots aloft. We talked about news and children and okra and cancer and how fat we were all getting and how little, in the end, we really cared.

After hours at the table, bellies full of garden tomatoes and bourbon, we headed to the piano in the foyer, where we began to sing. Leah played guitar, Peggy the accordion. Biz thumped her chest like a drum, while Lois swayed with my ailing dog, Milton, cuddling him like an infant. Julie picked the first few songs—long-forgotten old-timey murder ballads. We all joined in on the choruses, our voices swelling and warbling the pitch-black lyrics that somehow made us feel full of brio. My daughters snuggled together on a nearby couch, smiling at that darkness, seeing in real time how a group of women can turn tragedy into harmony, can leaven the sorrow of life by bathing it in light.

This is what Southern women do.

We come together to make the best of the world as it is, while nudging the world to be better than it has been, and we do it hand in hand, arms linked, voices rising.

To be a Southern woman is to be forever safe-guarded in a sisterhood that reaches hundreds of miles. One that will be there in the gloaming. And the dawn.

Singing.

—Allison Glock

I Cannot Talk about the South without Talking about Black Women

A GOLDEN SHOVEL AFTER LUCILLE CLIFTON*

BY ASHLEY M. JONES, FOR *SOUTHERN WOMEN*

My grandmothers made America,
                                made
                the fibers that made us
warm, made us invincible—heroines.

To tell you who they are, I must start with who they are not:
                servants, kitchen-bound mammies, silently obedient wives—
                                                                we
                                can't, in our modern comforts, imagine the survival they learned
                                was theirs to claim, can't hold the
                the light they burned through this colonial darkness, what tricks
                this nation, this American South pulled, minute by minute, to
                                                                keep
                                                my grandmothers convinced: the
                                body you're in is not enough, your race
                                and your gender work together
                                to mark you *less*, to mark you *takeable*, but
                                what they didn't know was that my grandmothers still had
                                an unmovable strength, enough to
                                build a bridge from here to Heaven. I know when I leave
                                this broken earth I'll find them there, sweetening every hour.

My grandmothers raised a generation of American men.
                There is no other way to
                                say this. Look at any Southern family and you'll find,
somewhere, in a past most will not claim, a Black woman. These men who call themselves
bootstrapping and self-made, somewhere there's a Black woman and
her unthanked hands who lifted them to where they are now.

My father tells a story of the sons of his grandmother's employers. How they,
instead of the pension she was promised, decided to give her a damned
old tire. An old suitcase, dusty in the yard. What
thanks is this for the years she raised that family, for the care they

---

*A golden shovel is a poetic form in which the last word of every line forms a line or lines from a poem by someone else; in this case, "Black Women," by Lucille Clifton.

                                                    cannot
                                forget? My father could never forgive
                those men, their Southern tradition. Their American tradition. Even
                now, they tell us Black women are going to save this whole
nation with votes or magic or our style taken and renamed. But this is no longer the land of massas
and mammies, and we are only superheroines for our own daughters and sons—
                my grandmothers did not give their lives
                for me to keep nursing this country, to keep shucking and jiving in
                                                                a
                                        bizarro American Dream—
                my grandmothers are worth more than this corrupt remembering.
Now, there is no room for the
                                Dixieland lie:
                                        we
                                        no longer hold these truths you made
                                        us accept. Under God, yes. We hear Him
                                        singing a song of powerful love
                                        despite the United Hate of America.

                Grandmothers, women made
                of salt and spirit, you are faith, continuous. Continue us—
                raise us to be heroes and heroines,
                to tell this country that we are not
                mules, not beasts. You, an army of workers and wives—
                                                        we
                                                        hid
                                                        our
                        fears and woes in your indestructible, ever-present ladyness—
                the blood you passed down to us is all we will ever need to
                                                        save
                                                        our
                                                        lives.

Ashley M. Jones is the award-winning author of two books of poetry, Magic City Gospel *and* dark // thing. *She lives in Birmingham, Alabama.*

PARAMOUNT
PARAMOUNT
PARAMOUNT
CHAMBER PLAYERS
BRISTOL BALLET'S MAY 12
ALICE IN WONDERLAND
PARAMOUNTBRISTOL.ORG

PERFORMERS
& PLAYERS

DANIELLE BROOKS

Nominated for a 2016 Tony for her breathtaking turn on Broadway as Sofia in *The Color Purple*, the actor Danielle Brooks says she is eager to play every role on offer—the rom-com lead, the action hero, the comic-book villain, the femme fatale. "I know I'm capable of doing all of that," she explains. "It's just a matter of people being open to seeing things differently." Brooks, who grew up in Greenville, South Carolina, helped alter just those types of perceptions as Litchfield inmate Tasha "Taystee" Jefferson in Netflix's Emmy Award–winning *Orange Is the New Black*—a series, she emphasizes, that owed its popularity to presenting women of all types and predilections.

What did you take away from being raised a Southern woman?

Oh, my manners. When I first came to New York at seventeen, I'll never forget being in class at Juilliard and calling one of the teachers "Miss Becky." And she was like, "If you don't stop calling us that!" I hold on to my Southern accent. I even have a few tattoos. A yellow jasmine on my body, which is the flower of South Carolina. And I have the number of my childhood address on my arm, a reminder of my family and the love that we have for each other. I just never want to forget where I grew up. When someone gets to really know me, they know I'm a Southerner.

You grew up singing in the church. When did you first realize you had a powerful voice?

I've been singing since I was young, but I've always been a hard critic [of myself]. I can hold a note, but I thought my voice was average. I didn't realize that people really enjoyed my singing until I got hired in my first musical. Growing up in the South, I know what it is when a person can *sang* with an *a*. You know? But I discovered my voice could actually take me places.

In what way?

In the church, I didn't get that many solos. My father sent me some tapes of me singing then, and when I look at those, I was super shy. I was holding back. The thing is, other people can feel like you have a voice, but until *you* believe it, it doesn't really matter. And I'm just now really believing it.

And did that make you feel powerful in other ways?

Finding your voice is crucial, because when you find yours, you really do help others find theirs. I didn't understand what level I was able to take it to until I was in *Orange Is the New Black*. That's when I was like, *Oh wow, this can go further than I ever imagined. I really can change things beyond my work.* For example, I became a spokesperson for the 67% Project, which is highlighting the fact that 67 percent of women in America are plus size and only 1 to 2 percent of them are represented in media. Women who are plus size—we do matter and we deserve to be seen.

And now you've been seen—on television, on Broadway, in fashion magazines. Do people still try to put you in a box?

Mhmm. But I think everybody gets put in a box, to be honest. I think white girls with blond hair are put into boxes. Their box might be a little wider.

It must feel good to shatter those expectations.

Women want to see themselves in every way. I want to challenge people to not limit their imaginations. Not to limit a *person*. And by extension, not to limit the world that we live in.

SISSY SPACEK

The beloved actor and Quitman, Texas, native Sissy Spacek won the Academy Award for portraying Loretta Lynn— who hand selected her for the role—in 1980's Coal Miner's Daughter. *When not starring in television series and films, she's at the Virginia farm where she and her husband, Jack Fisk, raised their two daughters, Schuyler and Madison.*

In the beginning, when I first arrived in New York City, agents and managers would say, "Oh, honey, with that accent get back on the plane to Texas!" But then, my Southernness gave me my biggest opportunities. [*Badlands* director] Terry Malick said I was just what he was looking for, and that was the best experience of my life.

When I lived in New York City, I loved it so much. But every six months I had to go home to Texas to remember who I was. Get filled back up. I have a little coffee cup that my daughter gave me that says, "What would you try to accomplish if you knew you could not fail?" My roots allow me to let go of the fear of failure.

I wanted to give my children roots. Have them grow up with animals and dirt between their toes. In 1978 my husband and I got the farm as a place to get away for a month or so. Then in 1981, I got pregnant with Schuyler, and the stays got longer. I love cities. I do. But nature is my refuge. A bug hitting a screen on a summer night is music to me. The wind in the trees, the creek running full after a storm. All of those sounds are a choir that fills me up and calms me. It took me a long time to realize that.

We are, as my mother said, a product of our choices. The world would be better if we taught our children those types of things. Not how to wipe your mouth with a napkin so much as how to become someone worthwhile.

When I took my girls to college, I was thinking I forgot to tell them this and that, but things we say to them stick. We all face adversity, but it is not so much what happens to you in life, but how you respond to what happens. Staying king of the mountain isn't important. It's all that stuff our mothers taught us.

TIG NOTARO

Having survived both a near-fatal intestinal infection and breast cancer in 2012, the same year her mother passed away from an accident, the Mississippi native Tig Notaro has grown adept at handling the unforeseen. Her comedy set about those tragedies became the stuff of legend and touched people in ways that stand-up rarely does. It was a gutsy move, one Notaro—who cocreated and starred in *One Mississippi*, a TV series based on her childhood home—says she owes to her Southern spitfire mother, Mathilde.

Your mom was unconventional.

Oh yeah, very much. She empowered me to be myself, to say to hell with folks who didn't get me. My mother was taught to be a pleaser, but she really rebelled against it and encouraged me to do so as well. I don't think I realized when I was young that it was unusual for a mother to be advising her kid to tell everyone to go to hell. My mother was very flawed, but the strength and confidence that she instilled in me are solidly there. I know I got that from her.

Was that confidence and autonomy the best gift she gave you?

That and my sense of humor. She was a wilder, louder version of me. But somehow still the same. We have similar sensibilities. My mother pranked everybody all the time. She loved to see a prank unfold, and I'm the same way. She used to send water shots to people at bars and restaurants. And you'd see people nod and thank her across the room, and then you'd watch them toss back a shot of water.

You quit school in the ninth grade. How did your mother react to that?

My mother wanted me to go to school, but when I quit, she accepted it pretty quickly, and then began bragging to people that I dropped out. "Yeah, Tig's off doing her own thing. She's doing great!" And people are like, "*She dropped out of high school!*" My mother just told them I was happy, to leave me alone.

You're a mother of twin boys, Finn and Max.

When I was a kid, I'd hear bad news, something happening in the world, and it would upset me and I'd want to tell my mother. And she would say, "Sweetie, please, I can't. I can't hear that." It really pained her. I've always been very compassionate and empathized with people, but it's a whole different depth of pain and cutting I feel as a mother when I know people are suffering. I see Max and Finn in everyone.

What do you and your wife, Stephanie Allynne, most want to impart to your children?

Having my health issues and losing my mother and experiencing fear of the end—they teach you what's important. And it's to spend time together, to be a family. Before the boys, life felt all over the place. I can't believe how responsible and focused and excited for my future I am in a way I've never been before. I can't believe this dropout failure could find so much joy and success.

You were raised in Pass Christian, Mississippi, and Spring, Texas. What defines the South for you?

The people. It took me a long time to realize these people were genuine, true characters. I'd bring home friends and their jaws would drop. *Oh my gosh, your aunt, your uncle.* And I was like, *What*? I didn't realize there was anything different about them. I couldn't see it. Once I went out into the wider world, I was like, *Yeah, I guess they are kind of interesting people.*

Do you see that eccentricity in yourself?

The way that I go about things, the essence of who I am, is Southern. When people go home with me, they're like, *Oh, right, this is why your pace, your sensibility, your delivery, is the way it is.*

In Her Own Words
CONNIE BRITTON

From 2006 to 2011 on Friday Night Lights, *the actor Connie Britton portrayed one of the most admired Southern women in television history: the by turns tough-as-nails and tender Tami Taylor, whose husband coaches a Texas high school football team.*

"My dad's family was from Tennessee. I grew up in Lynchburg, Virginia, where we lived at the base of the Blue Ridge Mountains. As a kid I was totally into Southern rock. Lynyrd Skynyrd. ZZ Top. It was so part of who I was.

I went to New York out of drama school, and I lived in California. But when the character of Tami Taylor in *Friday Night Lights* came along, it jogged something in me, like, I *know* this woman. It clicked. She felt very familiar.

Growing up in the South, there is that character of Southern women that I find to be so specific and unique. In many ways, the South can be very traditional and confining. And what is interesting to me is how women find their way around it. Those obstacles create an amazing sense of humor, of fun, and ultimately, of integrity. The fiercest and savviest women I have ever known are the women I grew up with. I love that and have carried those lessons throughout my life."

DIXIE CARTER & DELTA BURKE

Life lessons from Designing Women

BY HELEN ELLIS

When I was growing up in the eighties in Alabama, Mama would ban TV shows for two reasons: premarital sex or "It's just a bunch of people standing around insulting each other." *The Love Boat* and *The Jeffersons* fell under these categories. But *Designing Women* was in a class by itself. Its strong female leads were well mannered, kempt, and smart. And they promoted the values Mama thought her daughter should know.

Dixie Carter, a Tri Delt at what is now the University of Memphis, played Julia Sugarbaker, the president and owner of an Atlanta interior design firm—the kind of woman who'll stand, smooth the skirt of her candy-colored power suit, and then take off a gigantic clip-on earring to call a *New York Times* writer to correct his assertion that Southerners *eat dirt*. Delta Burke, Miss Florida 1974, played Suzanne, Julia's sister and *seemingly* superficial silent partner. Suzanne was thrice divorced and looking to marry for more money. She had a pet pig and a glass case full of beauty pageant crowns. She was a former Miss Georgia World. Or as Julia, her big sister, would say, "*The* Miss Georgia!"

I didn't know it at the time, but the Sugarbaker sisters were schooling me in feminism. For one, they taught me that women should support each other. In the episode in which the latest Miss Georgia World makes fun of Suzanne behind her back, it's Julia's ears that burn. Julia shuts the dressing-room door and gives the woman a dressing-down the likes of which haven't been seen on TV since. But Julia has the grace to confront her in private.

They taught me that women should be their own best advocates. When a photographer asks Julia to suck on her strand of pearls for a portrait he is taking, she suggests he find himself an oyster because she doesn't know any women who do that. She kicks him out of her house. When Suzanne wins Person Most Changed at her high school reunion because she's gotten fat, she accepts the award for her own reasons: Her *heart* has gotten bigger—and she loves trophies.

They taught me that your girlfriends can save your life, in ways big and small. When a gynecologist tells a friend to ignore a lump in her breast, you call your doctor and make an appointment for her to get a second opinion. When your friend's friend gets the nerve to leave her abusive husband, you give her money to help her get away. When another friend wants to pick up a man in a grocery store, you tell her to put pâté and flowers in her cart because men aren't going to talk to a woman who's wheeling around a twenty-five-pound sack of dog food and a big box of Kotex.

They taught me that you can create your own standard of beauty—and still be a strong woman. There were never two more gorgeous women on prime time. Julia and Suzanne had hot-rolled hair and full faces of makeup. If they were brands, they'd be Revlon's Fire & Ice and Cherries in the Snow. They showed their legs and always wore pantyhose. They went to health spas. As part of an exercise regime, Suzanne did her old pageant talent routine in a silk blouse and platform espadrilles. Bonus Sugarbaker tip: If you forget your baton, go ahead and twirl anyway.

SUTTON FOSTER

T he actor, singer, and dancer Sutton Foster's performances in more than a dozen Broadway shows, including two Tony Award–winning roles in *Thoroughly Modern Millie* and *Anything Goes*, marry earthy honesty with abundant talent. The Georgia native also displays that winsome combination as the star of the TV series *Younger,* for which she plays a forty-something woman so sunny and full of life she passes for a millennial.

How did your childhood in Georgia shape you?

I was born in a small town, Statesboro. Then we moved to Athens, then Augusta. My dad worked for General Motors, so we relocated every few years. I remember Augusta the most. I loved being outside. We had huge pine trees in our yard. My dad would plant azaleas, and we had marigolds in the summer. I would take pine cones—it's such a Southern thing—and I would make things out of them. I would play pretend, make pine-cone soup, whatever. I had a lot of energy. My mom put me in dance class really early, when I was four years old. She thought maybe dance classes would be good for me. I started getting involved with theater when I was around ten.

Then at age thirteen, you and your family moved to Detroit.

Detroit was a complete shock. Everyone thought I was from a foreign country. I had a really, really strong Southern drawl. I live in New York now, but I would say, fundamentally and morally, I'm Southern.

You've carried that value system with you.

Yeah. Like my aunt Mary Anne, whenever you stop by, she's always pulling something from the freezer that she cooked, and there are always fresh cookies. That Southern hospitality, that sense of community, that sense of family. And also, *man,* Southern food. I am such a sucker for anything that's fried or in a casserole form.

Do your Southern sensibilities translate to how you're raising your own family?

It's such a simple thing: I always say "yes, ma'am" and "no, ma'am." I was raised to give respect to people who are older or in charge. I still say it. I get made fun of, especially in New York, but I decided I want to raise my daughter to do that. It's something that I'm carrying from my Southern upbringing. It's a part of my mom too, what my mom taught me. She passed away in 2013.

Did your mom encourage you to follow your artistic ambitions?

She did. My mom grew up in a one-light town. She was born in 1947, and she had *aspirations*. She loved the movies. She was very beautiful. She thought about modeling. And her father, being a good old Southern boy, was like, *no*. So she eloped with my dad when they were nineteen years old, and had a family instead. As soon as my brother and I showed signs of liking anything unconventional, she fostered it.

What has been your most harrowing performance experience?

Oh, they're all harrowing in different ways. I would probably say *Anything Goes*. I didn't know if I could pull it off. I almost quit right before we started rehearsals. I was like, *This is going to be a disaster*. I was just so afraid of failure.

What kept you from pulling out?

It was one of those things where I felt it was a huge turning point in my life, in the way I viewed my work and my creativity. I grew the most doing that show. But it was definitely the scariest thing I've ever done.

Even with all the experience and success you'd had, you still felt that trepidation?

Honestly, I feel that way with every project, which I don't think is a bad thing. If you're constantly doing the easy thing, there's no growth. Every project I've taken on, especially in the last decade of my career, has been a new challenge, and I'm really interested in that. I want to exist where failure is a real possibility. That's where the good stuff is.

Where do you think your fortitude came from?

My mom. We had a very challenging relationship. My mom had a lot of issues—she was a very angry lady. I wanted to please her; I wanted her to be proud of me. Because my mom was so hard on me and so challenging, it made me resilient and also very ambitious. I was frustrated with her for so long. But I owe her a lot, because she made me incredibly strong.

Whom do you most want to make proud?

It's shifted. When my mom passed away, all of a sudden I was like, *Okay, why am I doing all this?* Because, for so long, I was doing it for her. I reflected on it and eventually realized my career does bring me joy, it's what I was born and meant to do. And so now, it's myself I want to make proud. I am doing it for me.

On Being Southern
BY BROOKE BALDWIN

I am a proud Southern woman living in New York City. It would be easy for me to dive right into the clichés I grew up with: demurely saying "please" and "thank you." Never being "too big for your britches" (my mother reminds me of this *to this day*). Going to an important place (e.g., the CVS around the corner) wearing a little makeup. I can still see my mom chasing me through our home in Atlanta: "Brooke, *please* put on some blush!" And, oh yeah . . . getting married in your twenties and having babies soon after.

When I was younger, I pushed back on so much of this. My family still pokes fun at me and my Southern woman "rebellion" during my sophomore year in college: my uniform of Birkenstocks, corduroy pants, and flannels. The fact that my hair didn't see a blow-dryer for a year. My crazy ear piercings. I didn't have a serious boyfriend. And there was no blush in my life.

After graduating from the University of North Carolina at Chapel Hill with degrees in journalism and Spanish, I dove straight into my first job, at the NBC-affiliated television station in Charlottesville, Virginia. This felt like the big time. I was a journalist. And suddenly, my Southern values became an advantage: I knew how to tell a good story, listen, show grace, respect my community, and, yes, even reacquaint myself with a curling iron.

Those values have never been more relevant than in my work at CNN. I have hosted two hours of live television every afternoon during a turbulent time politically. I deal with people who are upset, sometimes angry—and it is my job to listen, to be respectful, and to push back when necessary.

I also created a CNN series called *American Woman*, for which I've interviewed the likes of Ava DuVernay, Betty White, and Diane von Furstenberg—and dedicated it to my mom. When I showed her one of the first episodes, it brought her to tears. She reminded me that when she grew up, she wasn't encouraged to speak up or to speak out. And as I threw my arm around her, I had an important revelation: My mother and millions like her felt they couldn't use their voices but taught their daughters they must. I focused my next *American Woman* series on female candidates running for office in a year when an unprecedented number of women were doing so.

One of the biggest compliments someone can give me is that I am a "woman's woman." I believe part of my life's calling is to support other women, to give them a voice, and to inspire. And as far as being a Southern woman in Manhattan: As I've gotten older, I have never been prouder of my roots. I often find myself holding the door for others, complimenting random women on the street, and consciously slipping a "y'all" into conversation. I *want* people to know where I come from. In life, you test values because you're young, or you question them because you live somewhere else. Sometimes it takes leaving to fully appreciate what you miss, what makes you tick, *who you are.*

Most important, being a Southern woman is holding a contradiction within yourself: the need to be tough and soft, fierce and feminine. To be the embodiment of graceful . . . and to never, ever forget where you come from.

The Atlanta native Brooke Baldwin is a CNN anchor and journalist.

CAROL BURNETT

(1933–PRESENT)

The comedian with a Texas-sized sense of humor

Ratt: "You! You, vixen, you. Starlet, I love you. That, that, that gown is gorgeous."
Starlet: "Thank ya. I saw it in the win-dah and I just couldn't resist it."

And just like that the curtain-rod dress was born, on a Saturday night in November 1976. Earlier that week, *Gone with the Wind* had premiered on television, and the writers at *The Carol Burnett Show* were inspired to give their viewers a condensed version—"Went with the Wind!," an eighteen-minute goof on the nearly four-hour 1939 classic film. Today the green velvet Bob Mackie–designed costume that the comedian Carol Burnett wore that night as "Starlet"—her riff on Scarlett O'Hara—sits in the Smithsonian's National Museum of American History, but the woman who wore the dress (and the drapery rod) still has us laughing.

Movies had always been a source of inspiration for Burnett. It was in a San Antonio movie theater where as a girl she first fell in love with Jimmy Stewart, got into trouble with Mickey Rooney and Judy Garland, and sang along with Betty Grable. Those early films, the ones where the good guys always won, fueled both Burnett's desire to perform and her optimistic outlook. Her date to those many matinees was always her grandmother Nanny, who raised Burnett after her parents had left for California years prior.

Burnett's own Hollywood story began at age seven, when she and Nanny boarded a train in Texas and headed west. There awaited Burnett's mother and a one-room apartment with a Murphy bed, one block from Hollywood Boulevard—it wasn't glamorous, but it was glamour adjacent. Eventually, some good luck and coincidence pointed Burnett on her way. After seeing her perform at UCLA, a wealthy stranger offered her a loan of $1,000 so she could move to New York City. She arrived in August 1954, the same week Hurricane Carol battered the Northeast. True to form, Burnett chose to see it as a sign of good luck and quickly began auditioning. Soon she had her big break: She was cast in off Broadway's *Once upon a Mattress* and booked several television appearances, which eventually landed her a recurring role on *The Garry Moore Show*. By 1962, she had built enough cachet that when CBS wanted to sign her to a ten-year contract, her agent was able to include a canny clause: Within the first five years, if Burnett requested her own variety show, the network would have to give one to her.

Just as the five years were up, Burnett made the call. Network top brass discouraged her idea of a variety show—such shows were "a man's game," and a woman certainly couldn't carry one herself. But being contractually obligated, they green-lit the project. When *The Carol Burnett Show* went off the air in 1978, not only had she proved those executives wrong—the series lasted eleven seasons and won more than two dozen Emmy Awards—but she had forever changed the face of American television: It now wore many wigs and an occasional fat suit and brought America together to laugh, if only for one hour a week.

Over the years, her career has continued with films, more television, and Broadway, but no matter what roles Burnett plays, she'll always be most beloved for her signature Tarzan yell (perfected as a child), a tug on her left earlobe (a signal of *hello* to Nanny), and the hundreds of indelible variety-show characters, from Starlet O'Hara to Eunice Harper Higgins.

ALFRE WOODARD

A native of Tulsa, Oklahoma, with Texas family ties, Alfre Woodard is considered one of Hollywood's most versatile performers—she's received eighteen Emmy Award nominations (including four wins) for seventeen different roles.

I'm the "Southern police" on most of the projects I do. I say, "We're supposed to believe this is the South and you see women putting their purses on the floor? Or men putting their hats on the table?" Contrary to what many people seem to believe, there is no "stock Southerner." In fact, there is more variation in us than in other places. I don't want to talk bad about people, but this well-known actress was playing a Southern woman, and she was *cerebral*. She was acting from the chest up, when she should have been acting from the bottom. A Southern woman is not who you play. A Southern woman is who you are.

My mother was from a family of twelve. My father was from a family of twelve. My grandmother was from a family of seventeen kids. My grandfather was one of twenty.

They were all sharecroppers. We laugh, because when we'd visit my grandma in Texas, you had to be careful. We'd be eyeing some guy and she'd say, "Get away from that boy. He's your cousin!"

There was a vibrant African American community, a strong middle class [in Tulsa], and the working-class people all had jobs and houses and daddies. I was a Girl Scout. I remember every teacher I had. They cracked the whip in their pumps and suits every day. People looked at you and expected things from you, and when that happens in life, you deliver. I saw millionaires driving to work. I saw entrepreneurs and shopkeepers and lawyers. There were ballet dancers. Exotic dancers. Black kids back then got to see every kind of life and make their own choices. Now we are

economically segregated. And generations of kids are growing up without seeing people in their neighborhoods succeeding. Yes, our country was segregated. But I didn't know that as a child. Our communities were these enclaves where amazing things happened all the time. I wasn't called "the *n* word" until I was in college in Boston.

My kids get a kick out of the South. They've spent quite a bit of time there. When we go down to Texas and Oklahoma, my daughter will tease me. Normally when they ask to do something, I'll talk with them like, "I don't know, how do you feel about that?" But when we're down South, I'm like, "Oh hell no! That is *not* going to happen up in *here*!" Mavis just shakes her head and says, "Uh oh, Mom's gone Texas!"

LEAH NANAKO WINKLER

I n the play *Kentucky*, Leah Nanako Winkler's comedy about a young career woman returning home for her sister's wedding, bridesmaids sing a cheerfully addled rendition of "My Old Kentucky Home," then chow down on a snack of Japanese onigiri. This encapsulates Winkler's South. A Japanese American lauded as one of a new generation of Southern female playwrights, Winkler, who has also written for television, says she's just exploring the world she knows—a place that's more diverse than many other playwrights seem to recognize.

Your mother is Japanese and your father is a white American; you were born in Kamakura, Japan, and grew up in Lexington, Kentucky. What was that like?

Honestly, Lexington is a really diverse community. There are a lot of Asians, a lot of black people. There's a Japanese community because of the Toyota plant, and just by default there are half-Japanese people. I thought growing up as a mixed-race kid in Lexington was awesome.

You give two teachers at Tates Creek High School credit for getting you started in theater.

A hundred percent. I was aimless; I only joined drama club because I got kicked off my basketball team. But because of Lisa Osterman and Jason Meenach, I really found a passion. Lisa made me believe in my ability to make a career out of this—because she never told me I couldn't. She didn't push me to get a career in theater per se, but she was never discouraging and left me blind to the odds that were stacked against me.

After college you headed to New York.

I donated my eggs to do it. I come from a working-class family; it's expensive to move. I found on Craigslist someone who was looking for half-Asian egg donors, and they paid $4,500. I did that, and I bought a laptop and a Greyhound ticket.

Diversity is important in your plays.

It's the world I grew up in. My grandma has never gotten on an airplane, while my mom is an immigrant. It's important for me to reflect that narrative. Also, the optics onstage: Asian Americans constituted only 4 percent of casting decisions on and off Broadway in the 2015–2016 season. So I think it's really important to write modern roles for Asian women and also interracial relationships. Because that is the world that we live in.

Your plays Kentucky and God Said This are not autobiographical, but each was prompted by a seminal moment in your life.

The first one, *Kentucky*, I started writing at my sister's wedding. My sister had become engaged to this guy that she met in Bible school, and I didn't know him very well. We weren't really raised in a religion, but my sister and my mother had found Jesus. And I was just sort of feeling a little—it was just a big moment. I saw how happy my sister was, and I realized that my sister went to God and church as fervently as I went into the arts. I asked myself, *What if there was a version of me who was less empathetic, who was sort of an East Coast liberal who lives in the bubble and never went back to Kentucky?* And that's how the character Hiro was born. She's sort of a Bizarro World version of me.

God Said This, which features some of those Kentucky characters, came from a less happy family event—your mother's cancer.

I was going home to Lexington to oversee her chemotherapy treatments once a month for about five months. Chemotherapy is pretty boring. Just sitting there while the person getting chemo sleeps most of the time. So I was sitting with my laptop, thinking, *What would it be like to revisit this family again? How would they react if the matriarch got cancer?* That's how that play happened.

American Theatre magazine called you one of a new group of Southern female playwrights who are telling the story of today's South, minus nostalgia and mint juleps.

I'm just trying to depict Kentucky the way I experienced it. I don't really know what a julep is. I don't think I should represent what Southern life is, but I think I should present what the South isn't limited to. It isn't all *Steel Magnolias*. I want to explore my roots in Kentucky a little bit. There's a wealth of material, and I'm finding that more interesting now than writing about rich people in New York complaining about their problems over white wine.

HOLLY HUNTER

The one-of-a-kind voice that speaks for us all

BY ALLISON GLOCK

You know her first by her voice. That sugar gravel twang that lodges in your brain like a pop music hook. A sound both childlike and world-weary, her cadence mirroring the ups and downs of life's entirety in a single sentence.

My favorite of all of those sentences is from 1987's *Broadcast News*. After an unctuous male colleague tries to knock her down a few pegs by saying with a sneer, "It must be nice to always believe you know better, to always think you're the smartest person in the room," she replies to him, reconciled, forlorn: "No. It's *awful*."

With that single line, Holly Hunter became an instant touchstone for bright, spirited Southern women—all women, really—who find themselves habitually overlooked, or silenced, or sidelined, or misunderstood. In three words, she shed light with piercing clarity on generations of female frustration, and she did it while making us laugh.

It's a Southern habit to leaven hard truth with humor. To say the unsayable with a wry smile. Hunter, now in her sixties, has always brought this undercurrent of wisdom and wit to every role, her irrepressible humanity sloshing out even in her Oscar-winning performance as the buttoned-up nonspeaking Ada McGrath in the 1993 drama *The Piano*. (Only Hunter could make silence and clinical repression dynamic.)

She gave similar iconic turns in 1987's *Raising Arizona*, where her idiosyncratic charm allowed audiences to fall in love with a kidnapper, and in 1993's *The Firm*, where in a small, supporting role her quirky, brainy sex appeal instantly eclipsed the megawattage of costars Tom Cruise and Gene Hackman and essentially reduced the whole movie to an exercise in waiting for another scene with her in it, the way one anticipates a lion at the watering hole.

Hunter is indelible that way. A giant at five foot two. Deaf in one ear (a hurdle made invisible by her absolute commitment to her work), Hunter was raised on a farm in Conyers, Georgia, the youngest of seven kids. As such, she knows what it means to battle for space and attention, how to make the most of that attention when you capture it. Hunter is not one to squander a moment. Nor is she one to quash the vulnerability that gives that moment electricity, life.

"I always feel insecure and I always feel confident," she has said. "They're slammed up against each other and it's a constant balancing act."

Every woman knows intimately that same circus trick, and it is a profound relief when we get to watch Hunter walk the tightrope of her imperfections and transform them into art. She breathes grace and depth into every woman she portrays, reflecting feminine complexity with so much integrity, authenticity, and compassion she could probably make the Blood Countess seem like a fun lunch date.

For decades in the business, Hunter has lifted us all. It is why we feel we know her. It is why we are glad she exists. Because kinetic and singular as her voice may be, she still sounds like us.

OPRAH WINFREY

(1954–PRESENT)

A consummate Southern storyteller wields her power for good

You already know Oprah Winfrey's story. Everyone knows Oprah Winfrey's story.

But what's motivated Winfrey since she was anchoring the local news in Nashville is the opportunity to share other people's stories. And she's done it so well—with her signature combination of savvy and compassion—that speculation about her presidential ambitions now dates back decades. Not that Winfrey, who is a billionaire, needs the power and influence that come with the title—she already has both. But those anxious to cast a ballot just know they need her and her special way of uplifting women.

"Above all, it's a story," the *New York Times*'s James Poniewozik wrote of Winfrey's electrifying 2018 Golden Globes speech, delivered in acceptance of a lifetime achievement award, which, in soaring terms, recounted her history and inspirations. "And it's a story about stories. It moves from the personal . . . to the communal. . . . It tells the audience: I have my struggle, and I know you have yours, and that connects us all in the sweep of a global struggle."

Born in Mississippi, Winfrey was raised early on by her maternal grandmother, Hattie Mae Lee, whom she credits with teaching her to read. (Fittingly, she later found a "cocaptain" of her "angel team" in writer Maya Angelou, who became a trusted confidant.) Thanks to an oratory contest, she won a full scholarship to Tennessee State University. There, she studied communications, and then hopscotched between local television stations.

In 1984, Winfrey took over a low-rated talk show at Chicago's WLS-TV; not quite three years later, it was renamed for her and broadcast nationwide. Like her competitors, Winfrey at first interviewed celebrities and delved into salacious topics surrounding love and sex. But her approach grew more holistic with each passing year, and viewers became accustomed to hearing spiritual leaders, nutritionists, and charity workers come on *The Oprah Winfrey Show* to try to frame their life experiences.

Sometimes, the storytelling was more subtle: After the show aired a package about single fathers that included a clip of a black man putting his son to bed, "the white audience wrote letters saying, 'I didn't know black men did that,'" Winfrey once recalled. "Then I realized that the best way to show that black people are just like everybody else, or that gay people are just like everybody else, is not to do a show about gay people or black fathers raising their children [but] just to include them in a story about raising children."

In 1996, Winfrey launched Oprah's Book Club, a program that continues to stimulate the sale of millions of copies of books by previously unknown authors and great American writers, including Toni Morrison and Angelou. And while Winfrey ended her show in 2011, she supports and disseminates stories on her Oprah Winfrey Network and as the producer of films and TV shows: Since receiving an Academy Award acting nomination for 1985's *The Color Purple*, Winfrey has seen dozens of projects to screen, including Southern-centered narratives such as *Beloved*, *Selma*, and *Queen Sugar*.

"What more can I do to bring mercy, justice, and grace into this world?" Winfrey has said she asked herself after reading a former prison inmate's memoir. "That's the power of words—of a story told so well, you're enlarged by its meaning."

AMY SEDARIS

The sketch comedian, actor, author, and crafts enthusiast Amy Sedaris credits growing up in North Carolina—including two public access shows she watched there, At Home with Peggy Mann *and Bette Elliott's* Femme Fare—*with inspiring her love of hospitality and television.*

We belonged to a country club in Raleigh that didn't have any money. But I loved everything about it—buffet tables, families dressing up, greasing a watermelon and throwing it in the pool so everyone would chase it. My dad played golf, my mother was suntanning, and we were all in the pool. Everyone would bring their own liquor and extra fried chicken, and there would be a big meat spread with a meat carver. I loved that fruit cocktail mixed with whipped cream. We didn't go to a fancy country club, but it was fun being a member of a poor one.

When I saw [*At Home with Peggy Mann* and *Femme Fare*] on North Carolina public access when I was younger, I thought, *I'm going to do that one day.* It felt like somebody was playing house, and that was my favorite thing to do growing up—play house and turn my room into a soap opera. Those ladies on TV would say, "Welcome to my home," and it was clearly a set. They used that boring, monotone, old-money voice, which I loved. They would have a sewing segment, or Tammy Faye Bakker on for a cooking segment. She was the first

character that I remember on TV—she was a Southern woman making Southern food, wearing a lot of bad makeup, and I just loved her.

My character Patty Hogg comes from old money. She's a combination of every Southern woman I ever came across. Patty is me but much older, with more makeup, and raising my eyebrows because she's had a face-lift. I always think, *Wow, Patty looks good for her age; she's got great skin.* I celebrate people more than make fun of them. I really appreciate every misfit out there.

ASHLEY FLIEHR

W WE superstar Ashley Fliehr—who wrestles under the name Charlotte Flair—is a fearsome queen in the ring. But underneath her leather boots, bedazzling chest plates, and body slams, she insists she's a "sweet Southern girl" at heart. Born and raised in Charlotte, North Carolina, the daughter of wrestling icon Ric Flair moved back to her birthplace to be closer to family, literally. She's found a spot down the street from her mother and from her childhood residence, where long ago Fliehr spent hours playacting in her backyard dollhouse, a skill that presumably serves her well onstage.

You're very close to your mother.

She was born in South Carolina, and raised outside of Tallahassee in Havana, Florida. She's your typical Southern mom. I had to make good grades, follow the rules. My mom dressed me in Lilly Pulitzer throughout high school. I had a strand of pearls when I was young. She would always say, "You want to look classy" and "Less is more." When we went to church, we put on our Sunday best. It was hard for her, with my dad being on the road for months at a time, raising two kids and keeping the household together. Her strength as a woman was a huge influence on me.

How so?

She taught me to work hard and to treat others as you would want to be treated. To be thoughtful, respectful, to carry myself a certain way. To be classy and feminine and honest and disciplined. My mom wanted me to be at my best, because she believed that was what would be best for me. Oh, and she told me to keep my house clean.

Keeping a nice home is a point of pride for many Southern women.

Oh yeah. My aunt Francine, my grandmother's sister, would come to Charlotte and help my mom decorate. We would spend hours going to furniture stores, flipping through magazines for ideas, ripping out the pages. We had an antique dresser that had fake fruit all over it. And silk rugs we weren't allowed to step on, but we did anyway. My mom had my grandparents' china in a cabinet. I feel like it's a very Southern thing—to have a china cabinet. We also had a room with a piano and white couches that we weren't allowed to sit on.

What does being a Southern woman mean to you?

I love the unity you see among Southern women. The friendships, the close families, the traditions. I work with girls from all over the world, and our values are definitely different. My best friend is from Ireland, and she's always saying, "Southerners are the nicest people." She wants to move to Tennessee!

Do you think being raised in the South has helped you as you've traveled the world?

I do. Southern women really can do it all. My grandmother raised six kids. I've met so many Southern women along the way, especially before I left for WWE, who instilled confidence in me and showed me what life was really about. I remember a guidance counselor at my church, this tiny, soft-spoken brunette woman—if it wasn't for our meetings together, I'd never have left Charlotte and gone to train for professional wrestling. She encouraged me to believe in myself and gave me permission to follow my dreams.

Margo Martindale
My Grandmother's Rocking Chair

*The prolific theater, film, and television actor Margo Martindale has won three Emmy Awards
for her work on* Justified *and* The Americans. *She also played Truvy in the original off-Broadway production
of* Steel Magnolias, *a role written especially for her by Robert Harling.*

When my grandmother died, my mother put her rocking chair in our house, in Jacksonville, Texas. She would always have a cup of coffee and talk to her girlfriends sitting in the chair. Sometimes she sewed, or she'd look at magazines. My mother was the greatest woman on the face of the earth.

She collected antiques. She would drive around the countryside in a pickup, and she would find old pieces of furniture and redo them. And when she died, I put them all in storage, down the road from my hometown. My older brother, Billy, got the rocker and took it to his ranch. I went down after my middle brother died, and opened the locker, and *every piece was gone*—it had all been stolen. That haunted me.

She had always wanted me to have a house. So when I finally got a house, I thought, *I have to have something of hers*. My nephew Mart, Billy's son, knew I lusted for that chair. He cowboyed in and got it for me. My brother said, "Take it, send it to her." So he put it in his pickup, took it back to Dallas, and FedExed a huge wicker rocker to me! This is the only piece that I have of my mother's, and now it's sitting in my living room in Connecticut.

"The thing about the South is we accept our history. We don't push it under the rug. There is racism all over the United States. Most Southerners I know, we definitely find ourselves defending our heritage. But let me tell you something, whatever you think about the South, if your car breaks down in any Southern city, you're only going to be sitting on the road five minutes, max. You don't even have to pop up your hood! When my car broke down in L.A., nobody stopped. They just kept whizzing by."

—*Octavia Spencer*, Academy Award–winning actor and Alabama native

REESE WITHERSPOON

In addition to acting, the Oscar winner and Nashville native Reese Witherspoon produces and develops female-centric films, television series, and podcasts through her media company, Hello Sunshine, and helms the Southern-inspired lifestyle brand Draper James, named after her grandparents.

My mother always said, "If you want to get something done, ask a Southern woman to do it." It's so true. No matter what you need, within twenty-four hours, it has gotten done. [When] I shot in Georgia, I couldn't find summer camps for my kids. And I asked one friend, the phone tree happened, and before the day was over, I not only had a camp but also women volunteering to drive and pick up the kids. It's incredible how Southern women take care of each other.

Every Southern woman I meet is always so pulled together. I'm just saying you don't see a Southern woman standing in the airport in sweatpants. You just don't. Even when they are stressed and their kids are swarming around their legs, they do things with grace. It's how we were raised. We all have those lessons of what your mother or grandma told you was "appropriate" or "attractive." That idea is quintessentially Southern. My grandmother was always, always dressed to the nines. She was always put together. She had her hair done every Friday. It made her feel good. If you look good, you feel good. And that is an important part of life.

You can travel to so many places where you only see the same things, but you go to the South and you always experience something unique. It has *identity*. And in a world where "anything goes," sometimes it is nice to have a sense of respect. Events and occasions you need to dress for. It's about honoring the history of the people who came before you and created these traditions that became the cornerstones of our culture.

CHEFS & MIXOLOGISTS

MASHAMA BAILEY

As the James Beard Award–winning executive chef of Savannah's lauded modern-comfort-food destination the Grey, Mashama Bailey has embraced her influence after decades in the kitchen. "I'm getting really comfortable in my skin," she says with some bemusement. She has also found fresh inspiration in her Southern heritage. A seventieth birthday party for her father held in South Carolina underscored the point. "When you get with family, you see yourself as if looking in a mirror. I felt like, *Oh yeah, this is my part of the world. This is where I fit in.*"

You were raised primarily in New York City and made your bones under Gabrielle Hamilton at Prune—but you have deep Southern roots.

My family is all from Georgia or Alabama. My mom's Waynesboro, Georgia, born and raised. My parents have been together since she was nineteen years old. They live in South Carolina now, about two hours from me.

How did it feel to leave New York to open a restaurant in the South?

It brought on a lot of self-reflection. When I first moved here, I just saw the beauty of the place—it's very in your face, undeniable. It takes some time to see there's a distinct separation of people and class. It's a very different way of life than I'm used to. It's getting better, but, for example, the number of black people that come into the Grey is 15 percent, maybe 20. When they come, I'm so happy I want to impress them! As far as cooking, I've always felt like the South was the birthplace of the country for cuisine. I feel like Southern food is the start of it all. I knew I wanted to return to the South for its traditions. This place is so fruitful. Hot as hell, but fruitful.

What is the quintessential Southern dish?

Chicken and dumplings. In college, I lived with a bunch of people from the West Indies. One night I cooked for my mother and did a curried chicken and dumplings. She took one bite and said, "You should cook." The potential that I have, I didn't know that it was there. But my mom knew all along.

Your menus reflect a marriage of Southern cooking and the wider culture. Have you always valued the ability to build community and social awareness through food?

I really care about it. Even when I started, I wanted to cook for my family to expose them to the world. Because that's how I was exposed to the world—through food I tasted from fellow students from other countries and backgrounds. Back then I couldn't even pronounce half the shit I was making, but I'd say, "You need to try this because it's life changing!"

Food can be like going to church.

Yeah, totally! At the Grey, we work right behind this neighborhood, Yamacraw Village, and it's the projects. We've done so many events to try to bring out the residents, but no one really comes. Then this seventeen-year-old girl from Yamacraw rented the private room downstairs with all her friends. They ordered pasta and collard greens. They didn't eat a lot. I literally wanted to send them a rib eye. I wanted to give them the whole experience. I went down and said hi. They were very hesitant. They were stepping out of their comfort zone and trusting me with their money. When you're poor, that's a huge concern. But when they got their food, they were really happy.

That must have felt good.

For me, it was especially meaningful because I grew up knowing the value of that. As a kid, we never went out to restaurants. It needed to be, like, graduation. And we would go to Sammy's on City Island and eat

snow crabs. For those girls to choose to visit the Grey because I was the chef there? That felt incredible. And those girls are exactly the type of people I want to convert. I want them to feel they deserve great food. Not necessarily expensive food, but food made with love and care that challenges what you are used to.

How do you feel about having that influence?

Weird. Because I hadn't fully accepted that I have that power. I'm becoming even more invested in the community. Before it was an idea: *Wouldn't it be great if we changed the world?* Now I'm walking the walk. When you start to feed people, when you sit and talk with people, you understand people a bit better. And you understand what you can do to make their lives better. Feeding them a good meal automatically improves their quality of life, you know?

How else have you changed since you've moved south?

I'm a lot more confident. I believe you don't really know if you want to make an impact until you actually *do* make an impact, and then you realize what your power is. I've recognized I have power—in food, in culture, in my personal being. I accepted the fact that I have something to say, and I can actually make a difference in people's lives. In New York I would have been more competitive with others and less competitive with myself. This quieter environment allowed me to hear what I want more clearly. To listen to my own voice.

CARLA HALL

Carla Hall has become one of the most beloved food personalities in the country—a position that would surely have surprised her college-aged self. The chef, cookbook author, and television host lives in Washington, D.C., where she first moved to attend Howard University to become an accountant. It wasn't until she began modeling in Europe, having Sunday suppers with friends, that her passion for cooking took off. "The food made me think of home," she says. Hall decided to begin catering and attended culinary school before landing a spot on *Top Chef*. Her third cookbook, *Carla Hall's Soul Food*, brought her full circle, celebrating twists on the types of Southern dishes she grew up eating in Nashville.

What are your earliest food memories?

My grandmother on my mother's side, Granny, was a hairdresser. We would always go to her house for Sunday suppers. My grandmother wouldn't make the cornbread before she saw us on the inside of her door. Everything would be on the stove—she had been cooking slowly all day—but we couldn't eat because we had to wait for the cornbread. Then it would come out golden brown. Crispy around the edges. Just a bit of butter. It was just so good.

And greens, too, right?

One summer she was like, *Carla and Kim*—Kim is my sister—*I want you to go and pick the greens*. And I'm like, *I have to pick the greens? Ugh!* At dinner I said, "Well, you all may be eating weeds, because I didn't know the difference." It didn't dawn on me my grandmother would know the difference between collard greens and weeds, right?

How did you end up in accounting?

I was always that quirky kid—I liked numbers. But when I was doing accounting, I was so stressed out. I was in Ocala, Florida, doing an audit. And one of the accountants was folding this receipt. It took him about a minute; he was just focusing on the corners. And I'm like, *That can't be me. It just can't*. I was so afraid of being forty and hating my job.

You were modeling a little then, so you decided to go to Paris to do runway.

I went by myself. Paris ended up being the bridge between what I knew I didn't want to do and what I eventually wanted to do.

How so?

This woman named Elaine Evans would have Sunday suppers, all us models over. In the kitchen, they would be going back and forth, *Well, my mother does it like this* and *My mother does it like that*. And I was like, *I have no idea what my mother does, because all of those Sunday suppers at my grandmother's house, I was outside*. I was homesick. And it was wanting that connection to home that got me into cooking.

Then you returned to D.C. and began your catering business.

I walked door-to-door—to hair salons, doctors' offices, florists—and I sold sandwiches. I worked every single day for five years. Then I went to culinary school at thirty, and worked in restaurants for a couple years. I like catering because you get to create a moment for somebody, and it's all the food memories—you're in it with them.

You acted as a teen in Nashville. How did that training pay off?

Theater saved me from being bullied, because I was a quirky kid and really shy. Because I did acting, I was always comfortable on television. They would call me "quirky Carla" [on *Top Chef*]. I think most people are quirky—they're just afraid to show it.

Your public persona is always cheerful.

People think I'm like this all the time. I know who I am,

and I'm doing the thing I want to do. That helps. But every time I meet somebody, I'm thinking, *They've gotten to know me on television. And this is my opportunity to get to know them.*

How do you nurture chefs of color?

I say it to any person of color: Really honor your heritage through your food, because that's your North Star. And when you connect with your North Star, people can't help but be drawn in.

You've really embraced Southern food.

Why do authors use food in books? Because it's a shortcut to understanding where the character's coming from. To understanding who the person is and what they like and what they don't like. I am a proud, card-carrying Southerner.

"When I first opened a restaurant in New Orleans, I'd go out to the table, and it's maybe six people. They said, 'You're not the chef—there's no way that a woman would run a restaurant like this.' I shrugged it off, and said, 'I hope you had a pleasurable dinner.' Then I went back into the kitchen. I never saw myself as a role model, I saw myself as a chef. Nowadays, people are looking at chefs as role models, especially being a woman in the kitchen, a woman of color—there are not many of us in the kitchen. People are like, 'If she can do it, then I can do it too.'"

—**Nina Compton**, the Saint Lucia–born, James Beard Award–winning chef-owner of New Orleans' Compère Lapin and Bywater American Bistro

On Being Southern
BY VIVIAN HOWARD

I apologize.

If I putter around the kitchen all day in pursuit of serving a simple, satisfying dinner, and what I put on the plate ends up being fancy, I apologize. If in an effort not to be late, I'm a few minutes early, I make sure you know it wasn't my intention. When strangers appear at my door with a copy of my book and ask me to sign it, I say I'm sorry they had to lug such a heavy tome around while stalking me. No matter how benign it may be, before I share my opinion, I apologize for it. When fans of *A Chef's Life* say how much they appreciate my honesty and vulnerability on camera, I apologize for my realness and assure them I'm working toward a more polished persona. Before I reprimand my son for spitting on his gymnastics instructor, I make sure he knows scolding him hurts me, too. And if it's raining, or cloudy, or windy, or humid, or there are biting flies swarming your head, and I happen to be in your presence, please, please accept my apology on behalf of the universe and me.

These knee-jerk apologies are not a new thing. As long as I can remember, I've tried to soften the edges of reality with "I'm sorry" and "please forgive me." It's what my mom does. It's what my sisters do. It's a learned behavior.

My husband argues that I say "sorry" so much, my apologies mean nothing. In his opinion I'm a real-life, very prolific "boy who cried wolf." If saying I'm sorry suggests that I regret my grimace when I spot the smiling book holder at my door, or I feel bad for telling Theo he can't go through life spitting on people, then yes, I am not telling the truth when I apologize. I don't actually feel remorse for my actions in those circumstances. What I do feel is bad about how my actions might make people feel.

I've long thought my propensity for apology was just a female thing—a way to soften the impact of my voice. It's okay to speak your mind as a woman, just don't lend much weight to what you say. But lately, I've been thinking I apologize instead to support the infrastructure of Southern hospitality. As Southern women, the stewards of social grace and open arms, we have the mission to make others feel warm, welcomed, and validated. And I'm generally all for that. It makes me feel good to make other people feel good. Still, there are moments when for whatever reason I can't abandon my own will for the comfort of others. So I do or say what I want. Then I apologize. In a weird Southern woman kind of way, apologizing gives me permission to be myself.

I'm so sorry. I will try to stop.

Deep Run, North Carolina, native Vivian Howard is a chef, cookbook author, and the Emmy, Peabody, and James Beard Award–winning star of the PBS series A Chef's Life *and* South by Somewhere.

VERTAMAE SMART-GROSVENOR

(1937–2016)

The Renaissance woman who carried Gullah Geechee culture to the world

I n 2016, the world lost its "culinary griot," as Vertamae Smart-Grosvenor liked to call herself. If she had lived in the 1920s, she'd have been a madcap flapper. If she'd lived in the early 1800s, her adventures as a self-created African princess could have made her the prototype for Princess Caraboo. As it happened, she lived in the twentieth and twenty-first centuries, and she grabbed them with both hands and made them her own. Smart-Grosvenor crammed many lifetimes into one. She was a mistress of creative self-reinvention.

She was born in the Lowcountry of South Carolina in 1937, and that region would always influence her thought and her way of being in the world. At age ten, she moved to Philadelphia with her parents and dreamed of a life of travel and adventure. That dream became reality when she turned nineteen and bought a ticket on an ocean liner headed to Europe—destination, Paris. The move was a formative experience. In the City of Light, she met a group of expatriate artists and writers, including Allen Ginsberg, William S. Burroughs, and James Baldwin, who became a lifelong friend. She also met Robert Grosvenor, a New York–born sculptor who became her husband.

In the 1960s and 1970s, after her return to the United States, Smart-Grosvenor was a neighborhood fixture in New York's East Village during the years of the Black Arts Movement. She performed improvisational theater in Tompkins Square Park and became a "moon goddess," a backup singer, in Sun Ra's avant-

garde music collective, the Solar-Myth Arkestra. Most important, she cooked for her fellow artists. Her dinners were legendary, both for the meals served and for who might turn up at her table. James Baldwin, Maya Angelou, Yoko Ono, the scholar and cultural critic Larry Neal, the poet Quincy Troupe, and other luminaries all feasted there.

Her career as a culinary anthropologist began in 1970, with her groundbreaking cookbook *Vibration Cooking: Or, the Travel Notes of a Geechee Girl*. Proudly reclaiming the word *Geechee*, previously considered pejorative, the work established her as a Lowcountry cultural force. The book's recipes did not conform to traditional methodology—a cup of this, a tablespoon of that. Instead, she rendered them in vignettes about their origins—who created them, where the recipes came from—as well as how to prepare them. She followed the cookbook with *Thursdays and Every Other Sunday Off: A Domestic Rap*, a mordantly humorous look at the world of domestic work. She also contributed to *Essence* and *Elan* magazines.

In 1980, Smart-Grosvenor began a career at National Public Radio that would span three decades and earn her many accolades, including James Beard and National Association of Black Journalists awards. Her commentary covered social, political, and cultural issues as well as food. Her expertise with food also spawned an opera, *Nyam*, a compilation of traditional and original music and commentary that she performed around the country. In the nineties, she acted in films, appearing in the Lowcountry-set classic *Daughters of the Dust* (1991) and *Beloved* (1998), based on the Toni Morrison novel. She also starred on the small screen, with a public-TV show called *The Americas' Family Kitchen with Vertamae Grosvenor.* The show, one of few with an African American host, prompted two more cookbooks (*Vertamae Cooks* and *Vertamae Cooks Again*) and brought her acclaim.

At the time of her death, Smart-Grosvenor was a full-fledged culinary icon—her list of awards lengthy, her life and work the subject of two documentaries, *Travel Notes of a Geechee Girl* and *Vertamae Grosvenor, Always Already.* But it's impossible to catch the whirlwind. The remnants she left behind are only a pale shadow of this vibrant, opinionated, amazing woman, who saw the world, savored it, and made it her own.

VON DIAZ

The Puerto Rico–born, Georgia-raised journalist and radio producer Von Diaz's cookbook, Coconuts & Collards: Recipes and Stories from Puerto Rico to the Deep South, *explores the two cuisines of her childhood.*

My grandmother was a really unusual woman for her time. She was independent, fearless, and an incredible champion for her children and her grandchildren. As in so many other families where a male figure is suddenly gone, the women in my family had to take care of kids and each other on their own. My grandmother instilled this sense of purpose and independence in my mom, who later put those same values in my head.

When my grandfather was still in the picture and there were plenty of resources for the family, my grandmother was a homemaker. The stories about her always end with people showing up at the house right at dinnertime, conveniently available to have a meal. When he left the family, her ability to be this incredible hostess and the quality of ingredients available to her also shifted. That's when my mom had to pick up cooking and housekeeping. That same scenario replicated itself in my family later when my parents split up: My mom was on her own, and I subsequently took on some of the household duties in a stronger way.

I was five when we moved to Georgia for my father's job in the army. When I'd visit my grandmother as a child, I'd gorge myself on Puerto Rican food almost in this attempt to feel connected. I'd be on my way to Puerto Rico and start imagining the taste of *besitos de coco, sofrito,* meat cooked on the side of the road, or cod fritters. I could taste them as the plane was landing, and then later I would go back to the South and be thinking of these flavors still.

It was hard to imitate them with what we had access to in Georgia in the eighties and nineties. I didn't have the best ingredients, but I did have a really strong sense of what tasted good. That's how I started cooking. I wanted food that was as delicious and interesting as I'd seen prepared by this incredible person who was really important to me.

A lot of things served to me in school or in a friend's kitchen or at church were very bland. As I got older, I began to understand the diversity of Southern food. When I left the South, those same longings and connections I had felt as a child to Puerto Rico I now also felt for the South. When I'd go back home, I'd imagine fried catfish served on cheese grits with a side of greens, and when I'd get to eat them, I'd feel really complete. The dishes and ingredients that make up the cuisines we grow up eating become this incredible lifeline that we can never deny.

After some time as a public radio producer and writer, I kept finding myself really attracted to the moments when someone would talk about what they ate or how they cooked. Telling a person's story through food gives you an opportunity to explore where they worked, where they grew up, what was going on there. I became addicted to that process of pulling back the curtain on someone's food history as being a way to tell someone's larger story. And I started with my own because I knew it best.

LUCILLE BISHOP SMITH

A groundbreaking Texas chef and entrepreneur

BY TONI TIPTON-MARTIN

On June 19, 1865, enslaved African Americans put down their hammers, garden hoes, and cook pots and gathered in Galveston, Texas, listening intently as General Gordon Granger made an announcement: The Emancipation Proclamation's General Order Number 3 had brought an end to the system that forced them into the unpaid, backbreaking labor that built this country's cities, tended its crops, cooked its meals, and nurtured its children.

On the 150th anniversary of Juneteenth, or Emancipation Day, as the date is also known, I hosted "Soul Summit: A Conversation about Race, Identity, Power and Food," an unprecedented gathering of the nation's top African American chefs, food historians, writers, authors, farmers, and scholars in Austin to celebrate African American culinary freedom. For two days, on the campus of the city's historically black college, Huston-Tillotson University, chefs, caterers, mixologists, and winemakers delighted the group with Afrocentric food. In between, panels and presentations explored the ways African American cooking has been confined to the slave cabin and proposed ideas for disentangling it. And we also raised a glass to honor one underappreciated chef and businessperson in particular: Lucille Bishop Smith.

From her socially conscious kitchen in Fort Worth, where she ran a catering business and coordinated a vocational program for African American domestic workers, Bishop Smith fashioned a reputation around culinary proficiency and professionalism during the mid-twentieth century, spurred by the ambitious aim of "lifting Culinary art from the commonplace," as

she once put it. Her cooking prioritized variety, easy and enjoyable preparation, efficiency, seasonality, reliability, and eye and taste appeal at a time when those virtues were unheard-of as far as black cooks and cooking were concerned. Despite laws—both written and unwritten—that limited her career options, she created projects that disputed the myths associated with black people and food: that our experience is limited to survival cooking and the myriad iterations of soul food, or that the food we prepare while on the job is "white people's food."

Each time I lift the lid on the recipe collection she published in 1941, a bright red and pale blue recipe-card file entitled *Lucille's Treasure Chest of Fine Foods*, its musty aromas transport me to her kitchen, where my own desire to use food as a mechanism for change was awakened. Her cheerful recipe writing for the likes of mushroom fondue and sweet potatoes on the half shell; encouraging letters to family and students; the teacher training manuals she created; and the ingenuity of the packaged hot roll mix—the first of its kind—she manufactured and sold across from her husband's barbecue restaurant, making her one of Texas's first African American businesswomen, challenge me to reimagine, then to reclaim, my ancestral ways as values, and to encourage my readers—women and girls especially—to choose the type of healthy eating she advocated; to pursue new ambitions like food styling, photography, or restaurant design; to be unbridled from a bitter stereotype.

Chris Williams, a Le Cordon Bleu chef and Bishop Smith's great-grandson, embodies all of that today. In his fine-dining restaurant called Lucille's, a cozy bungalow in Houston's Museum District, black-and-white photos of Bishop Smith adorn the walls: Bishop Smith pictured with the boxer Joe Louis and with Martin Luther King Jr.; the three hundred fruitcakes she baked and sent to Vietnam servicemen; the chef regally posed in a pristine uniform. And in the menu, Williams has knitted together classical training with cultural diversity in a way that honors her memory. He refines his mix of iconic Southern dishes with global flavors from Vietnam, West Africa, and East Asia. All of it set off with one of Bishop Smith's special appetizers, Lucille's Famous Chili Biscuits—puffy hot rolls that are light, airy, and not too sweet, topped with ground meat laced with a hint of dark chocolate, aromatic spices, the peppery punch of hot peppers, and a crown of shredded cheese.

Anywhere else, the dish might seem out of place in a lineup that includes agrodolce and gremolata. But Williams's menu and style display his heritage and training as *he* understands them, not as outsiders have defined them—an ultimate expression of culinary freedom that would make his great-grandmother proud.

MARIANNE EAVES

W hen she was growing up, Marianne Eaves's interests were wide-ranging, from fixing cars to decorating sitting rooms to studying chemical engineering, her major at the University of Louisville. But an internship at the historic spirits company Brown-Forman—home of Old Forester, Jack Daniel's, and Woodford Reserve, among others—drew her into the bourbon business. Within five years of joining the company, she became Brown-Forman's master taster. In 2015, at the age of twenty-eight, Eaves left the global giant for the newly formed Castle & Key Distillery, which opened three years later in the turreted former home of Old Taylor Distillery in Frankfort, Kentucky—a move that made her the first female master distiller in the state's bourbon industry since Prohibition.

You opened a little shop with your mom after high school, because you couldn't settle on a career path.

I thought about linguistics and interior design and auto mechanics. I was talking it over with my dad, and he was looking at all these online lists of best salaries, and he suggested chemical engineering. I was like, actually, this is pretty cool: You can go make peanut butter or fuel additives. Or, it turns out, you can make bourbon.

And did you like chemical engineering school?

They make engineering school really hard. Every class is a weed-out class your first year. Even in my junior year, I had a crisis and called my mom, saying, "Maybe it's not for me. Maybe I should go into social work or dentistry." She was like, "Just keep at it, you can do it." So I kept pushing through and finally made it. But I think working for Brown-Forman was my saving grace, because I could see a future. They were already talking to me about opportunities.

How did you decide to make the leap from Brown-Forman to Castle & Key—to go with an upstart over a long-established company?

It wasn't an easy decision, because I loved working with Brown-Forman. But after meeting my now partners, it was clear Castle & Key was their passion, and they were going to make it happen, one way or another. I really wanted to be part of the project, and almost felt kind of a responsibility to the site itself and to help bring it back to life. The way they approached me was "We have this facility that used to produce a thousand barrels a day, and now it's your playground." That was a pretty exciting proposition.

After you were hired, you had to endure unfair rumors that you were hired for your looks.

There's an obvious difference between my appearance and that of the other, more established master distillers, but I just don't let it bother me. I wouldn't say I necessarily ignore it, because I'm very aware it exists. But I think it's kind of fun sometimes, when you're approached by someone and they're like, "Who are you? What do you do here?" and I'm like, "I make the bourbon." I believe once people start listening to me and hearing me speak about the process, it's pretty evident I know what I'm talking about. I tend to lean toward a little more technical way of describing things, but because of the training I had at Brown-Forman, I also understand how to get on someone's level. It's been an effort on my part to develop public speaking skills, because I'm naturally an introvert.

And now, you've said, you have become a role model for little girls.

My business partner has two little girls. Bishop—I don't know how old she was, she might have been five or six—motioned to her friend, like, *Hey, come over here, I want to show you something.* She had one of her parents' cell phones. And they were just sure she was going to show, like, a cartoon video. Instead, she pulls up a video of *me* talking about the distillery.

LEAH CHASE

Until her death in June 2019 at the age of ninety-six, Leah Chase reigned as the Queen of Creole Cuisine at Dooky Chase's, the storied New Orleans restaurant where the famous (Mahalia Jackson, Beyoncé, several presidents) and the familiar (her neighbors in Tremé) came to dine and pay homage. But Chase was more than the sum of her gumbo and fried chicken—she embodied the city and its history, and earned just about every culinary honor possible. During the segregated civil rights era, Dooky Chase's was one of the few public places in New Orleans where activists such as the Freedom Riders and Martin Luther King Jr. could meet with people of other races. "You did things back in those days and you didn't consider yourself changing anything," Chase said in this interview with her friend Jessica B. Harris, pictured here with the legendary chef in Dooky Chase's kitchen.

You say of growing up in Madisonville, across Lake Pontchartrain from New Orleans, "I guess we were the poorest things there."

A lady called me on Sunday, and she said, "Leah, I want you to see this across the street." And the sign on the little building said, VEGAN SOUL FOOD. I said, "Well what the heck is vegan soul food?" I guess that's what I came up on, vegan soul food. I was six years old when the Great Depression came, and there was no meat—there was no meat for anybody. So I was a vegan when it wasn't fashionable.

You graduated from high school at age sixteen, and took your first job in New Orleans two years later.

I went to work for this woman—I had never been inside a restaurant in my life. And she put me on the floor the next day. We were selling breakfast and lunch, making hamburger sandwiches. And after that, we said, *Our people are tired of eatin' sandwiches—let us cook one meal.* Now, we don't know one bloomin' thing about what to cook, but we all knew what we ate at home. And one of the dishes that the Creoles of color always put together when they didn't have much money was wieners in a Creole sauce. So we called it Creole wieners and spaghetti.

But you still weren't sure you wanted to do that for the rest of your life.

You get restless as a young person—you want to try new things. So I went to work for a bookie. I used to

like boxing, too. One day my grandfather showed me a picture of Joe Louis. And he said to me, "This man can beat anybody in the world." And I thought that was the most fascinating thing I ever heard: how strong you could be, that you could beat anybody in the world.

So you were hanging out with boxers at eighteen?

I knew all those boxers. I met Joe Louis. You were single, but you knew how to take care of yourself. When people would say, "Leah, I want to take you out," okay, you put on your best clothes you have, and you go out. But I'm not going with you in any dark corners. I'm going to sit at my friend's little bar—they had plenty of women who had bars in those days. You'd sit there and you'd have a little Tom Collins and you'd talk and you'd go back home.

When you met your husband, Dooky, and started working at his parents' restaurant, Dooky Chase's, it was a sandwich shop.

I came in, and I said, "We're gonna change. We're gonna do like the folks on the other side of town. There's no difference in people but the color of their skin." Now, that was stupid. When you're young, you don't know from nothin'. I'm gonna put lobster on the menu, lobster thermidor. Well, my dear, those people called my mother-in-law and said, "That girl is gonna ruin your business. Nobody wants lobster thermidor." They had never had the chance to eat it! That to me was the worst thing about segregation: Black people were not

allowed to learn. But [my mother-in-law] allowed me to go ahead [and start cooking dishes like gumbos and jambalayas]. That was the strangest thing. She allowed me to do it.

Maybe she saw something in you that you didn't see in yourself.

She was stubborn as a blue-moon mule, but she knew what she knew. She started this little restaurant because her husband was sick. He used to sell lottery. Well in New Orleans, we very sophisticated, so we don't say a numbers runner—he was a lottery vendor, dear. We had class about it. And he had all these clients. So when the poor man got too sick to go to all his clients, she had them come to her, and she would take the ticket, you see, and sell her sandwiches. She was a smart cookie.

Then everyone started coming to Dooky Chase's— musicians such as Ray Charles, writers such as James Baldwin...

Everybody came here because there was nowhere else for them to go. It was segregation. If they wanted to sit down to a table and eat, they had to come here.

There were no other black restaurants in New Orleans?

Not like this. Not with tablecloths. Dooky used to say to me all the time, "You're never satisfied." It isn't that I'm never satisfied. But I think as long as you're living, you should try to grow, try to raise yourself up. Raise somebody else up with you.

You raised three daughters. What does being a Southern woman mean to you?

Southern women have an air about them. You could be poor as Job's turkey, but you knew you had some culture. We may not have all the silver white people had, but you had a good piece you saved. During the week, you ate on an oilcloth. But on Sunday, you had a starched and ironed tablecloth, made of flour sacks. Your mother made you embroider the corners and crochet the edges. So you had a little culture, you had a little class. And I always say, a good woman ought to know how to talk her way out of hell if she has to.

What do you hope your legacy will be?

I was taught that your job was to make this earth better. I hope my children will carry on [Dooky Chase's]. I hope I've taught them enough to keep trying to grow, keep trying to make people understand how to enjoy life. Look at all the beautiful things around you, look at the progress. You gotta enjoy that, you gotta appreciate that, and I do.

CORNELIA BAILEY

(1945–2017)

The protector of Sapelo Island and its Gullah Geechee traditions

lthough she lived to be seventy-two, the Gullah matriarch Cornelia Bailey died once, when she was three. To the visitors and writers she invited to her Sapelo Island, Georgia, home, she often recounted the story: Little Cornelia fell deathly ill after eating unripe pears. Her mother and father, already heartbroken over the loss of two baby boys, had a pine coffin made and a grave dug. But her aunt Mary sensed something within the child, crushed cloves of garlic, and placed them in cold Cornelia's mouth, nose, "and God only knows where else," Bailey later remembered, "and I came around." That legacy of being reborn for a higher purpose followed Bailey the rest of her life in the small Gullah Geechee community of Hog Hammock on Sapelo.

Bailey called herself a Saltwater Geechee, and her life was as deeply rooted to the fertile Georgia barrier island as the sour oranges, Purple Ribbon sugarcane, and red peas that grow there. Like those crops, Bailey's origins traced back to slavery, when her towering ancestor, the African Muslim called Bilali, oversaw hundreds of slaves and the nation's first sugarcane production. After the Civil War, the island of freed African Americans watched as speculators and investors tried to reshape the land, and the tobacco-famous Reynolds family built neighborhoods and consolidated the black population

to the Hog Hammock community. It was there that Bailey was born in 1945, raised in a wooden cottage, died at age three, and was resurrected for a reason to uplift and protect the island's Gullah Geechee foodways, traditional medicines, gardening practices, and social customs. Cornelia Bailey *was* Sapelo Island.

"On high tide, you'd smell the salt more and on low tide, you'd get a whiff of the sea and everything in it," Bailey recounted in her delightful 2001 memoir, *God, Dr. Buzzard, and the Bolito Man*. "'Just smell that marsh,' Mama would say proudly. 'It smell so marshy.'" Bailey spent her entire life on Sapelo, directed by the seasons, supporting anyone with any cultural project that would uplift the Gullah community and its ties back to its West African traditions. She invested in agriculture and brought back the peas and sugarcane on her own terms—to be sold at Southern markets and to enable a new generation of folks to make a living on the speck of earth in the Atlantic.

"There's always been a part of Cornelia who could see Sapelo's culture slipping away, and she wanted to make people aware of the story," said Michele Johnson, the author of *Sapelo Island's Hog Hammock*, after Bailey's death in 2017. "She didn't want it to be something you read in a book or saw in a museum. She wanted it to be alive."

LEAH WONG ASHBURN

In 2015, Leah Wong Ashburn took over for her father, Oscar Wong, as the family owner, president, and CEO of Highland Brewing Co., Asheville, North Carolina's first legal brewery since Prohibition, making her one of the few female heads of a brewery in the South.

Highland Brewing started in a basement in downtown Asheville [in 1994]. Now we can fit thousands of people at the brewery. The market has revolutionized in front of my eyes. I have to be humble, because I don't brew. So my professional life, and my personal life, now, are completely in the hands of the brewing team; the quality team; the packaging team; the distribution team. There is no one job here I can do better than they can, by design.

It takes people a minute to figure out I'm approachable, because I have my mom's formality. I don't mean to, but it's just ingrained. I gravitate toward people who have a looser energy, that are more fun than I am. I've been in Asheville just since 2012, and it takes a long time to form really deep friendships; I feel like I've just started to get my groove.

You can't script your life—I wouldn't have scripted I was going to be a stepmom when I turned forty. But I went to a Highland dinner in Charlotte to keep our brewmaster company; a local bottle shop owner was there, and he brought one of his most frequent customers. He never told me if he was setting us up, but yeah, I think he had it in mind.

My husband and I live in our house with two cats. He has two daughters: One is in college and one is in high school in Charlotte. To say I feel fortunate doesn't begin to describe it: These two girls are wonderful young women. They're smart and accomplished and funny.

Family is very important. I work with my dad, and my sister is across the street. A lot of folks don't know I have a sister. She's just eighteen months younger. She's developmentally disabled, so she couldn't fully be a part of the running of the brewery, but she comes and dances. No matter what the band is, she's in front of the stage, dancing. She keeps us grounded.

EDNA LEWIS

(1916–2006)

The legendary cookbook author imbued Southern food with elegance

Perhaps because the cookbook that would define her career—and help redefine American perspectives on Southern cuisine—was called *The Taste of Country Cooking*, some food fans who have only just discovered Edna Lewis assume the Virginia native brought a touch of bumpkin to her dishes. Like the man who recently asked one of Lewis's old friends whether she was close to smothered biscuit specialist Mildred Council, they figure she was folksy in her work and attitude.

As anyone who sampled Lewis's acclaimed chocolate soufflé can confirm, however, those conjectures are flat-out wrong. "In Miss Lewis's kitchen, braised meats are called ragout, stewed fruit is a compote, potatoes are whipped not mashed, and steamed rice goes to the table molded and shaped into a ring," explains the culinary historian Toni Tipton-Martin in the essay collection *Edna Lewis: At the Table with an American Original.*

Lewis was the epitome of sophistication: Nowadays, people can get a sense of that quality from the stamp that features her portrait, issued by the U.S. Postal Service in 2014. Lewis has lately begun to receive the recognition she's long deserved, with her 1976 *Taste* book shooting up the best-seller list following a *Top Chef* episode devoted to her legacy. She was the subject of a 2018 book-length anthology and continues to be celebrated at themed dinners and panel discussions.

Central to Lewis's sophistication was a fierce belief that Southern food and the people who produced it were dignified and deserved to be treated as such. "It's not all fried chicken and greasy greens," she told the *Washington Post* in 1990. Rather, in her recollections, it was fig jam when the tree fruit turned swollen and ripe, fried shad for breakfast in the spring, and blueberry cake when there weren't enough berries left to fill one more jar at canning time.

All of those dishes were served in Lewis's childhood home of Freetown, where she was born in 1916. In 1932, she left the farming community settled by once-enslaved people and landed in New York. There, Lewis worked for a communist newspaper. And because Lewis and her friends didn't believe their politics were at odds with pleasure, Lewis got into the habit of throwing dinner parties. In 1949, she opened Café Nicholson, serving Southern-inspired dishes and her chocolate soufflé to guests including Truman Capote, Tennessee Williams, William Faulkner, and Harper Lee. Lewis left the restaurant in 1954 but remained a partner, and published her first cookbook, *The Edna Lewis Cookbook*, in 1972.

The legendary cookbook editor Judith Jones thought there was another, more personal cookbook in Lewis. So she encouraged Lewis to write the book that would cement her standing as "the South's Julia Child." (Financially, her cookbooks were never windfalls: Lewis worked kitchen jobs, including at Middleton Place, in Charleston, South Carolina, for some twenty years.)

In 2003, three years before she died, she published her last cookbook, with her frequent collaborator, friend, and fellow chef Scott Peacock, called *The Gift of Southern Cooking*. And that gift, rendered down to a philosophy, was perhaps best expressed by Lewis in a 1989 piece for the *New York Times Magazine*: "As a child in Virginia, I thought all food tasted delicious. . . . It has been my lifelong effort to try and recapture those good flavors of the past."

ASHLEY CHRISTENSEN

Nearly single-handedly revitalizing downtown Raleigh via her charitable social outreach and her multiple restaurants (including the renowned Poole's Diner), chef Ashley Christensen keeps giving back through her food, her activism, and her refusal to give up on places, people, and politics. The James Beard Award winner jolted the conversation forward by instituting a sexual harassment policy that extends to anyone who sets foot in her restaurants to work, promoting progress in an industry not known for generosity to women. "We also put a sign in every restaurant window that says, DON'T FORGET KINDNESS," Christensen adds, smiling. "To me, you can't argue with that."

What does Southern hospitality mean to you?

Making people feel welcome and comforted. Finding a way in a room full of strangers to make people feel really at home. I think there's a real openness in the South, and certainly in the restaurant community, for sharing and being a part of everyone's growth. Fostering community, basically. Most of us find a lot of joy and reward from that.

You've said being a chef is a huge responsibility.

It's a giant responsibility. I'm not just a chef, I'm an employer. It's up to me to create an environment that challenges people to be better, even outside of work. When I think about the issues that I want to speak up for, which are generally for people who don't have enough strong advocates, that's not just something that I enjoy being a part of, it's something I view as vital.

What do you say to people who argue that food and politics don't mix?

It would be insane to think that we should be left out of those conversations. Food has always been a tremendously important part of what defines our com-

munities and what celebrates the cultures that make up those places. When you have that kind of light and attention, it's up to us to take that spotlight and use it for great causes.

What feels intrinsically Southern to you about your upbringing outside of Greensboro?

Growing up close to a couple of big gardens. That was sort of at the center of our chores as kids. Being a part of watching something grow, and then to experience it right out of the garden, or to preserve it. That's very much at the core of why I cook the way that I do, and

it's probably the biggest part of my inspiration and my love for cooking food specifically in North Carolina.

You've always stayed very close to home.

I never got on an airplane with my family until I was like, nineteen. We had this pretty magical life where we lived. We would entertain—I would have friends over or my parents would have a big party. They didn't entertain to keep up with other people, they entertained to give something to people. I think that is the deepest part of our Southernness, and what I think is one of the most special parts of what I get to do every day.

Your parents are both incredible cooks.

My mother being from Memphis, her grandmother taught her how to cook and she shared that with me. Cooking wasn't something she had to bone up on. It was just a part of who she is. These Southern traditions—like, too much squash in the garden was never a challenge. When I'm thinking about food, I picture it from my childhood kitchen. My mom still lives in the same house. To me, that's the biggest part of my South. Everything evolves, but it is really rooted in this experience of what I grew up with.

What would you say is your most Southern dish?

Tomato pie. That's something my mom loves so much. I was telling her what I was thinking for my riff on it, how I season the tomatoes and put them on racks so the excess liquid drops off, and she's like, "That sounds great, but it probably takes a while. I just put mine in that thing that you gave me for spinning my lettuce and then I take the liquid and I make pasta sauce out of it." I was like, that's so fucking brilliant!

What other Southern women taught you about life?

A home economics teacher, Helen Prince. I was the kid who was throwing dinner parties in high school, which was unusual. She was the first person who asked if I'd ever thought about culinary school. I didn't end up going, but she put it in my head that cooking is something that I could do, because I felt this special connection with food. She set the example for me to be a better listener and to understand what it means to people when you pay attention to them, because she paid attention to me.

KELLY FIELDS

It didn't take long for New Orleanians to fall in love with the griddled banana bread, fried chicken biscuits with Tabasco honey, and cornbread with cane syrup at Willa Jean, the bakery Kelly Fields named after her grandmother and opened in 2015. National adoration soon followed—among other accolades, the James Beard Foundation named her a finalist for Outstanding Pastry Chef twice before she won the award in 2019. When her mentor and partner at the bakery, the dining magnate John Besh, stepped down from his restaurants amid sexual harassment allegations in 2017, Fields decided to stay and use her position to help effect change—and to build an empire of her own.

You set up the Yes Ma'am Foundation to help women in food and beverage, even before the allegations against Besh. What led you to do that?

It started as an idea of how to bring women together and create a network of mentorship that was missing for me when I was coming up in this industry. We realized we can offer unique, personalized, hands-on education to women in the South, and hopefully one day we'll get to a place where we can invest in bigger and better things for the women who nourish the South.

So what does that look like for someone who's a beneficiary?

I had women in my kitchen who had never been to culinary school, who were phenomenal cooks—probably better than what they would be coming out of culinary school. They didn't necessarily fit into any of the options for scholarships that are available in New Orleans. So I was trying to figure out a way: If this one cook wanted to go spend a month in San Francisco working for chef Traci Des Jardins, how do I make that possible? Like, where she gets to go, she gets to learn, she doesn't have to worry about the money—because San Francisco is not cheap, let's be honest. How can I help that be a reality for a bunch of different women doing a bunch of different things from wine to service to cooking?

You've really sought out mentors yourself through the years. The chef and baker Shuna Lydon, of Gramercy Tavern and the French Laundry, for one.

I didn't understand mentorship as a young cook. I didn't understand the importance of it. You know, I got put in a pastry chef position a little bit earlier in my career than I probably should have. So nobody taught me how to be a mentor, and I didn't take it seriously, and I didn't understand the power of that role for someone else until I left New Orleans with Hurricane Katrina. I went to San Francisco and sought out [Lydon], who had worked in every kitchen I had ever dreamed of setting foot in. And she came to define mentorship for me, and really showed me the power of the influence you can have on someone else.

How did she do it?

She just *was* it. That was her thing. She understood that her responsibility as a chef was to make me the best version of myself for the long term, and not just for her in that moment at that particular restaurant.

Being a mentor can be like a full-time job. How do you manage it?

I wake up thinking about it. I wake up in the morning thinking about if someone on my staff isn't performing up to my standards or their own, what am I doing to help them? Or what am I doing to stand in their way? How do we all keep getting better? It's as natural for me as breathing—probably more so sometimes.

How did mentorship figure into what happened with the Besh Restaurant Group turmoil and how women like you came through it?

I'm in the position now where I'm trying to navigate restorative conversations that move us and push us forward; where the weight of what has happened doesn't rest on my shoulders, or on any other innocent woman in this company. That's a time-consuming goal, right there.

Pardis Stitt
My Samovar Lamp

Pardis Stitt is the James Beard Award–winning co-owner of four Birmingham, Alabama, restaurants, for which she also oversees the front of house: Highlands Bar & Grill, Chez Fonfon, Bottega, and Bottega Café.

My parents are from Iran. They came to the States in the early sixties, and I was born here. My father bought this Russian-made samovar in an antique store in Kermanshah in the mid-seventies. It's probably about 120 years old now. I thought it would be great to make it into a lamp, something more useful.

I feel like a Southern woman; I don't look the part, but I feel that every day. When I think about my identity, I grew up very much with one foot very deeply in Persian traditions. My mom would get the samovar going in the morning, and we would have Darjeeling tea, and we ate Persian food; Persian culture is a very hospitable culture, which paved the way naturally for what I do now in my business.

But then there was the other side. Here I am, this Iranian American growing up in Birmingham, Alabama, in the seventies and eighties, coming of age with questions of *who are you?* and *what are you?* As a teenager, I didn't want the connection. I wanted to be blond. I wanted to fit in with everyone else.

After going to college, things turned around; I started to appreciate my parents' insisting that we speak Persian, that we have that connection to the language. I feel like I owe it to myself, to my niece, my nephews, my stepkids, to learn more and to pass it on to them. The lamp is a connection to that Persian heritage; I'm so happy and proud that I have these pieces that speak to that part of my life.

ALBA HUERTA

Bartender and aspiring perfumer Alba Huerta, a Monterrey, Mexico, native raised in Texas, has garnered national acclaim for the Southern riffs on cocktails she crafts at Julep, the bar she owns in Houston.

I started working in a bar when I was nineteen years old, because I ran up my credit-card bills in college. I had no idea what I was doing: I was the worst bartender on the planet for three months. I couldn't use a jigger. But they kept with me, and I got better and I got better and I got better. I'm constantly aware of the things I don't know. I'm constantly making myself better in the fields I'm not very strong in.

I always have a lot of projects outside of the bar. I've been distilling perfumes for quite some time, and training in that. Distilling is a matter of flowers and different kinds of organic materials, so I'm not really creating anything. The difficult part is blending. Learning which components are good partners with others—that takes years. I'm at the I-know-nothing stage. But it's a very romantic way of doing things.

Allowing yourself to learn something completely new is probably one of the best things you can do for yourself professionally. You put yourself in a very vulnerable position and you acknowledge that you don't know things, and you make yourself a student again. It's really important to be a teacher, but never forget to be a student.

NATHALIE DUPREE

When the most well-known of Nathalie Dupree's fifteen cookbooks, *New Southern Cooking*, debuted in 1986, the soon-to-be best seller redefined for many what Southern food could be. Dupree, who grew up in Virginia, trained at Le Cordon Bleu in London and worked as a chef in Majorca, Spain, before opening her own restaurant just outside of Social Circle, Georgia, in the 1970s, and for ten years she directed thousands of students at the Rich's Cooking School in Atlanta. It all led to the creation of her own cooking program on public television and her emergence as a personality—she would go on to film more than three hundred episodes, the most after Julia Child. She also founded both the Atlanta and Charleston, South Carolina, chapters of the women-in-food group Les Dames d'Escoffier. "I have this thing called the pork chop theory," she says of the countless women she has mentored. "If one pork chop is in a pan, it goes dry. If two or more are in a pan, the fat from one feeds the other. So there's always room to move over for another woman."

When did you begin to work with food?

I didn't want to settle down, so I lived all over. I studied at Harvard's summer school in 1958 and stayed in an international student house. Everybody had a job, and my job was to deal with the mail. I can write a letter, fold it, and maybe get it into an envelope, but the whole stamping and mailing a thing out—it's just too much for me. These two Mormon boys came back in the middle of the summer and they were supposed to show up for the draft the next day. But I hadn't forwarded their draft stuff to wherever they were on mission. So they took me off that job and put me in the kitchen.

I loved the kitchen. I couldn't cook then, but I learned fast. There were eighteen of us at the house, which is a fair number of people to get mad at you if you didn't cook a good meal. I discovered a lot during that summer. I was never good at anything until I became a cook.

Was your family supportive?

When I was cooking in the international student house, I called my mother and told her I loved the job. It was really the only thing she ever asked me not to do. My mother didn't want me to be a cook, because she said I'd have to work at night with men and be on my feet. She said if I could find any woman cooking, and this was in 1959, other than one who was slinging hash in a diner, but who was actually cooking, that she would give me her blessing.

Did you have a role model?

I never had a mentor. Back when I was just getting started, I couldn't find one woman who ran a kitchen or was in charge of the cooking. When I studied at the Cordon Bleu cooking school in London, I met Julia Child on the day I left. I was the house American, so they trotted me out to meet Julia. I had never heard of her, because I really didn't watch television when I was young. I asked her what I should do next. She said I should open a cooking school. You see, even Julia had never worked in a restaurant, which is what I wanted to do.

Eventually, you opened up your own.

My favorite former husband and I had an opportunity to move to Social Circle in Georgia. The banker who loaned us the money for my husband's antique shop said that none of the money could go to a restaurant—my restaurant inside the antique shop. So I ran the largest paper route in Covington, Georgia, all summer in order to make the money to open my restaurant Nathalie's at Mount Pleasant Village. I was throwing papers. But I never could throw them very far. I hit some geraniums once.

You've seen the nation's interest in Southern food fall and rise again.

A lot of the time, chefs get the flavor right. But frequently, it's too complicated and precious. Male chefs can't stop adding something that's unique or that will cause a little comment. It's like you get a dollar more per adjective on the menu. Sometimes I just wish they would serve a really good plate of butter beans. That, to me, is the essence of something that's new Southern—not gussied up, just fresh and well dressed but not overly done.

You have such a long view of the industry—have you ever compared notes with your peers and mentees?

I've always believed in telling everybody what you make. Once I was talking with Edna [Lewis] about books we'd written and I said, "Isn't it nice when those royalty checks come in twice a year?" And she said, "I never got a royalty check." I was furious for her. Here she was, touted, but she never collected a royalty.

Lewis has been coming back into focus recently for her contributions to the Southern culinary canon. What was your relationship with her like?

Edna was a good friend. I would call her every time I went up to New York, and we would go out to eat. We'd go to the Four Seasons or the '21' Club and the chefs would walk in, see Edna, and then rush over and be so excited to see her.

But I have conflicted feelings about the way people treated Edna and the way she's being treated even now. She was young, sweet, naive, and she always had a quiet quality to her. But she knew her own style. She wore African dresses and set herself apart. She was very active in the Communist Party. But the way she's remembered now is almost . . . too safe. It's safe to just remember a few things about her and say, *Edna is wonderful*. But what about other black women, women who cooked more and might have cooked more Southern food but didn't have Edna's sweetness? I just feel like we could go further with whom we recognize. Edna is a stepping-stone to the rest of the story. She's heating the fat in the pan.

INNOVATORS & ICONOCLASTS

NIKKI HALEY

Nikki Haley isn't interested in playing by anyone's rules—especially when it comes to gender. "When I became a legislator, South Carolina had one of the lowest rates of females in office," says the former United Nations ambassador, who also served as South Carolina's first female governor from 2011 to 2017. "At the UN, I was the only woman on the Security Council. Let's just say there were no lines to the women's bathroom in my world. Ever." Born Nimrata Randhawa in Bamberg, South Carolina, the Indian American politician and career public servant charted a professional course that spiked glass ceilings from the very beginning—a feat she credits to lessons learned from the steely-sweet women she grew up emulating. "Southern women kick with a smile," she says.

What was the moment that set you on your path to public service?

I was a member of the National Association of Women Business Owners, and we'd get together once a month and talk about different issues and challenges, and we'd have different speakers come in each time. One time, we were discussing an issue that was government related. There were a lot of complaints but not a lot of solutions being offered, so I spoke up and told the group what we needed to do and how we needed to do it and that we had to not whine about it. They listened to me, and when I saw them listen to me and I saw that I made a difference in that moment, I thought, *I have to do something with my life to move the ball.*

What do you think when you hear the word ambition?

Used too often for women and not for men. I think it's been given a negative connotation as it relates to women. In career-oriented places, men will refer to a woman as "ambitious" when she speaks out and does her job well and gets something done. What I tell young women is, whatever you do, be great at it. And make sure people remember.

How does being a Southern woman shape your worldview?

I think women have the ability to see the overall picture in a way that they can prioritize and balance. Women bring a lot to the table because they are very much a part of their finances, running their families, making sure they're a support system for their spouse, and often they have a job to do, too. Women today do it all. And we don't just want to do it all; we want to do it all well.

When you have a high-profile, high-pressure job, how does it affect your home life?

I don't talk about work at home for two reasons: One, I don't want to relive what just happened that day. And, two, my family doesn't necessarily want to hear about my day. I'd rather start off the dinner-table conversation with "What was the best thing and the worst thing that happened to you today?" And we all go around and talk about our day. It's important for me that my kids understand that life is more than just a certain time or facet of the day. In South Carolina, I always said, if I'm a good wife and a good mom, I'll be a good governor. When we moved to New York, I said the same thing about being an ambassador. If home is good, I can do anything.

You often wear a pendant of a palmetto tree and a crescent, the emblems of the South Carolina state flag. What does the idea of home mean to you?

The necklace is about staying humble and remembering where I came from. I wear it so I always remember what it was like to be that young Indian American girl in a small Southern town. I remember the challenges I went through. I remember what it's like to live in a rural area, where education isn't always top priority and people don't always have money. I know what

racism feels like. That's what I try to remember when I go out and do my job. The one thing you never forget after growing up in the South is neighbors helping neighbors, people helping people, and taking care of each other.

Who are your greatest influences?

I love how hard Margaret Thatcher pushed for things. I always quote her as saying, "If you want something said, ask a man. If you want something done, ask a woman." And then my mom. She has literally pushed through every challenge throughout her life. The other Southern women who influenced me were all around my town growing up. Being Southern gives you a different swagger, and these women had it. They were doing everything in their personal and civic lives, and you never knew how to read them. I mean, if you can read a Southern woman, you can do just about anything.

ROSALYNN CARTER

(1927–PRESENT)

A committed advocate beyond the White House for those in need

Eleanor "Rosalynn" Smith was born in Plains, Georgia, on August 18, 1927, the oldest of four children. When she was thirteen, her father died of leukemia, leaving her to help her mother with raising the rest of the children and to work as a dressmaker in order to help make ends meet—so began a lifetime of caring for others.

That little girl would grow up to establish commissions to advocate for the mentally ill, to fight the effects of poverty, and to eradicate vaccine-preventable diseases. She would be instrumental in passing the Mental Health Systems Act of 1980. The small-town Georgia woman drove policy discussions and reshaped the way public officials do their jobs, but her name was never on the ballot—her husband's was. As First Lady to Jimmy Carter, Rosalynn Carter paved the way for generations of leaders to come.

Long before he was the thirty-ninth president of the United States, Jimmy was just the cute older brother of Rosalynn's friend Ruth. He was in Annapolis at military school when the two began dating in 1945, and it wasn't long before Jimmy proposed marriage. Rosalynn turned him down—it was too quick, she thought. But two months later, when he asked again, she said yes, and the two were married in July of 1946. Jimmy's naval duties moved the couple all over the country until 1953, when his father passed away. Jimmy resigned from service, and the couple—now with three children in tow—moved back to Plains, Georgia, to take over the family peanut business.

As Jimmy made his way, first on the farm, and then as a politician, Rosalynn proved a vital part of the family's success. She ran accounting for the peanut business, handled political correspondence, and campaigned for his governorship. On the campaign trail, Rosalynn saw the need for mental health advocacy firsthand, and in the governor's mansion she began her lifelong crusade for the mentally ill, serving on the Governor's Commission to Improve Services to the Mentally and Emotionally Handicapped. Her resolve only strengthened when Jimmy made a bid for the White House. The first candidate's spouse to make a campaign promise of her own, she swore she would advocate for those affected by mental illness, and though her policy aspirations and involvement in the president's work rubbed some the wrong way, Rosalynn never abandoned that mission.

In the decades since the Carter presidency, Rosalynn has continued to fight for underserved members of the community, especially women and children. Through the Carter Center, which the couple founded in 1982, she promotes advancements in the mental health field. In 1991, she helped launch Every Child by Two, a campaign to eliminate preventable diseases by spreading awareness about vaccination. Her alma mater, Georgia Southwestern State University, has established an institute in her name to support and train caregivers—something that the thirteen-year-old Rosalynn would certainly have found a worthy cause. Her life has come full circle in many ways, not least in her love for her hometown: Today, the Carters have found themselves back in Plains—living in the same modest home they left when Jimmy won the presidency.

IDA B. WELLS

A barrier-shattering muckraker and activist

BY BRONWEN DICKEY

The year is 1883, and a smartly dressed young schoolteacher has just boarded a Memphis-bound train in Woodstock, Tennessee. She is twenty-one years old, but you'd never know it. Even with her hair piled gracefully atop her head, she is so physically tiny—not even five feet tall—that some brush her aside as though she were a child.

Shortly after she takes her seat, the conductor informs her that she will have to sit elsewhere. He simply cannot have a black woman in the first-class ladies' car. Not even an elegantly dressed black woman who has traveled in that car dozens of times over the past two years.

Hoping she will follow him out, the man grabs the teacher's bag.

She stays right where she is.

The conductor then grips her arm, thinking he can just lift this little troublemaker out of her seat. He has no idea whom he's about to tangle with.

The passenger he is manhandling was born into slavery in Holly Springs, Mississippi, in 1862, the height of the Civil War. When she was sixteen, both her parents and one of her brothers died of yellow fever and she was left alone to raise her five remaining siblings. To do so, she gave up her own formal education and took a teaching job at a rural school far from her home. In the early mornings, she rode a grouchy old mule named Ginger to work. Late at night, she read by the fireside because she could not afford extra wax for candles or oil for lamps. Men pursued her; women gossiped about her. She let neither get in her way. Hers is the kind of tenacity that the Greeks wrote into their myths—to say nothing of her temper, which is legendary among those who knew her well.

On this day, that temper could probably power the sun. Once that man dares to put his hands on the person of Miss Ida Bell Wells, he gets what is coming to him: His skin is memorably, painfully introduced to her teeth. Wells puts up such a hellacious physical fight, in fact, that it takes three grown men to remove her from the car. She then goes on to sue the railroad—*twice.*

She wins her case, too, at least initially. When the Tennessee Supreme Court overturns the verdict, Wells continues speaking out and writing about the injustices of segregation. The writing suits her spectacularly well. By the time she is only twenty-seven, she is both the editor and part owner of an African American newspaper, Memphis's *Free Speech and Headlight,* for which she pens bold, graphic editorials about the horrors of lynching. In retaliation for her forthright commentary, a mob of enraged white men soon destroys the paper's printing press while Wells is away on business. Should she ever publish the paper again, they tell her, she herself will be lynched.

Does that shut her up? No. Does it even slow her down? Hardly. But it does require her to keep a pistol in her purse and flee the South. Wells moves to Chicago, where her crusade to expose the brutality of Jim Crow expands across the country, then across the Atlantic. Her 1892 investigation into the real causes of lynching, *Southern Horrors: Lynch Law in All Its Phases,* will obliterate the absurd lie that black men habitually prey upon white women. Four years later, the ardent suffragette helps organize the National Association of Colored Women's Clubs. In 1909, she helps found the National Association for the Advancement of Colored People, though that fierce temper of hers will cause her to part ways with the group's leadership soon after.

Finally, after a lifetime of muckraking journalism and international renown, the woman once called "the princess of the press" runs for the Illinois state senate at the age of sixty-eight, making her one of the first black women in the country to run for public office. She doesn't win, but the loss pales in comparison to what she has already accomplished.

"The way to right wrongs is to turn the light of truth upon them," Wells wrote in 1892. And while she lived, the truth never had quite so bright a beacon.

SIMONS WELTER

Simons Welter leads fly-fishing excursions for Brookings Anglers, out of Cashiers, North Carolina, making her one of the few female guides in the South.

There's a growing number of women in fly fishing, but we're still in the vast minority in the sport. It's just taking a little time for it to really sink in that fishing has absolutely nothing to do with gender. I was a full-time mom and homemaker before this. If at any point in my life [someone] had said, "Someday you're going to be a fly-fishing guide," I'd have laughed. I would've said, "You're crazy."

It's really kind of funny. My dad was a huge bass fisherman. He would take me, and I hated it. I backlashed every reel he put in my hand, so it was just nothing but frustration for both of us. I did not pick up another rod until I was in my late thirties. That's when I got introduced to fly fishing. I picked it up very quickly, and all I could think was, *Man, why haven't I been doing this the whole time?* The first time I ever went and actually had my feet in the river casting, I was just like, *Okay, this is home for me. This is where I belong.*

Back in the seventies, it was still very much a "this is what girls do, this is what boys do" world. I can distinctly remember being at a vacation Bible school as a kid, and they had the boys build and paint wooden trucks and the girls make dolls. And I didn't want to make a doll. I wanted to make a truck. And they wouldn't let me!

I've had several clients who have told me they keep coming back to me because I'm a woman, because I pay attention to detail. Little things. I bring chairs. I bring a mat to stand on so your feet don't get filthy dirty when you're changing your shoes. My mentor Spider Littleton always said that women were much better fly fishermen than men were. Because casting a fly is more about finesse than power, and women just have more finesse.

Fly fishing is so unbelievably therapeutic. When you're standing in a moving river and the sun's shining, and the trees are around you, and the sound of the river—it's just the most wonderful, relaxing, peaceful place on earth. My favorite type of river is a small mountain brook trout stream where it's a very physical day. Where you have to hike in a

ways, and you're on the river, and you're climbing over rocks and you're bushwhacking around waterfalls, and by the time you come out, you're at least bruised in one or two places and bleeding in another and so tired you can barely get back to the car. That's my favorite day of fishing.

DR. VALERIE MONTGOMERY RICE

D r. Valerie Montgomery Rice's childhood in Macon, Georgia, wasn't easy. Domestic violence, racism, and a rare infection that necessitated a months-long hospital stay were just a few of the challenges that could've slowed her down as an inquisitive young girl. Instead, they motivated her. Montgomery Rice is now the first female president and dean of Atlanta's Morehouse School of Medicine—and the first black woman in the United States to be named to lead a freestanding medical school. And throughout her career as a renowned reproductive endocrinologist and the founding director of the Center for Women's Health Research at Nashville's Meharry Medical College, Montgomery Rice has prioritized studying medical issues that disproportionately impact women of color and creating more diverse leadership opportunities.

How did growing up in Macon influence your identity?

I grew up in a single-parent household. My father was abusive. I had osteomyelitis when I was young. I was in the hospital when my mother left my father and my life totally changed. I started riding this bus called the Lucky Duck Bus [after that infection]. That was probably my first lesson in humility, riding with kids who were mentally challenged, and being teased initially on that bus. I worked with those kids, helping them learn to read.

How did you do in school after that?

I graduated as valedictorian in the seventh grade and had a teacher, Ms. Betty Davis, who made me repeat the word *humble* over and over and over again in my speech. And when I didn't get it right, she just made me keep saying it. I said, "Why do you keep making me say this?" And she said, "Because you're going to need some humility as you get older. You just don't know it yet."

Why do you think she said that to you?

I have no idea. Maybe she had aspirations for me that I didn't know about. And she used to make me say, "God grant me the serenity to accept the things I can-not change, courage to change the things I can, and wisdom to know the difference." I just never forgot that.

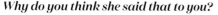

You went to Georgia Tech, but you weren't studying medicine—you were studying engineering. How did you end up switching?

I recognized I didn't like engineering. I always tell people this story about me having on this new outfit, and I had to go into this little plant in the back and check the readings on this machine. I had to put on this bunny suit, and this hat, and go through all the slush. I looked at my reflection and my life flashed before me. I could see myself with this bonnet on and these goggles and I said, "I'm really too cute for this. I'm not doing this for the rest of my life."

There's no premed program [at Georgia Tech]. I went over to Spelman and talked to the premed counselor. I told her I wanted to go to medical school. She said, "You don't seem like you know a lot about going to medical school." And I said, "Well, I didn't know a lot about being an engineer, and that seems to be working out all right." And the rest is history.

You've talked about what it was like to be in these spaces as the only black person or the only woman, and the importance of diversifying the medical field.

It started when I was in high school. If you look at my high school yearbooks, I was the only black person for many, many years in the honors program. I never looked at it as an honor, though. Some people get confused—they begin to think they're special because they're the only one of something. I think it's a problem when I'm the only one.

Have you ever felt like you were obligated to look at medical conditions that disproportionately affect minorities because there aren't many other women or people of color in the room to do it?

I think there's always some level of obligation. It does matter what you do when you sit in the seat. If not you, then who? I always tell my team we are the ones that we have been waiting for. There is nobody else. If there's a problem to be solved, then who else is going to solve it? I think that sometimes, though, we set about trying to solve the problem without being inclusive enough, and we assume that solving the problem is only working on it ourselves and not being inclusive of other people.

When you reflect on your relationship with the South, how do you feel about it?

I am a Southerner by nature. I don't think I've ever forgotten that. I love the gentility. I love when I'm getting ready to take my suitcase down and someone asks me if I need help. I don't mind people opening doors for me. I am comfortable with people saying "yes, ma'am" and "thank you" and "can I help you?" I don't have any problem with that. In fact, I prefer it, okay? I've lived up North. I've lived in the Midwest. I've lived lots of different places. I am a Southern person at heart. I believe in kindness.

MARY McLEOD BETHUNE

The leader who used education to empower

BY JESSICA B. HARRIS

When Beyoncé gifted scholarships to four historically black colleges and universities in 2018, she also honored the legacy of a woman born in 1875 in Mayesville, South Carolina, the daughter of former slaves: Mary McLeod Bethune, for whom one of the schools, Bethune-Cookman University, is named.

As an observant young girl, Bethune had noticed that the ability to read and write was a fundamental difference between blacks and whites. As she recalled it, "The whole world opened to me when I learned to read." She became the only child in her family to attend school and pursued her education with a vengeance, continuing through college hoping to become a missionary. Told that there was no need for black missionaries, she changed her focus to teaching and eventually did social work and taught in mission schools throughout the South.

Her teaching career flourished, and she realized that educating young black women and girls could benefit the population at large. In 1904, she rented a house in Daytona Beach, Florida, and with little more than an idea and a wellspring of grit, opened a school furnished with castoffs and discards. Initially, there were five students and a rigorous curriculum; within a year, there were thirty students. Bethune had found her vocation. She transformed herself into a tireless fund-raiser, garnering money for her school from a list of notable benefactors, including John D. Rockefeller.

As she became active in fund-raising, she moved into a more public arena. Her role as a champion for the rights of African Americans and women grew, and she was named president of the National Association of Colored Women in 1924. She was appointed to a number of national committees under presidents Coolidge and Hoover and by the 1930s had become a member of the inner circle of Franklin and Eleanor Roosevelt.

The school she founded blossomed along with her career; in 1923, it merged with a neighboring boys' school, and she became president of what would become Bethune-Cookman College—making her one of the few female college presidents in the country at the time. Indefatigable and relentless, Bethune was also a community activist and a women's rights advocate before the terms were invented. She founded the National Council of Negro Women in 1935 as an umbrella group for the numerous black women's organizations working to secure basic civil rights for African Americans. She also became a special adviser to the Roosevelt administration (many referred to her as the unofficial leader of Roosevelt's "Black Cabinet") and the director of the Division of Negro Affairs of the National Youth Administration; lobbied for African American women to be able to join the military; and was the only black woman present at the founding of the United Nations, among other honors.

By the time she died in 1955, Bethune had carved a path that remains unduplicated. Her words "World peace and brotherhood are based on a common understanding of the contributions and cultures of all races and creeds" resonate as much today as they did when she wrote them in 1939. A statue depicting Bethune with two children in Washington, D.C.'s Lincoln Park celebrates her life and legacy. The inscription on the pedestal simply says, "Let her works praise her." May we all have an epitaph as true.

Queen Quet
My Homeland

Queen Quet is the elected Chieftess of the Gullah/Geechee Nation, a body formed in 2000 to protect and promote the culture of the Gullah Geechee people—the descendants of enslaved Africans and indigenous Americans along the sea islands of North Carolina, South Carolina, Georgia, and Florida.

"De wata bring we and de wata gwine tek we bak. Disya chillun ain unstan and caan see. We da de land and de land da we."

More oft than not, I find myself telling people, "The land is our family and the waterways are our bloodline." As I look out at the waves hitting the shoreline of St. Helena Island, from which Gullah Geechee ancestral roots sprang from Sea Island soil, I look back to the Motherland whence my people came. Yes, "de wata bring we."

The sounds of the waves are perfectly synchronized with the polyrhythms that we shout in the bush arbors and brush arbors and in the praise houses and churches on the land of the sea islands that stretch along the coast from Jacksonville, North Carolina, to Jacksonville, Florida, where most of the Gullah/Geechee Nation still reside. We shout because our ancestors endured the chains of enslavement that cut into their skin and caused their literal blood to spill into this soil. We shout because the cotton that was king and the rice that was queen—often picked in our sweetgrass baskets tied with indigo-blue bows—no longer reign. We thank GOD that we do! Yes, de Gullah Geechee still dey pun de land!

As I go out into the fields to plant tomatoes, okra, peanuts, watermelons, sweet potatoes, and more each year, I can hear those rhythms reach me there on one-hundred-degree Sea Island days, and I keep pushing on as my ancestors did with the earth pulsating under my every step. At the end of the day or the end of the row, I stop at the hand pump that my grandfather drove into the ground and pump out water until the mason jar sweats from the coolness. I sit down there beneath the oak tree with its Spanish moss beard and I hear my ancestors continuing to speak the ancient wisdom: *Hold pun de land. Hold pun de culcha.* When I rise, I go forth to do what a good Southern girl raised with manners does—listen to my elders!

MADELINE JORDAN

Nothing seems to faze Madeline Jordan. Not hurtling across a field on her mare to sail over a downed live oak on her family's Tallahassee, Florida, farm. Not waiting at the show-ring gate to perform against the top young riders in America. And not recalling her accident, when an impaired driver struck her while she was trick-or-treating in 2015. That night, she broke her femur and suffered a traumatic brain injury. Doctors told her parents she might never ride again. But the determined Maddie, as she's known, was back on her pony in less than six months. A little more than a year later, the teenager clinched a first-place finish in the national pony finals.

Your horse's name is Tribecca. But you call her something else.

When we got her, they were calling her Becca, and I didn't think it fit her. So one day at breakfast, I was like, "You know what would be a really cute name for a horse? Bacon. Because everybody loves bacon."

You got Bacon after the accident. What happened that night?

My friend had invited me to a small neighborhood off one of these beautiful canopy roads. My friend's parents had a hayride, but none of us were in it because we were out trying to get candy. I went to cross the street, and then I don't remember anything after that, until I was lying on the ground. My parents were right there. But it was a blur. In the ambulance with my mom and dad, it was obvious my leg was—well, it wasn't a compound fracture, but the bone—it was obvious it was broken.

What was the recovery like?

I did a lot of physical therapy. My pony, Ben, helped me too. My parents would bring him up to the porch so I could pet him. I was in a wheelchair and then a walker and then crutches. Once I got stronger, my physical therapist had me doing bear crawls and lunges, and then things like one-legged squats while throwing a ball—it was insane.

So who decided when you could ride?

We had a doctor's appointment with my surgeon, and my mom told him she didn't know about letting me ride. Another surgeon had said he'd never clear me to ride. But the doctor said, "Don't Bubble Wrap her. You let her ride before—why would she stop now? I mean, she has titanium in her leg—she's not going to break it."

What was that first time back like?

I was really excited. We went to a show just planning to watch Ben. But then we decided I could get on. I started by walking, and then trotting, and cantering. My leg was a lot weaker than it had been, but it didn't hurt. I didn't feel like I was riding as best as I could, but I was trying. Then I ended up getting fourth place out of twenty ponies. I was like, *What in the world? Well, this is awesome. I'm going to have to do this more.*

Did the accident change your attitude?

Before the accident, I always wanted to win, and if I didn't win, I felt defeated. But now I know how quickly something can be taken away from you, and so now I can just go out there and not even get a ribbon, and I'm fine. But when we win, it's amazing.

Are you ever scared of falling off?

Not really. I've fallen off of Bacon once or twice. My old pony, Louie, I would fall off of him like every day. When Bacon bucks, it's nothing. When Louie bucked, it was like I was in a bull-riding competition.

Which women inspire you?

My mom, because she's really determined and she works really hard. She tells me every day: Whatever you do, do what you love. She was like, *You could be the booger-eating champion of the world and I'd still support you.* And I was like, *Okay. I don't want to be that, but whatever.*

What advice would you give someone going through a challenge like you did?

Just try to be optimistic and enjoy knowing what your life was before and what it will be after. I just had to grasp the fact that you can't control things. Yes, if I would have been two minutes late walking across the road, none of this would have happened. But if this wouldn't have happened, I probably wouldn't have gotten Louie, and if I hadn't gotten Louie, I wouldn't have won pony finals, and if I hadn't won pony finals, I wouldn't have gotten Bacon.

MADAM C.J. WALKER

(1867–1919)

A beauty mogul whose influence went beyond skin deep

Surely you are not going to shut the door in my face," Madam C.J. Walker shouted to Booker T. Washington, who was standing at the podium of the 1912 National Negro Business League Convention in Chicago. "I am a woman who came from the cotton fields of the South. I was promoted from there to the washtub. Then I was promoted to the cook kitchen. And from there I promoted myself into the business of manufacturing hair goods and preparations. . . . I have built my own factory on my own ground."

Walker had asked Washington to include her on the agenda for the conference. After all, she was a successful entrepreneur—she would one day be considered the first female self-made millionaire and one of the first black millionaires. When her request was ignored, she seized the opportunity to tell her truth. She was indeed heard that day. The following year, Washington invited her back to the conference as a keynote speaker.

From the day she was born in 1867, Sarah Breedlove was different. Her parents and five older siblings had been enslaved on a plantation outside Delta, Louisiana, but she was born free. Her life would be extraordinary, but the journey would not be easy. Orphaned by the age of seven. Married at fourteen and widowed at twenty with a daughter, A'Lelia. Determined to provide for her child, Breedlove left Vicksburg, Mississippi, where she had moved with her husband, and joined her four brothers in St. Louis.

At the time, many African American women suffered from hair loss due to scalp disease, as a lack of indoor plumbing and electricity affected hygiene practices. In the 1890s, Breedlove's own hair started falling out. She began to pray, and to experiment with remedies. Her prayers were answered in a dream in which she said a large black man told her a formula that would help regrow her hair. This miracle tonic—a healing scalp conditioner—did more than that. It grew an empire.

Breedlove took her savings of $1.50 and her daughter to Denver. There, she married Charles Joseph

Walker, whose name she took to brand her line of hair and beauty products for underserved African Americans, and she became Madam C. J. Walker. The business expanded, and after a few years of traveling and selling across the South, Walker relocated the company's headquarters to Indianapolis and opened a factory to manufacture her products.

Walker's business not only celebrated black women but empowered them—she employed them as sales agents, stylists in her hair parlors, and behind the scenes in the running of her company. She pioneered a system of multilevel marketing that rewarded her employees with a competitive salary. Her daughter helped expand the company into Harlem, New York, the cultural home for the Harlem Renaissance.

When she died in 1919 at her thirty-four-room Italianate mansion in Irvington in New York's Westchester County, Walker was lauded as an entrepreneur, a philanthropist, and a champion for African Americans. But her influence didn't end with her death. In 2016, Sephora stores began carrying a hair-care product line honoring her, and two years later, Netflix green-lit a series based on her life, inspired by a detailed biography of Walker, *On Her Own Ground*, written by her great-great-granddaughter, A'Lelia Bundles.

DARLA MOORE

Even sitting still, Darla Moore exudes an energy that makes it easy to imagine the Lake City, South Carolina–raised businesswoman commanding a boardroom of Wall Street bigwigs. Moore's success in the eighties and nineties, when she specialized in what were essentially bankruptcy takeovers, led to a $2.3 billion net worth and the cover of *Fortune* magazine, the first woman to land there. These days, the focus of Moore's razor-sharp smarts is less on making money than on giving it away. Among other donations, she's granted more than $75 million to the University of South Carolina School of Business and $10 million to Clemson University's College of Education. But it's Moore's transformative efforts in Lake City—a faded tobacco boomtown—that bring her the most joy.

What was it like growing up in Lake City?

I spent most of my time with my grandparents on their farm. Tobacco was the great cash crop and produced what prosperity there was for a long, long time. I loved it—being on a working farm. The activity of it. My poor grandmother's good silver. I would take spoons out and dig mud holes. It was the happiest place of my life—the most comforting, peaceful place.

After graduating from the University of South Carolina, you left—first for Washington, D.C., then for New York.

I had a strong urge to leave from a very early age, primarily out of curiosity and innate drive. What I always knew, and had a sixth sense about, was that my life would be different. You know, at eight years old, I could never have defined what that meant, but I knew it was going to be different.

How did you end up in banking and investing?

Everything I have ever done has been in steps—gradual. I think it is a mistake to try to plan too much. If somebody asks, "What are you doing in five years?" and you have an answer, I think there's a good chance you aren't going to get there. If you pick one thing, then you've neglected all other opportunities. I tended to make decisions based on where I could achieve the most personal and professional independence. That was the driver.

That couldn't have been easy on Wall Street in the 1980s.

It was challenging, as you might imagine. While I was never sexually harassed, I was certainly sexually discriminated against. A lot of areas in finance were off-limits to me just because I was a woman.

So you struck out on your own, financing companies going through bankruptcy. You turned heads by booting powerful businessmen out of their companies.

The only reason it was interesting was because I was a female. When you've got a CEO putting shareholder value at risk and potentially damaging the company—a guy would have been in there elbowing all over the place. I only did the same thing.

The 1997 Fortune cover called you "The Toughest Babe in Business." How would you describe yourself back then?

Disciplined. Direct. Not a lot of gamesmanship. Just deliver what you say.

In 2012, you became one of the first women, along with fellow Southerner Condoleezza Rice, admitted to Augusta National.

I was shocked. When they came and presented the idea, I put my hands over my face and thought, *My God, my life is going to be the answer to a trivia question.* It is an extraordinary honor. Augusta has this aura that is otherworldly. You know, grown men . . . I'll take them

there—successful, accomplished, confident men—and they become like Twizzlers. Just overwhelmed. The most joyful thing about being a member of Augusta is the ability to share it.

You moved part-time to Lake City, opening Moore Farms Botanical Garden on your grandparents' land and starting ArtFields, an annual art competition that gives away upwards of $120,000. What brought you home?

Love of this place. Lake City was one of the country's largest tobacco markets—all that is gone now. There was no reason for anyone to come to town. Today the botanical garden is part of the new economic engine, along with ArtFields. There was a guy here working for us, and he said, "There's an art competition a family does in Grand Rapids, Michigan, called ArtPrize." This was one of those periods in life when you're too dumb to know any better. Nobody in town knew anything about art. But the success is based on authenticity. The town puts on ArtFields, I don't. If people want to see art, they've got to go in every shop—the barbershop, the gift shop, the mattress store. For the businesses, the nine days of ArtFields is their Christmas.

How did giving money away become your full-time gig?
I did well in banking and finance. Married my husband, and we went on to invest and do very well. Then you get to a point where you have enough—where you say, "You know, I really want to give it away now." It's the hardest work you will ever do. The check writing is not the end. You've got to follow through and be attentive. You develop pretty strong opinions about things. Where your interest lies. Where you can have the most impact. What's the most gratifying.

And what is the most gratifying part?
Seeing the lives affected. Individual lives.

MICHELLE DORRANCE

A native of Chapel Hill, North Carolina, the MacArthur "genius" grant-winning choreographer and dancer Michelle Dorrance has been credited with revolutionizing the art of tap.

Improvising is the closest thing I do to meditation. I have to respond honestly to what's happening in the music, and in the moment. If I do that honestly, I'm in the realm of the purest form of improvisation.

My mentor, Gene Medler in North Carolina, tells a story about the first time I auditioned for his company, at about seven years old. He always gives dancers the opportunity to do a little something extra at the end of their auditions. Some people might sing or do a flashy step. He said I took the opportunity to improvise. It was something that felt natural, and something that he encouraged me to keep doing. Improvising is at the root of tap dance.

My newest work is focused on brain function and our nerve fibers. The more you do something, the better you become. There is a lot of abstract character development that is part of everything we practice. Our behaviors, whether good or bad, form patterns and become pathways we fire on. I think that relates to a lot in the world right now. When there is tremendous darkness and negativity, you sense that in all directions. Our behaviors are practiced in the ways we move. You have a choice if you want to be a destructive force in the world or a productive one.

SIMONE BILES

(1997–PRESENT)

A superstar gymnast and world-class role model

In Spring, Texas, on the outskirts of Houston, an early 2000s home video shows a little girl flipping through her family's living room. Backflip, walkover, handspring, split. "That was ugly," her little sister's voice says from behind the camera.

"I don't care." The child on-screen smiles.

Now no one considers Simone Biles's gymnastics ugly. By twenty-one years old, the four-foot-eight Biles had claimed the title of the most decorated American gymnast in history and was deemed one of the world's greatest athletes. She first became a household name during the 2016 Rio Olympics, at which she won gold medals in vault, floor exercise, individual all-around, and team all-around. In 2018, she became the only woman to win the all-around title at the U.S. Gymnastics Championship five times, and at the World Championship four times. She's accumulated world medals in every event and has two signature flips—one used in floor routines and one on vault—so difficult they've been dubbed "the Biles."

Her life's view hasn't always been from the top of the award podium, though. Biles was born on March 14, 1997, in Columbus, Ohio. Throughout her early years, her father was not present and her mother was in and out of jail, struggling with drug and alcohol addiction. Child Protective Services placed her and her siblings in the foster system when she was three, and in 2000, she and her younger sister, Adria, became Texans when they went to live with their maternal grandparents, Ron and Nellie Biles, in Spring. When Biles was six, the couple legally adopted them.

Six was a formative age for Biles. That same year, she took a field trip to a local gym. She became so entranced by the gymnasts that she began imitating their moves on the sidelines. The coaches noticed and sent her home with a note asking Ron and Nellie to let her join. After that, there was no stopping her.

Due to her prowess and her perpetual positivity, many have come to regard Biles as the leader of American gymnastics. When Larry Nassar, a former USA Gymnastics team doctor, made headlines in 2017 for molesting hundreds of young female gymnasts, Biles came out as one of the survivors, championing her friends and teammates.

"I have promised myself that my story will be much greater than this and I promise all of you that I will never give up," she wrote to her legion of fans on Twitter. "We need to make sure something like this never happens again." She then took to wearing teal, the color of sexual assault survivors, and uses her position of power to demand accountability in the administration of the sport.

Her indomitable spirit knows no bounds. In 2018, just twenty-four hours before the World Championships in Qatar, Biles was hospitalized for kidney stones. Not only did she compete the next day, but she secured gold for herself and her team, claiming a spot in the 2020 Olympics in Tokyo.

LAURA BUSH

The former First Lady with Texas grit

BY JULIA REED

Her Secret Service name was Tempo, and much has been made of her own remarkably measured one. "She's got a reassuring calm to her," then governor George W. Bush told me during his first run for the presidency. "As a man who goes a hundred miles an hour, I find that very attractive." So attractive that when he was introduced to Laura Welch by mutual friends at a backyard barbecue in Midland, Texas, it was, he said, "love at first sight." After dating only three months, on the day after her thirty-first birthday, they were married.

Typically, she downplays the instant fireworks: "We were both thirty and really ready to get married." There was also the not unimportant fact that she could hold her own with the formidable Bush clan. When she was introduced to her new beau's notoriously imperious paternal grandmother, Dorothy, the matriarch gave her a long look and asked her what it was, exactly, that she did. The self-possessed schoolteacher didn't miss a beat: "I read and I smoke."

Her mother, daughter Jenna's namesake, said she was born "a happy little kiddo," and her almost Zen-like ability to be content in whatever situation she finds herself in seems to have stuck. Says lifelong friend Regan Gammon, "When George decided to run, Laura's approach was 'Yes, it's stressful, but this is the task at hand and I'll get it done.'"

She got it done with such enormous grace that her approval ratings were higher than those of any First Lady in modern times other than, briefly, her own mother-in-law. But the affection she enjoyed was little solace for the vicious attacks on her husband during his second term. During one of her many post-Katrina trips to the Gulf Coast, she asked a small handful of friends to join her for what she hoped would be a relaxing dinner at Galatoire's, in New Orleans. At first, the restaurant's patrons were courteous, asking for autographs or a quick snap. But once those barriers were broken down, a stream of diners—all male, as it happens—stopped by to offer up such appalling sentiments as "I hope they do to your husband what they did to the prisoners at Abu Ghraib" and "I want you to know that I hate your husband, but I really like you."

The latter elicited an ironic "And that's supposed to make me feel good?"—but not until the speaker was well out of earshot. The rest of the time, she managed not just to be in the moment, but to be funny and charming and generous enough to put her mortified tablemates at ease.

The evening is a perfect example of what her son-in-law, Henry Hager, means when he says, "She carries a charming confidence. In this totally quiet way, she goes about including everybody and looking out for everybody." When she asked Hager's family to spend Thanksgiving in Crawford, Texas, for example, she immediately went into high gear, outfitting one of the cabins so that it would be wheelchair accessible for Hager's father.

When I visited her at the ranch just after the main house had been completed, she was planning an Easter lunch of ham, cheese grits, and asparagus, and making baskets for the family. Her husband brags on her "fabulous taste" as well as her lack of ostentation, and the house, he says, is the clear reflection of both.

Made of the usually discarded rough end cuts of limestone, it is utterly chic and seems to rise up organically from the landscape. It is also entirely eco-friendly. Rainwater falls off the tin roof into gravel troughs that channel it into a cistern for irrigation, and a geothermal system heats and cools the house.

While her inner Al Gore is not something the former First Lady would ever trade on, she has a remarkable ability to break the mold, while still filling it perfectly. Jenna and Barbara were in the first grade when she took them to a stop on Paul Simon's *Graceland* tour; their care packages at camp consisted of Bob Dylan tapes. At the ranch, they plundered their mom's collection of Jimmy Cliff and Bob Marley—on *The Oprah Winfrey Show*, Jenna "outed" her mom as a "secret Rastafarian."

"Everybody always describes her as 'so gracious' and 'a class act,'" Hager says. "She is those things, but I'd put it a little differently: She's real."

In Her Own Words

ELIZABETH LANIER FENNELL

In addition to organizing events for the women's sporting group she founded—Girls Really Into Shooting (GRITS), which has more than a dozen chapters across the country—Elizabeth Lanier Fennell co-owns Fennell Shooting School in Sharon, South Carolina.

I was married previously, and I gave my then husband shooting lessons. I went with him to the first one and the instructor said, "Oh, why don't you give this a try?" I pulled the trigger, and I broke a few clays, and I really liked it. I liked it so well, I went in and took the rest of the lessons that I'd given my ex-husband. I just found it very therapeutic. It was something I got to do for me. And when you're raising three small children, you don't have very many of those moments.

We got asked to go hunting in Argentina, and I thought, *Well, I'm not gonna stay behind.* So I went with sixteen men, and I shot there for a couple of days, and I couldn't hit anything. The bird boys were all making fun of me. I thought, *Well, shoot. I'm just gonna sit down and drink beer. Forget this shooting birds thing.*

Two years later, I went to the Homestead [in Virginia] for a weekend and I decided to shoot skeet targets. David Judah, who runs the Homestead gun club, watched me shoot and he said, "Liz, do me a favor and shut your left eye." And the clay just exploded. I was left eye dominant, so I had been

shooting the gun wrong from the beginning.

I did it on and off, and then we got invited to go to Scotland on a driven shoot. I was totally addicted at that moment. I loved the scenery, I loved the dogs, I loved the clothes, and I mostly loved the gun going "bang."

I'd been everything—I'd been the room mother, I'd been the team mom, I'd been president of the Parent-Teacher Organization, I'd chaired the auctions. And I thought, *You know, it's okay to have a little time for me.* So I invited a couple of women who had been on this trip to Scotland to go shoot a clay course with me, and that was the evolution of the GRITS. We got a few more women, and a few more women. One was a lawyer at the largest law firm in Richmond. Another lady sailed and raced boats. We had a schoolteacher. There just weren't lots of women out doing this—not actively seeking it out like a garden club or book club or tennis club.

I went through a pretty brutal divorce. That's what was happening to me at the point in my life where I decided to launch GRITS nationally. I was trying to support my kids by

teaching shooting lessons. My mother would say to me, "You know, you could always go back to being an interior designer." That's what my degree was in. To my mother, this was a gentleman's sport—not what your fifty-year-old daughter made her living doing.

I don't allow score keeping. I went to a competition in Rhode Island, and this woman came up to me, and she goes, "You need to make the GRITS competitive. It's not fun unless it's competitive." I said, "Well, think of how you could mentor women in this sport. But we need a comfortable place to enter." And if you keep score, there's intimidation.

I've seen so many women who are afraid—afraid of their own shadow. My best friend—her father would not let her drive a golf cart. He wouldn't let her do anything. She came to me for shooting lessons, and became my helper, every lesson I ever gave. She would drive the Gator, she'd drive the tractor. She went everywhere with me, shooting guns. It was amazing to see the transformation. It's empowering. It gives us a sense of independence, and a can-do attitude.

MINNIE LOU BRADLEY

Some little girls want dolls or pretty clothes. Minnie Lou Bradley wanted a book on livestock judging—so she cleaned chicken roosts till she'd earned enough money to buy it. By nine years old, she was showing lambs; at thirteen, she got her first Angus cow. Bradley eventually became the first woman to major in animal husbandry at Oklahoma State University (then Oklahoma A&M) and, later, the first female president of the American Angus Association and a National Cowgirl Hall of Fame inductee. With help from her father-in-law, Bradley, and her husband, Bill, she started the Bradley 3 Ranch in the Texas Panhandle in 1955, where, even in her eighties, she still lends a hand.

When did you decide you wanted to work in animal husbandry?

All I can tell you is that I think you're born with some of it. I had an uncle who was still in high school and was in Future Farmers of America. These boys would go out to one farm or the other to look at the projects, and my uncle took me with him. We moved to the country when I was about nine. I read where they had a junior livestock show in Oklahoma City, and my granddad said, "Here's a thousand head of lamb. You pick out the ten you want, and we'll go to this show." I won with that count of ten, and the race was on.

Whom did you look up to?

When you look back, you really appreciate a lot of people that you didn't at that time. My first animal science class, I walked up to the professor, who I knew was the coach for the judging team, and I said, "Sir, I'm going to be on your judging team."

When it came time—I knew I should go to Denver [for a judging contest, where students are scored on their ability to evaluate and rank groups of livestock]. But my name wasn't on the list. My heart was broken. The coach called me into his office and he said, "You know you deserve to go—but we've all talked about it, and they're not used to any girls." I was hurt. Two weeks later, he called me in and said, "We can't find anything in the books that says you can travel with six young men and a coach. But we don't see anything that says you *can't*."

So you went to the next contest, in Fort Worth?

We got out to the show grounds and here came the head of the department—and he was one of those who would scare the bediddling out of you. He said, "You are the first girl to ever represent Oklahoma A&M on the judging team. You will be the last if you don't come through today." I did okay, and from then on, he was my friend. I had a couple of really great days at the right places. We came out of Chicago and I felt pretty good—and of course, that's the biggie.

That was when, at twenty years old, you won the International Intercollegiate Livestock Judging Contest?

Oh, my kingdom—it made headlines everywhere. It was a great experience. It is what has bounced me into the rest of my life.

What is the biggest challenge you've faced?

I guess you're getting around to the fact I went into a man's world. But I just never gave it a thought. I would earn my way in. When I asked them, "If I am good enough, can I be a part of this?"—they were all men, and every one of them said, "If you're good enough." And that's the way it's been.

What advice would you give to a woman starting her career in ranching?

You have to have a passion for work. Be honest with everybody, including yourself. Integrity is the most important thing, and if you lose that, you've lost everything. I was raised to believe there wasn't anything greater than people trusting you.

What's your favorite part of the life you've built?

I always said I'll never have a very big ranch. I just want it to be the best, as far as improving the grass, the environment, the water, the wildlife, and have the best cattle running on it we possibly can. That was my dream. I'll never realize that dream, because I keep reaching out for more.

I sit out on my front porch and I can see for twenty miles in either direction—can't see a human being. Just wildlife and cattle. I get to thinking, *How can there be strife in the world when it's so quiet and peaceful out here?*

EUNEIKA ROGERS-SIPP

The Stone Mountain, Georgia, multidisciplinary designer and activist Euneika Rogers-Sipp has founded organizations that center on sustainability and agriculture in the South's Black Belt region, including Destination Design School, a professional design, arts education, and consulting firm that specializes in planning for rural communities, landscapes, heritage areas, and historic properties.

When I think about growing up in Reidsville, North Carolina, it's of the juxtaposition between my mother and my grandmother. My grandmother was very traditional and old-fashioned, and very much a homebody—all I know about living off the land came from her. My mother was the opposite; she was a rolling stone. Very eccentric. Very bright. The head of her class. She wanted the world.

Particularly with African American families and migration, their relationships to the land were formed by economic opportunities and the sociopolitical conditions. My grandmother was born in 1906, in the more rural Caswell County, and that's where my mother was born. They moved toward the city where the textile mills were, for more opportunity. But my mother had a real desire, fire even, to go beyond that. Being of the next generation, I missed my opportunity to be a laborer to that degree on the land. I remember playing, and having an incredible sense of freedom compared with those who had gone before me.

I've had to—out of respect for those women in my family, and for the African American journey, here in the South especially—help put ourselves in the places that did not want us. That were not ours, and to try to make them ours. That started

in fashion school. I realized early on that there were no places for the workers—the people who worked in factories and the people who actually sewed the clothing. They were being excised out of the equation. That was a wake-up call for me, because that was why my mother didn't want to stay in a place like Reidsville and work at a factory. That was where I first felt like I had enough knowledge of a system, and the power of a system, to be able to shift it because I was informed.

As soon as we begin to ask a question, become informed, that's where our opportunity is to change it. It's very specific to the Southern experience, the way in which people have to navigate the landscape as a result of our history. And for me as an African American, it absolutely means access to markets, accessing the skills and intellectual capital that I'm blessed with, and to be able to utilize that so that I can create long-term sustainability for my family.

That's what all families want. We're fighting to not be pushed off of our land that we are stewarding and that we inherited since emancipation. We are fighting some unfair battles, environmentally, because our communities have been totally disregarded. That's why this whole solar irrigation project in Alabama I worked on with my project Sustainable Rural Regenerative Enterprises for Families was really important, because the conversation those families were having was *we really would like to do things better*. That was an opening for me to be able to introduce new technology.

We have things we need to repair and restore—righting the wrongs of the land, through restoring the soil [that's been overworked]. And the management of our waterways and our soil, particularly around the Mississippi Delta. Regardless of whether you think climate change is real or not, the way in which we as a species are able to manage our climate—that we're falling short on.

I've always wanted to be led by the community, but now I'm much more confident in my own projects—*I know this, there's evidence that shows this, and I want to show it. So join me.* I will always be a community organizer, but I want to focus more on the organizing aspect as an artistic practice. Where I can show more of my creativity so people can see that, instead of it getting buried in the pile of papers.

So I am working with a lot of my artist friends, collaborating with them around some deep questions around our historical relationship to soil. Some of it is theater based. Some of it is film. But it's all design. And we're also looking through the literature of W. E. B. Du Bois and his travels during his Reconstruction research, and the conversations he was having with families on the land—reimagining those today, remixing them. And visiting those places again. It's important for us to have a knowledge of how things got to be, how they've evolved over time, in order to kind of understand our evolution and how we might evolve.

FANNIE LOU HAMER

An undaunted voice for civil rights

BY BRONWEN DICKEY

I n 1962, there were many things Fannie Lou Hamer did not have. A seventh-grade education, for one. As the youngest of twenty siblings born to share-croppers, she had picked cotton for white plantation owners in the Mississippi Delta since she was six years old. The backbreaking work of that job kept her out of the classroom after sixth grade, and the debt her bosses claimed her family owed kept her from leaving the plantation altogether.

Running water and adequate health care were two other basic ne-cessities Hamer's family lacked. In fact, she walked with a permanent limp from either childhood polio or a bad fall early in life, though the exact cause was hard to determine since her parents couldn't afford proper medical treatment for either case.

As Hamer passed her forty-fourth birthday, she and her hus-band, "Pap," also did not have any children of their own. In 1961, a white doctor removed Hamer's uterus without her consent when she only asked him to re-move a small tumor. Forced sterilization was yet an-other barbaric cruelty that poor black women in the Jim Crow South often felt powerless to stop.

But, despite everything that she had been denied, Fannie Lou Hamer did have one source of immense personal strength. She had a voice: a deep, booming, almost tenor-range voice strengthened over decades of singing in the cotton fields and in church. It was un-trained and unpolished, even a little husky, but every time she tipped her head back and belted out one of her favorite spirituals, she channeled the power and pain of every sharecropper in the Delta. Her friend Harry

Belafonte once said that the only other person who commanded that level of soul was Mahalia Jackson.

Hamer learned to use that voice in an entirely new way one fateful August night in 1962, when a neighbor urged her to attend a church meeting hosted by some hopeful, hardworking college kids from a new group called the Student Nonviolent Coordinating Commit-tee who were traveling across the South registering African Americans to vote.

At first, Hamer wasn't inter-ested. *Voter registration? For blacks? In Sunflower County, Missis-sippi?* Were these children *insane*? Folks like her had been murdered for less, much less. Sometimes they were murdered for no reason at all.

After thinking it over, though, Hamer decided to join the meet-ing. She was, as she would famously testify alongside Malcolm X two years later, "sick and tired of being sick and tired." The more she worked and gave and ac-commodated the inhumane demands of segregation, the more was taken away from her. She was done living like that.

Once committed, Hamer then began a long, difficult journey of community organizing and political leader-ship that would inspire generations of like-minded civil rights activists around the world. Those who thought they could write off an unassuming middle-aged woman had never heard the way Hamer could both enthrall and comfort a crowd. She didn't prepare her speeches, because she didn't need to. She was powered by an extraordinary and undaunted love for humanity, and her example drove others forward in an often perilous battle for justice.

Hamer never backed down. Not after she and Pap were evicted from their home because she refused to take her name off the county's voter rolls. Not after a storm of bullets tore through the room she slept in. Not after she was arrested in Winona, Mississippi, following an incident with her fellow activists at the bus depot's lunch counter, then beaten so badly while in jail that she could barely walk. And certainly not after President Lyndon B. Johnson grew nervous enough about her testimony during the 1964 Democratic National Convention, where she spoke as a cofounder of Mississippi's Freedom Democratic Party, that he gave his own speech in order to turn attention away from her. So compelling was Hamer's story, told with tears in her eyes and sweat on her face, that networks played it on a loop all weekend anyway. The microphone in front of her might as well have been the flaming sword of an avenging angel.

By the time of her death at age fifty-nine from breast cancer, Fannie Lou Hamer had made her way from the fields of Ruleville, Mississippi, into the pantheon of America's greatest leaders. She was a heart, a spine, a conscience, and a compass.

But more than anything, she was a voice. Whether shouting her message on the courthouse steps or singing it from a jail cell, she forced the world to listen. The sound of freedom could not be silenced.

VICKI SMITH

Vicki Smith holds the distinction of being the "world's oldest mermaid" at Weeki Wachee Springs, one of Old Florida's most beloved roadside attractions.

I was born in Tampa in 1939, and raised in Brooksville, Florida, just east of Weeki Wachee. Back then you got married or went off to school or you became a Weeki Wachee mermaid—that was about the only industry there was around here. I swam my first show on July 7, 1957, and I was only in training about a month. Today they go through extensive training, six months to a year, and I am so respectful of these women today. Back then there were no strong codes—they pretty much just kicked me in the water and as soon as I learned to breathe off the air hose, they put me in a show. We did not swim to music, and no one could talk to us—if there was a gator in the spring or a snake nearby, they could motion to us and we knew to get out.

I started raising my family, and moved to Knoxville, Tennessee, for twenty-seven years, but whether you've been a mermaid for only six months or for thirty years, whenever you leave you want to come back just one more time, to get on that air hose and sink beneath the surface of that beautiful spring water. There's a freedom in that water. There's a group of us called the legends— we're all over sixty—who had dreams of coming back. The legends came together in 1997 at

the fiftieth anniversary of Weeki Wachee's opening, and we've been swimming together ever since.

I might not have the stamina I had when I was a teenager. But I can still dance, eat a banana, and drink a pop underwater. Once a mermaid, always a mermaid.

MELINDA GATES

(1964–PRESENT)

The philanthropist improving women's lives around the globe

Melinda Gates—one of the most powerful and philanthropic people in the world, thanks to a fortune she helped build at Microsoft—can trace her path of success directly back to an Apple III computer. Her father, an aerospace engineer at NASA, brought the machine to their Dallas home when she was sixteen, and encouraged the budding computer scientist's obsession with the then-nascent discipline.

Growing up, Gates, born Melinda French in 1964, was the type of girl, as her sister has said, who "always knew what she wanted," whether it was becoming valedictorian of the Ursuline Academy of Dallas, or graduating from Duke University with two degrees (including one in computer science) and an MBA in five years. But she also proved to have vision, and an appetite for risk: In 1987, after turning down a postgraduate job at IBM, Gates took a chance on a product manager role at a smaller, lesser known company that had just gone public: Microsoft Corporation. A pre-Encarta, pre-Publisher, pre-Expedia Microsoft.

That same year, she met the CEO of the company, Bill Gates, at a work event in New York City, and they began dating. The couple eventually married in 1994—fellow Texan Willie Nelson played the rehearsal dinner—and Melinda left her job as general manager of information products to have and raise their three children. In 2000, though, Melinda began a new chapter of important work, as the cofounder and cochair of the Bill & Melinda Gates Foundation.

Under Melinda's supervision—she steered it virtually by herself the first handful of years—the foundation's philanthropy has improved millions of lives in ways great and small. She has contributed billions of dollars to address health, sanitation, and poverty issues around the globe, including the eradication of malaria and polio in developing countries, as well as to education initiatives and scholarships in the United States. In the name of reproductive health, Gates even set aside her Roman Catholic beliefs to promote female contraception. In 2016, she turned her attention to the lack of women in technology, vowing to address the problem.

She has garnered just about every honor and honorary doctorate to be had in the process, including the Presidential Medal of Freedom, the Most Excellent Order of the British Empire, the Legion of Honour, and *Time*'s Person of the Year, along with Bill and their frequent collaborator, the musician Bono. In the end, she hopes to be remembered on a much more intimate scale, too: "On the day I die," she once told *Fortune*, "I want people to think that I was a great mom and a great family member and a great friend."

DANICA ROEM

Virginia delegate Danica Roem often jokes that she talks too much, but she swears she comes by it honestly: Her late father's family was originally from New Jersey, and her mother's hailed from the Bronx. In 2017, when the thirty-three-year-old former journalist and lifelong Manassas resident bested an incumbent for the right to represent the state's 13th District, the world sat up and listened. Her opponent had occupied his seat for more than twenty-five years, and Roem had no previous experience in politics. She was, however, deeply informed about the issues that most affected the daily lives of her neighbors, as well as a tough, passionate civil rights advocate for the LGBTQ community—now she is the only openly transgender official to serve in a U.S. state legislature. "You should be who you are," she likes to say, quoting Saint Francis de Sales, "and be that well."

How did growing up in the South shape who you are?

Making sure that we're protecting the environment for the next generation is extremely important to me, both politically and in terms of how I personally feel about Prince William County, and Virginia as a whole. The South is inherently gorgeous. I hate seeing our wilderness get destroyed as we rapidly expand our development.

At the same time, I had no political role models who were LGBTQ when I was growing up in Prince William County. It was extremely popular to stigmatize LGBTQ people in my community, instead of welcoming and celebrating them. The version of the South that I'm working to help create is a more inclusive Commonwealth of Virginia, a more inclusive region, for the South as a whole, and a more inclusive America.

Who were your childhood heroes?

Publicly, it was very easy when your gender expression is male and you're too scared to come out to anyone to just fall [back on] sports. I looked up to a lot of baseball players. I was a Los Angeles Dodgers fan.

What about privately?

Seeing how affirming and embracing of LGBTQ people Gwen Stefani was, I had a lot of respect for her. Arch Enemy [who had a female lead singer] had the power, the speed, the absolute aggression I loved in heavy metal. Then I got into Lacuna Coil, and their vocalist Cristina Scabbia is by far the woman in heavy metal who has inspired so much of my life.

You've said that your grandfather's love for his daily newspaper motivated you to become a journalist.

He told me once, "The basis of my knowledge comes from reading the newspaper every day." So I would read the newspaper every day.

What are some of the most useful lessons you learned as a reporter?

Number one is the phrase "Tell me a story." The great commonality that human beings share is that we are storytellers and we are story sharers.

What does "courage" mean to you?

I think of a line from George R. R. Martin that I'll paraphrase: You can't be brave unless you're scared. I've been scared my whole life. I've been scared since I was running to my next-door neighbor's house as the fire engines were approaching my house, when my dad killed himself. I've been dealing with fear, and dealing with intense fear, prior to my transition, and through my entire transition. I've done it in journalism, driving down to watch Paul Powell get electrocuted in the electric chair, which is another one of our Southern traditions. I was nervous as all hell, because I knew I was on my way to watch a human being die.

What scares you most at this point in your life?

Apathy. If people get so nihilistic about their government that they tune out, then the only voices left are the last ones you want.

How do you want to be remembered?

Number one, I'd like to be remembered by my family for being a good stepmom, and being a good girlfriend, and being a decent human being. Number two, I'd like to be remembered publicly as someone who took care of her constituents, and was herself while she was doing that. I have never shied away from who I am. I've been very public and very forward about who I am.

ARTISTS
& ARTISANS

MAYA FREELON

Maya Freelon's artwork is alive, constantly making and unmaking itself depending on the light—no surprise, considering the Durham, North Carolina, native constructs the pieces she is known for out of tissue paper. An amalgamation of collage and sculpture, they allow joy and urgency to exist side by side and are steeped in the philosophies of the African diaspora. She often meditates on the concept of ubuntu, a shortened version of a Zulu proverb that means "I am because we are" or "my humanity is tied to yours." Freelon's message of collective strength has resonated around the world, with exhibitions and permanent installations in places such as the Smithsonian, Ghana, Rome, Paris, and Jamaica.

You encountered your medium of choice by accident.

The tissue paper idea came from my grandmother's elementary class. I lived with her during graduate school, and one day I went into the basement and discovered this paper—it was water damaged, and the droplets pushed the color outward. When I saw it, I said, "Oh my God. That looks so amazing. How do I reproduce it?" It's so funny—the more you try to mimic an accident, the harder the goal is to achieve. It just takes that organic nature out of it. That's how you know you have a gift—when you can't replicate it, because that moment has come and gone.

Your relationship with your grandmother seems like it is central to your sense of self, and your work.

Her name was Queen Mother Frances Pierce, and she passed in 2011, when I was twenty-eight and she was eighty-two. She was born in 1928. I was born in 1982. When she died, it was like she passed the mantle—an eclipse happened, and I started turning into her. She had such a presence, and she showed me how to take nothing and make something.

My grandmother would have been an artist, if she could have. She didn't have the means, resources, or support. For her to see me do it gave her so much joy. I feel like I would be doing a disservice if I did not heed the call to action. She constantly said, "You see my hands? You see how they look? You see the scars? I did this for you, so do something."

She was giving me life advice and showed me how to move in the world and not to take no for an answer. The most important thing she taught me was to have faith and confidence in what you're doing. All of these lessons are constantly going through my head, and I'm passing them on to my children. They helped me form my mantras as an artist, my ways of moving as a business woman.

Your heritage means a lot to you.

We were a family of sharecroppers that never got their fair share. Everything was a history lesson. Everything was "remember where you came from." It was always "be proud of yourself—do you know we're the ones that refuse to die?" I owe my ancestors an enormous amount of gratitude. I pay homage to them because they didn't have that.

We come from a long line of first-born daughters that goes back at least five generations. There's this honor and also responsibility to this first-born daughter, the idea that you're teaching the ones behind you. That you're bearing fruit for the next generation.

That contrasts with your artwork—because you use tissue paper, there's a temporal nature to what you do. How do you come to terms with your work continuing to evolve, even after you considered it finished?

My artwork can be a little volatile. I really do mean on that verge of destruction. When I make spinning tissue ink monoprints, I work on a pottery wheel and get a lot of movement and motion. It's complicated because it's wet, spinning, hard to manipulate, and a lot of times the paper flies off and gets destroyed. There's strength in the process, and power in this relationship with the paper and water. I've always embraced this contradiction

that we become obsessed with preserving things the exact same way, but we're all aging, we're all changing, and we're all in a state of flux. I appreciate that this art reminds us that it has a natural evolution, too.

You lived in Baltimore for a while. What led you back to Durham?

I remember the smell of tobacco here in the streets when I was little—it's a very weird, sweet smell. I became nostalgic for the North Carolina State Fair. There's roasted corn and you get to play games and you leave with dusty shoes. I missed the smells of being outside and really feeling the shift of seasons. I missed that Southern charm, the food, feeling like people missed you, even though they didn't know you were gone. I really like being able to bike ride with my brothers and saying, "y'all." I love feeling like this is where I learned how to treat human beings.

On the other side of the coin, how do you deal with the complicated history of this place?

Well, I go to the rallies, I'm right there. We're still hot, the South. It's very backward and weird, but there's this sweetness here. You can walk by a Confederate flag and that person might even hold the door for you. I understand that everything isn't harmonious, but I find faith in the times that we can come together. Around here I've found those times usually happen around the water, like Jordan Lake or Falls Lake. Regardless of race, to be there you strip yourself of everything, and you're all coming to this water, this space that renews. You put your feet in there and you stop, because you're in collaboration with the earth at that point. Whatever the problem is has been grounded, and it flows away from you.

CLEMENTINE HUNTER

(1886–1988)

The prolific painter whose folk art celebrated everday life in Louisiana

In a story Clementine Hunter once related to friends, her husband called to her from bed: "Woman, if you don't stop painting and get some sleep, you'll go crazy." "No," the self-taught artist replied. "If I don't get this painting out of my head, I'll sure go crazy." Beginning in her fifties, Hunter was moved to paint at all hours and on all surfaces—bottles, gourds, cardboard boxes, window shades, and jugs all went under her paintbrush, and she eventually created more than five thousand pieces. Until her death in 1988, Hunter painted her way into becoming one of the most recognizable folk artists in the world.

Born two decades after the end of slavery, in 1886, Hunter never traveled more than a hundred miles from Melrose Plantation in Louisiana's Natchitoches Parish, where she and her family picked cotton and harvested pecans. In her life, she attended only ten days of school. Using tubes of paint left by artists who had visited Melrose, Hunter was already a grandmother when she began painting the patchwork moments of community that sustained lives in the early and mid-1900s. In saturated colors and with confident, bold shapes, she conveyed scenes she knew from her life: a riverside baptism; friends hanging clothes on a line; church meetings, weddings, and funerals; and the simple beauties of the rural Cane River region, such as an overflowing bowl of garden-gathered zinnia flowers.

At first hesitant to sell her work, she hung a sign outside her small house near Melrose: CLEMENTINE HUNTER ARTIST 25¢ TO LOOK. She sold pieces for a few dollars or gave them away to friends. After François Mignon, the curator at Melrose, and his friend the writer and naturalist James Register became early collectors and patrons, they also helped publicize her work, submitting pieces to art shows and seeking out press coverage.

Hunter showed her work in Oklahoma and Texas, and then in 1955, two prominent Louisiana galleries hosted solo shows: The Delgado Museum of Art (now the New Orleans Museum of Art) gave her its first solo show by a black artist, and Northwestern State College (now University) in Natchitoches also celebrated its native daughter. This was nine years before the Civil Rights Act, and Hunter had never been allowed to view her work in a gallery alongside white art patrons. So a friend, college faculty member Ora Williams, took her to the gallery on a Sunday and unlocked the door. For the first time ever, Clementine Hunter turned and turned among her painted worlds. "She would throw her head back, laugh, and say, 'Where did you get that one . . . I don't remember that one,'" Williams once recalled. "Gradually, it all came back to her." Thirty years later and two years before her death, that same college awarded Hunter an honorary doctor of fine arts degree.

AMANDA MATTHEWS

A Lexington, Kentucky–based sculptor and painter, and the CEO of Prometheus Foundry, Amanda Matthews also founded the Artemis Initiative, a nonprofit that funds and creates public sculptures honoring women and minorities such as Alice Dunnigan, the first African American female journalist accredited to cover the White House.

I'm not sure I ever actually decided I wanted to go into foundry work. My initial college degree was in studio painting. Sculpture was born out of my need to have more depth in my paintings. Once I started sculpting, I thought, *Wow, where have you been all my life? I feel at home*—all the things that people say when they know they've found their calling.

I didn't realize how male dominated this field was. When I became an owner of the foundry, I just thought, *This is a business.* I didn't realize I'd be, as my father says, "as rare as hen's teeth" in this industry. I have had some wonderful things happen because it is such a rarity, and I have had some things that have been troublesome happen. I am the one involved in writing our proposals for large projects. Once, I reached out to contractors and actually had men tell me they absolutely will not work with a woman-owned company.

When I was researching for a project for a conceptual sculpture, I came across an article in the *Courier Journal*, a paper in Louisville, that contained a statement to the effect of: There are no women honored with statuary on any public land in the entire state of Kentucky other than Carolina, which is Colonel John Breckinridge Castleman's horse. It wasn't even a woman—it was a horse! And I just thought, with our company and what we do as sculptors, *we* can change this. That's really when I set out to make sure there was a sculpture in the Kentucky State Capitol honoring a woman.

My life is about honoring other women. I want my work to create a dialogue, and even if that is a difficult dialogue, I still want it to be one that unites and elevates the conversation and our understanding. It pushes you beyond where you might be comfortable in the hopes that people will at least give thought to the fact that we all have a shared history.

I have two daughters who are sixteen and nineteen. A lot of my reasons for wanting to change the dialogue and honor these women is to give people like my daughters the opportunity to have these icons and symbols. I have been inspired not only by these women that came before me but by my daughters, for whom I want to leave a better world.

WILLIE ANNE WRIGHT

Whether it's a shot of young ladies sunbathing languidly by a pool or pregnant women with fecund bellies sitting beside overripened melons, nearly all of the images captured by the Richmond photographer Willie Anne Wright are encircled by a dark area that creates what she calls "the pinhole magic." Wright, who is also a painter, pioneered color-Cibachrome-pinhole photography in the 1970s, and today her lensless photographs and paintings are in collections ranging from the George Eastman Museum to the High Museum of Art. Time and again, she has interrogated Southern history and narrative by focusing on the people and places surrounding her—even in her nineties, she still wields her camera.

You didn't decide to attend art school at what is now Virginia Commonwealth University until your thirties, following your family's return to Richmond after years away for your husband's job. That was quite a leap for a mother of three in the early 1960s.

I had never done what I really wanted to do with myself. I had taken art classes everywhere we lived. I wanted to see what I could do as an artist, remembering I had been an art star at William & Mary. I took night classes at first, and then I went to see the head of the department, and he said, "If you come back to school, why don't you try for a master's?" This was just the beginning of women going back to school. I think they were looking me over to see if they thought I was really true and if I was going to work out. I was determined. I went there feeling that I had a chance to prove myself.

Was there anyone there who influenced you?

Theresa Pollak, who started the art school in 1928. She came into my life when I really needed somebody who had dedicated themselves to their art. I admired her greatly, and she really wanted me to succeed. Theresa was the only woman teacher then. The rest were male teachers, and that was a whole 'nother thing because they weren't too anxious to see ladies coming back to school.

When did you get your first big break?

I joined the Richmond Artists Association, and my work got around the city a little bit. I was fortunate that Dick Cossitt, the art critic for the local paper, liked and wrote frequently about my work. When I painted *One Night at Jimmy's We Saw the Supremes on Color Television*, that was 1966. The Virginia Museum of Fine Arts purchased the painting, and it is currently hanging in the pop art gallery. I had changed my medium to acrylic paint, and it was like a new birth. I rented my own studio. I took it very seriously—I would go and work all day. I would try to get my works in shows, and I did that for eight years.

When did you turn to pinhole photography?

In 1972, we moved to [Richmond's] Fan District, and everything changed because my husband, Jack, who was a photographer, established a darkroom in the basement and gave me a 35-millimeter Canon camera. I had no idea it was going to be meaningful to me particularly. The first thing we did in [photography] class was make a pinhole camera. Nobody wanted to do it because everybody was like me—they wanted to get into using their new cameras! Little did we know, but in college photography classes all over the States, pinhole photography was being introduced. I was part of that new wave. I have never stopped painting, but it became obvious that people responded to my pinhole photographs. It was just like something was on my shoulder, pushing me.

You're well known for your color pinhole photography.

I devised a way to photograph on Cibachrome color material, which was developed for printing color photographs with enlarger light. I thought, *I wonder what would happen if I put Cibachrome in a pinhole camera and exposed directly on it?* I was one of the first ones, but I don't think I'm the only one who did it. But I did an awful lot of it, so my body of work is probably one of the ones that gets noticed because of the amount I did. Now Ilford no longer manufactures Cibachrome. It ended. It had a life.

Many of your photographs feature women—by the pool, at the beach, alongside architectural ruins . . .

Women in or near pools was a good subject because they could be still. I learned what I was doing, how to control it, what would be good subject matter, and what time of the year the sun would be right, because the photographs would take a long time to expose. You couldn't get guys to go in the middle of the day when the sun was right—they just were not available. Women liked to pose and swim in the pools. Once I got into this thing and exhibited the photos, women would either hear about it or I'd hear about them, and often pool owners would ask if I could come to photograph.

How does it feel to be a practicing photographer for almost fifty years?

I don't like to be called a photographer because honestly, I don't think I know a lot about photography. I mean, I know a lot about what I did, but when people ask me technical questions about photography, I often can't answer them.

Do you call yourself an artist?

Yes. It took a long time to say that, too. It's hard now to say it out loud! But I think I've tried to be. I think I tried hard.

MARY MARGARET PETTWAY

One of Boykin, Alabama's storied Gee's Bend quilters, Mary Margaret Pettway is an Alabama Humanities Foundation fellow and an instructor at the Black Belt Treasures Cultural Arts Center, and also serves as board chair of the Souls Grown Deep Foundation, a nonprofit dedicated to preserving and promoting African American artists in the South.

I can tell a person by their stitches. By looking at a quilt, I can tell who did which parts. I have small stitches, like my mom. Our stitches could pass as twin stitches. I'm a fourth-generation Gee's Bend quilter. I started out as a little girl, sitting underneath the quilt and passing the needle back up. I was four or five. The boys had to learn, too. They know how to sew and quilt.

Those first stitches I did were *ugly*. But these were what we call "house quilts" at that point. That means you wouldn't show these quilts, these are ones you would keep right at the mattress. Only time it got shown was when you washed it. All of these were house quilts before Gee's Bend got known. You would put what you thought was a pretty quilt on top of the bed.

But all of them keep us warm.

I'm drawn to pattern. And I love color. The best palette I've seen so far is nature's palette. I love poppy red and kelly green. I love a vibrant blue, too. It all depends on what fabric I've got. The fabric we use is a little of everything. Cotton, scraps from old dresses. *The Beverly Hillbillies* reminds me of how things used to be. Using meat grease from a hog killing to make soap; pulling water from a deep pump. You take what you had to make what you need.

Now, when I see a pretty quilt, I'm going to ask who did it, look at the stitches, ask if I could take a picture. I laugh when I have my quilts hanging on a line and I'll see a person drive their car past, turn around, and drive by again. Then I realize they're taking a picture.

Usually that's fine, but they could just ask, "Do you mind if I take a picture?"

One of my favorite quilts is hanging at the High Museum of Art in Atlanta. You can also see part of it in the new portrait of Michelle Obama. Her skirt is made up of quilts from Gee's Bend. One of them was one my mom kept on her bed. I'm gonna make one just like it, but bigger.

We've always been a quilting community. Somebody in every house is quilting. Or they can do really, really good cooking. Around here, you can either be a quilter or a good cook. To be honest, I can cook enough to keep me and mine, but I hate cooking. I'm a sandwich person. I would rather quilt any day than cook.

LINDA ANDERSON

The memory artist who illuminates Appalachia

BY CANDICE DYER

Linda Anderson no longer drives. She has totaled three cars because her all-consuming visions distract her on the road. "I start seeing pictures in my mind just like photographs—some clear, some not," she says, brushing a curl away from the crescent moon tattooed on her forehead, a tribute to her favorite MoonPies. "A strong feeling comes to me as if I'm right there, even though it may have been fifty years since I've been there."

At that point, she must retreat to her studio in Clarkesville, Georgia, where she enters a trance-like state and renders these tableaux into art.

Anderson is regarded as one of the Southeast's premier folk artists and "memory painters," drawing on her personal experiences of a bygone Appalachia. She relays scenes of women quilting, of home births with a stout-armed midwife, of church congregants speaking in tongues. The crude human figures in her brightly colored landscapes have a kinetic quality; everyone—men, women, children—bustles with a mulish work ethic. To take in her paintings one by one is to be transported over the mountain, into her singular, uncanny Southern gothic imagination.

"Although my paintings show a bucolic peacefulness on the surface, my life was not like that," she says, noting the edgy sense of foreboding that shadows some of her work. A painting titled *Mad Dog* shows an animal foaming at the mouth and treeing a boy in overalls. There are guns aplenty. One oil-on-linen is a graphic representation of a hog slaughter. She creates mixed-media pieces from found objects, too—when her favorite calico cat died, she allowed ants to clean the bones and made jewelry from them.

Anderson is what people mean when they say "salt of the earth." She was born in 1941 in a dirt-floor house to a family of tenant farmers in Clarkesville. They were poor, Pentecostal, and "quare," she says, using mountain slang for "peculiar." Her daddy was a moonshiner, and one of her chores as a child was to climb a tree with a .22 rifle and shoot at any revenuers who came sniffing around. She dropped out of school in the eighth grade.

In 1977, her daughter Betty Jane, or B.J., suffered an aneurysm and required round-the-clock care. "One night I felt such despair," Anderson recalls. "I thought I really can't endure any more of this. That's when I felt a reassuring presence, sort of an apparition that is hard to explain. It told me I would receive a gift."

Anderson had never taken an art class. Nevertheless, at age forty, she began to paint. She sold a piece at a county fair, and it found its way to Judith Alexander, who had established the first folk art gallery in Atlanta. Anderson was "discovered."

Since then, her work has shown in New York City, Chicago, San Francisco, and Rome, Italy. Her one-woman exhibit at the High Museum in Atlanta set an attendance record, drawing more than seven hundred admirers. For that event, Anderson giddily wore a tiara she had made herself.

She and her partner, Susan Shlaer, live in a house for which Anderson built all the cabinets—she's also a certified carpenter. "I never thought I would be the sort of person who would receive a gift like this," she says of her art. "I'm just a human with flaws."

Gogo Ferguson
Her Primitive Jewelry

Janet "Gogo" Ferguson is a jewelry designer with galleries on Cumberland and St. Simons islands in Georgia, as well as Martha's Vineyard. The High Museum of Art in Atlanta exhibited a retrospective of her designs in 2013.

Being inspired by nature's beauty comes naturally to Gogo Ferguson. When she was a girl, she and her grandmother Lucy hiked and rode horseback around Cumberland Island, Georgia, adorning their hair with feathers found on their jaunts. After returning to raise her own daughter on Cumberland in the 1970s, Ferguson—among the fifth of seven generations of the iron-and-steel Carnegie family to live there since her direct ancestor, Thomas, brother of Andrew, bought much of the island in the 1880s—began crafting jewelry created from organic materials like rattlesnake ribs she found on the large sea island.

Ferguson was walking through the Cumberland forest in the early 1980s when three conch shells, along with a ceremonial ear plug, or earring, caught her eye. It's difficult to drill through conch shells, even using modern tools, says Ferguson, yet these pieces had been expertly pierced and strung together to create a necklace. The jewelry—most likely the work of a member of one of the indigenous tribes such as the Timucua, who occupied Cumberland for centuries before the island was colonized by the Spanish, French, and British—resonated. "It's thousands of years later, and I'm incorporating nature into my life, too, and particularly into my jewelry," she says.

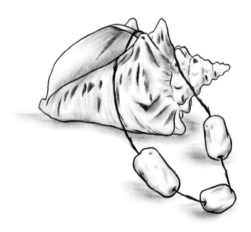

TEMPLE ST. CLAIR

Temple St. Clair's jewelry—gold amulets, owl-shaped lockets, celestial pendants—is as elegant as it is global, influenced by the places the designer has worked over her three-decade career: Florence, Italy, where she founded her company in 1986 and, recently, opened her first boutique on the iconic Ponte Vecchio; Paris, France, where she became the first American woman to be added to the permanent collection of the Louvre's Musée des Arts Décoratifs; Japan and Kenya, where she concentrates her dolphin and lion conservation efforts; New York City, where she lives. Her creativity, though, began during her youth in Virginia's Blue Ridge Mountains. "When you're from the South, you have a very strong foundation," St. Clair says. "Other Southerners I know in New York refer to it as the 'Magnolia Mafia.' There's a connection to this place that you hold, and people recognize it in you."

What was your childhood in Roanoke, Virginia, like?

It was an incredible place to grow up. It's something special to be a Southerner, but on top of that, a Virginian. Its heritage and legacy and its characters like Thomas Jefferson and [George] Washington; the architecture; the nature—so many things [there] have infused my view of the world.

And your jewelry designs?

Absolutely. I think about this all the time. People get very literal about how a design comes to be. But often, it's a blend of our experiences and our life stories that ultimately influences what we produce. I lived in Virginia from [age] zero to fourteen, and then my parents moved to South Carolina, and that's all part of my foundation. I come from a family that wasn't necessarily in creative fields, but they were very creative people and had a deep appreciation for culture, art history, and architecture. At a very early age I visited Monticello, Mount Vernon, and the University of Virginia many times. I lived in and spent time in homes—my own parents', my mother's sisters', and my grandparents'—and there was history running through those houses in terms of how they collected furniture, objects, and art, and what it meant to them. It's more of a sensitivity that was born out of tradition that certainly has its roots in the South.

Many of your collections are inspired by nature, and benefit causes like coral reef preservation, marine mammal advocacy, and lion conservation. How did that interest originate?

I love cultural things—the Renaissance, dance, literature. But I *love* nature. I spent a lot of time climbing trees in my youth, hiking in the Blue Ridge Mountains. And even more so when we moved to South Carolina—getting to know the Lowcountry and the tidal creeks and spending time out on boats watching the dolphins. All of that was really magical for me.

After college and graduate school, you moved to Italy, where your mother inadvertently got you started in the jewelry-design industry.

It was very serendipitous. She was visiting me in Florence and wanted an ancient coin to be set into a piece of jewelry. She left me with this assignment, and it was a natural catalyst. I had just finished graduate school studying Italian Renaissance literature and art history, and these coins held all this great history. My first commercial endeavor, though, actually started in Charleston. My parents had moved to Hilton Head after Roanoke, and then they separately ended up in Savannah and Charleston. My first sales—to my mother's dismay—were off her dining room table in Charleston. I have a nomadic merchant gene in me. I *like* business. I'm very naturally entrepreneurial as well as being a creative.

In that business world, have you found that anything was different for you as a woman than it would've been for a man?

Sure. Always. People just don't realize there are so many strong, incredible women in the world. I've even run into that lately in Italy. The mayor of Rome is a woman. In Florence, one of the top people in local government is a woman. Women are getting into these more influential, powerful positions, but still, even in the Ponte Vecchio right now I'm running into a very patriarchal system. And that's tough. You do have to work extra hard as a woman. I feel that in this country, too.

In 2017 you became the third American and first American woman to be included in the Louvre's Musée des Arts Décoratifs.

That collection and the collection at the Victoria and Albert in London are probably two of the greatest representations of the history of jewelry in the world. To play a little part of that huge arc of human history is amazing.

MARY JACKSON

The MacArthur "genius" grant recipient Mary Jackson has been acclaimed not only for her contemporary sweetgrass basket designs but also for working to reestablish sweetgrass in the South Carolina Lowcountry.

I used to say to my mother, "Take these ugly grasses from the marsh and make something beautiful from them." When I lived in New York, I did not think about baskets. But my mother used to say, "One day you might want to know how to do this, and it's good to know how to do more than one thing." And sure enough, I came back to this. It was like I was supposed to be doing this. When I left work to stay home with [my son], to have something to do, I made baskets. On weekends I went to the market and sold them. That's how it started.

I didn't want to have something somebody else had. I had learned the traditional designs and mastered the traditional technique. I thought, *I know all this*, and I wanted to try something new.

When I came back, the ladies were complaining that they couldn't find grasses. The only answer was to learn how to grow sweetgrass. That was something unheard-of among basket weavers. Lots of people thought we would never do it. But I'm one who was willing to try. I remember my mom always said, "Oh try, try hard. Nothing beat a failure but a try." And we tried it, and it worked.

LAUREN HAYNES

W alk into the Early American Art Galleries at the Crystal Bridges Museum of American Art in Bentonville, Arkansas, and you'll come upon an installation that re-creates the U.S. Constitution preamble's opening words, "We the People," in . . . shoelaces. "Has its meaning changed?" the wall text asks. "How do those words still apply to our society today?" It's an idea that intrigues Lauren Haynes, Crystal Bridges' curator of contemporary art, a native of LaFollette, Tennessee, who was drawn to Arkansas from her decade-long post at Harlem's Studio Museum in large part because of Crystal Bridges' commitment to telling the *whole* American story, not just the part that's typically celebrated in the annals of art history. To be American is to be many things. And to be Southern, Haynes says, is to recognize that we have this "loaded and complex history and present and future."

When people ask you where you're from, do you define yourself as "Southern"?

It definitely makes up a huge part of who I am. But, you know, I would never describe my *mother* as Southern, even though she lives in Atlanta now. She's from New York, her family before that was from Barbuda, so if anything, she's Caribbean to me in certain ways. And then with me . . . It's not clear where I picked up certain things, and where it all just kind of combines.

You're an amalgam.

If someone asks me and I say, *I was born in Tennessee and then we moved to New York*, they immediately think, *Oh, well you're from New York*. And I'm like, *Okay, am I?* It's one of those things where I can't give a quick answer. When people here in Bentonville find out I lived in New York, they're like, *Oh, what's it like? Arkansas must be so strange for you*. But then I tell them I lived in Tennessee the first twelve years and it gives them some context. I'm not a fish out of water. It's different for sure, but for me, it's familiar.

What spurred you to make the leap to Bentonville in 2016?

I was excited about this idea of a different audience. I think sometimes when you work in museums that are on the coasts, you're just talking to each other, right? You're talking to other institutions. I knew I needed to be somewhere where that wasn't the case. And I really found it interesting to think about what it meant to do this job in the middle of the country.

And what does it mean?

Where I grew up there wasn't this . . . this *access*. I don't even know where the closest world-class collection would be to LaFollette. Being exposed to art that first time can change your life. Access to the arts helps build empathy, and it helps you better understand other people and other cultures. That's something that can't be underestimated. Especially now.

How are you hoping to be a part of that process?

I think a lot about the me that was an eight-year-old growing up in Tennessee. How can I make Young Lauren feel like, *Oh, what's a museum? Is this a place for me?* Not to say that everyone needs to be a curator, or everyone needs to want to work in a museum when they grow up. But I want them to know it's an option.

Even in Arkansas.

Yes! People here have such a sense of ownership around this place, it's fascinating. When I got here, even my Uber and Lyft drivers—because I couldn't drive!—would go on and on about how the museum being here had set off this series of changes in terms of culture and growth and everything else that's going on. That's not to say everyone loves everything we do—especially as it relates to contemporary art. When I arrived, people were like, *We're so glad you're here—now you can explain contemporary art to us!*

You're also exposing them to fresh voices. In the Georgia O'Keeffe exhibition you curated, The Beyond, you pulled in work from twenty new artists—many of them women and people of color—whom she inspired.

We're trying to really be more open and not just think, *Oh, if we put this work up by this well-known white artist, we've done our job.* Have we? Or could we think a little deeper and put that work in conversation with a work of art by a lesser known artist of color or a female artist? Sometimes that means more work, or putting up works that people might not understand. But it's really saying, there's more to this story. Because there's not just *one* story. There's not just one way to be an artist, one way to make art. And if we can show our visitors that, I feel like that's what it means to think about inclusion.

What other Southern artists do you admire?

I don't know if I so much think about where people are from when I think about their work. With a lot of African American artists, we have this really interesting thing about migration, about how people sort of move around, and so we have artists who were born in the South but then spent their lives elsewhere—artists like Alma Thomas or Jack Whitten or Mel Edwards. For me, and for a lot of artists of a certain generation, the South made a huge imprint on the early part of their lives because that's where they grew up. And at that time, it was a really difficult place to be black and to try to live and exist. So just thinking about the impact a place can have, even years after you lived there—that intrigues me.

SALLY MANN

A lens that reflects the South

BY ALLISON GLOCK

Sally Mann's photography is a study in mourning. Every image—be it of her three children, Emmett, Jessie, and Virginia; of her beloved Lexington, Virginia, farm; of opaque Southern landscapes; of her husband's body as it bends and bows to progressive muscular dystrophy—conjures loss. Loss of the present, of innocence, of certainty, of this sweet, thorny life.

Mann is keenly aware (as most Southerners are) of the fleetingness of all things and the folly of trying to hold onto them. Which is why (as most Southerners do) she thumbs her nose at that reality and endeavors to capture and collect as many moments as she can.

"It shouldn't come as such a big surprise to me that I'm suddenly old, but it has, and I'm getting a little panicked about it," she told an interviewer in 2017. "If I want to deal with what's left of my photographic life, I'm going to have to get on it."

A prolific artist for more than forty years, Mann, now in her late sixties, has wasted nary a second. Born in Lexington in 1951, she grew up "benignly neglected" in the Shenandoah Valley, describing herself as "a feral child," often naked, dirty, running wild with her dogs and horses. Even then she gravitated to the elegiac in the ordinary. Her father, Robert, a doctor, did not coddle his three children. Death was something to reconcile, respect. The inevitable ruin of living things became both a spur and a beacon to Mann.

By age sixteen, she'd begun taking pictures, studying photography in high school at the Putney School in Vermont, then later at Bennington College, where she met Larry Mann and married him, at the age of eighteen. It was while raising her three children with Larry

in the 1980s that Mann honed her approach, training her lens on her family, a practical necessity with three young ones under ten.

The resulting photos—dreamy, unsettling, intimate to the point of discomfort—made Mann a sensation. Her subsequent book, *Immediate Family*, showcased sixty-five of those black-and-white shots, featuring her children as feral and naked as Mann had been in her Appalachian youth. Its 1992 publication catapulted her into mainstream success and controversy, as some of the photos were deemed exploitative by critics. In 2001, *Time* named Mann "America's Best Photographer." She has since been the subject of two documentaries and published a dozen photography books, as well as a 2015 memoir, *Hold Still*, in which she describes herself as, among other things, "some ungodly cross between a hummingbird and a bulldozer."

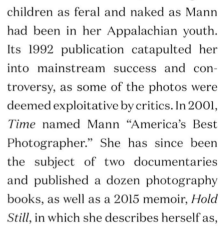

Through it all, the South has held Mann captive. She has never moved from her farm, nor from her focus on the region—its people, its stained legacy, its rites, its rigors. She muses often and candidly about how photographs displace and destabilize memory, even hers.

"I don't remember the things that other people remember from their childhood," she told the *New York Times*. "Sometimes I think the only memories I have are those that I've created around photographs of me as a child. Maybe I'm creating my own life."

As she does, she is also creating ours. Introducing images, showing us ways to see, prying open hidden worlds, alerting us to what we take for granted. Her vision shared, then blossoming in our hearts and minds, blinding us with light before the inevitable dark.

AMANDA CROWE

(1928–2004)

The carver who revived the art among the Cherokee

"With little more than a pocketknife, a block of wood and a few basic instructions, you can be on your way," Amanda Crowe, the legendary Cherokee carver, assured young women in a 1966 article for the Girl Scouts' national magazine, adding, "If your brother has a good, sharp pocketknife, he may be willing to lend it to you. But you'll probably want to invest in your own."

Inspiring students to carve was Crowe's proudest achievement, her relatives recalled after her 2004 death. Crowe, who was born in 1928, herself started carving at the age of four; former classmates later remembered being scared of her because she carried a knife to school. When she moved to Chicago in the early 1940s to finish high school, she'd already been selling animal sculptures for half her life.

"I knew what I wanted to do, so I just whittled away," she said once.

Although she went on to study at the Art Institute of Chicago and Instituto Allende in San Miguel, Mexico, Crowe felt she belonged back in Western North Carolina. In 1953, she set up a studio in the Qualla Boundary's Painttown community there and started teaching carving at Cherokee High School, where she remained for forty years.

Prior to Crowe's return, wood carving was considered a minor craft by the Eastern Band of Cherokee. But once she showed students how they could pry money and pride from blocks of cherrywood, carving became a cultural touchstone for the community. She and partner Doris Coulter produced poplar-and-knife sets for aspiring carvers for decades.

Museums, including the High Museum in Atlanta, the Mint Museum in Charlotte, and the Smithsonian Institution, exhibited Crowe's geese, rabbits, and deer. It was the bears, though, that defined Crowe's body of work; she joked that "everybody in the country" owned at least one. As a sportswoman, Crowe had seen her share of bears. But the versions she created behaved in different ways than the black bears that lumbered through the Great Smokies: Looking content and partly human, Crowe's bears ran, reached, danced, and cheered. Friends thought they conveyed the joy Crowe felt when she had a carving knife and wood in hand.

"I carve," Crowe said, "because I love to do it."

NATALIE CHANIN

From her hometown of Florence, Alabama, Natalie Chanin has brought Southern handicrafts into the twenty-first century through Alabama Chanin, a sustainable, organic cotton clothing line that has expanded since she moved back in 2001—after years working in the fashion industry, in New York and abroad—into a series of instructional books, the School of Making, a flagship store and café, and a machine-made design and manufacturing division.

My grandmothers were very accomplished makers, as a lot of women were, living in rural areas at that time. I grew up believing anything could be made. My father's mother, she had three girls. She made everything from underwear to prom dresses. My mother's mother also had three girls and was a very accomplished seamstress, and good at knitting and crocheting as well.

I remember my father's mother taking me to the fabric store very early on and letting me pick up fabric and buttons for the dress she was going to make me. She empowered me at a very young age to make those decisions. So sewing seemed like the most normal thing to do in the world. It didn't seem fancy or special somehow. Of course, looking back, it was very special.

I knew that making made me very happy. But in the era I was growing up, this idea of design was something that seemed ethereal. The idea of textiles being a career— I'm not sure I fully understood it, even though I loved fashion magazines. Then I found out about the school of design at North Carolina State University. It was the first time where I really thought, *Oh, that's a place I could study.*

When I left the South, a kind of shame about our history is something I always carried with me. When I got out into the world, I realized that that kind of hate can exist anywhere. We own our part of it, but we are not the only region in the world that has experienced that deep hatred in the very recent past. It took years of coming to terms with my own beliefs, and figuring out what I could do to change this history that's attached to me.

I thought I was just coming back South for a few months. I didn't anticipate I was coming back forever. The initial impetus was to find these women who had quilting skills who could work with me to make garments. Almost twenty years later, I'm still here.

Textiles in America traditionally have been women's work. The building we're in was an old sewing plant, and it was part of this empire called Tee Jays, the largest of the T-shirt manufacturing companies here in this community, which was known as the T-shirt capital of the world. I was asking the man who still owns the building and had this giant organization, what percentage of the organization was women? And he said, 100 percent of the sewers were women, 80 percent of management were

women, and then 50 percent of the administrative side were women. So there is a deep legacy for women working in this industry, in this region. Sometimes I get credit for having started this woman-run business. But we're just building on ideas and talent that were already here. I'm proud we're carrying that on.

My daughter is a crafter. She has a different idea about cooking than I do, and she has a different idea about sewing than I do. I think a good analogy is that my father's mother was an avid gardener and just grew the most beautiful flowers. I never understood all of that, but as I've gotten older, I love gardening and horticulture. It's something that brings me great pleasure, and it's a way that I relax. That's something my grandmother instilled in me, but it didn't catch up to me until I was in my forties and started having this sense that I needed to put my hands in some dirt. I think there are lessons that we learn like that. We may not adopt them straight away, but they travel with us. And I would imagine that my son, my daughter, and my granddaughter—making will continue to travel with them.

DOROTHY SHAIN

Dorothy Shain has fashioned a career for herself any young artist would covet. The Greenville, South Carolina, native infuses her paintings with a vibrancy inspired by her travels—collages that echo the jungles of Vietnam; an oil of a street dog she encountered in Guatemala; mixed-media bikinis painted with Lowcountry herons. That soul-stirring sense of place has landed her exhibitions and artistic collaborations across the country, including with Anthropologie for a swimwear line based on her series of bikini paintings. Even the actor and writer Mindy Kaling has commissioned a piece.

When did you first feel a creative spark?

My mom always dabbled in painting. When I was little, she had a studio in our garage. She could tell I was interested, so I took art classes, and loved it. In high school, I started to get more serious. I had a teacher, Susanne Abrams, really push me. At the time, we butted heads—we did not get along.

What was the problem?

She recognized if I worked hard, I could excel. That hadn't hit me yet. I was struggling with friendship stuff—high school girls can be mean. I wasn't doing well in school. Then one day, I took her advice, and just poured myself into art, and everything else got better. Probably because it's so therapeutic. I landed in a different, positive group of friends. My grades started turning around; I was applying myself, and seeing results, which helped my confidence.

So you decided to pursue art at Southern Methodist University, in Dallas.

I had this college counselor who was like, "You're probably not going to get in where you want to, because you haven't done well till now." That was the first instance

of someone really fueling my fire. So I was like, *Screw that!* I applied everywhere she told me I couldn't get into, and I got into every single place.

What was the first year as a full-time artist like?

It was so hard. I had so many side gigs. It took a really long time for things to get to a point where I could pay my rent just from the art. I had a family member come into my studio in the first two weeks, when I was just figuring things out. They said, "Nothing in here will ever sell. You need to get a real job." I had just worked on this tiny little series, and they were like, "I hate to say it, but these are just dumb." The next week, twelve of those little pieces sold.

You've collaborated quite a bit with other artisans. What have you learned?

You need to be choosy about whom you work with. In the beginning, my thought was, *Say yes to everything.* But you want it to be a true reflection of you, too. The person you work with, you want them to understand and value your work; and they want *you* to value theirs. You need to know what you're both bringing to the table, from an art perspective and a business perspective.

Your parents played into your move back to Greenville, right?

My dad—he and his dad had an auto-parts store in Greenville for a long time, then my dad went into finance. He has the coolest approach to business. Everyone he works with becomes a friend—he knows their birthdays, he knows their children are graduating, he goes to their grandmothers' funerals. He taught me the value of relationships. He used to say, "Never think of a meeting as a meeting. Think of it as sitting down to catch up with someone. Because the people you work with, you want to genuinely know about them, and you want them to be interested in you, too."

You call your mother your "momanger" because she helps you make business plans, and a "powerful Southern woman."

She's the epitome of that. Her dad passed away when she was little, and her mother raised her—my mom saw how hard she worked. When she married my dad, she came to eat dinner with his family one night. His mom had cooked this beautiful meal. Afterward, Dad and Granddad left the table to watch football. Mom was like, *What?* She washed dishes for hours. She was like, "That night, I slam-dunked his ass. I told him I wouldn't have any more of that." To this day, my dad is at the sink at night washing everyone's dishes.

You believe in networking as an artist—the Mindy Kaling commission happened after you chatted up her assistant at a dinner.

I was probably one too many margaritas in. I was like, "If she ever needs art, let me know!" Three months later, [the assistant] reached out. It was a good lesson to me to always talk to whoever's around you, because you never know. There's a fine line when it comes to self-promotion—but if you want to make a living doing this, who else is going to do it for you?

us was the vehicle through which
we spoke our creative genius, our ho
and our dreams....The sense of belon
and confidence that *us* imparted
upon me remains within
my psyche today and continues
to provide community and acceptan

-Monica Manuel

MARIE T. COCHRAN

Marie T. Cochran is a mixed-media artist, writer, and curator in Toccoa, Georgia, whose work has been featured in exhibitions at the Studio Museum in Harlem, Spelman College, the High Museum of Art, and the Georgia Museum of Art. Cochran also founded the Affrilachian Artist Project to seek out and curate the artwork of people of color living in Appalachia, as well as to create a network of those interested in diversity in the region.

When it was time to send me to kindergarten, my parents made the decision for me to integrate our local elementary school [in Stephens County, Georgia]. The first civil rights activity I remember was integrating the Coats & Clark textile mill swimming pool. Segregation was no longer legal, but they still kept the races separated. My mother refused to take the tickets they offered her so that we could use the colored pool. Mom elegantly strolled to the regular pool wearing her sunglasses, and we followed her. Some people left. People started taking their kids out of the pool, holding them on the sidelines. When my brother noticed we were the only children in the pool, he said, "Look, we got the pool all by ourself." After a while, the people who stayed got tired of holding their kids back, and that was the integration—without any protests, without any placards.

My mother is ferocious. She has no fear—none, and she's not easily impressed. My parents were sharecroppers' children. Mom was a feminist before the word was even known. She has no interest in art. Even though she loves me, she gives me grief about making it. Nobody had finished college in my family. I started off at what was then West Georgia College in Carrollton, and we did the whole orientation thing as a family. When my family got ready to leave, my mom realized she didn't have to take out her checkbook. That was when she realized that I could take care of myself.

I was always involved in student activism. I started the first black history program in my high school. When I was an undergrad, I helped found black student organizations. I was the news editor for the newspaper while I was a graduate student at the School of the Art Institute of Chicago. It was more important for me to do those things than my culminating thesis. I knew I could make an impact on the institutions and open up doors that hadn't been open before. That's the gratifying part—the feeling that I wasn't just making pretty pictures about social justice. Art is a tool.

I'm interested in triggering something in the viewer's memory, to get the conversation going.

I didn't learn about black artists in the classroom. My paternal grandmother received calendars from the Atlanta Life Insurance Company, and they used African American art. When the calendar was old, Grandma would give it to me and I would cut those pictures and tape them up all around my room. I went to the library and I looked up black artists in the encyclopedia, and that's how I found out about people like Jacob Lawrence and Romare Bearden.

Malcolm Gladwell uses the term *pollinators*—that's what I am. I know people who should know people. Bringing folks together is like putting these fibers in a collage— it builds. Initially you don't know the infrastructure, and people on the outside only see all the stuff on top, but there's something underneath the polymer, other adhesives and things. It's intoxicating to know the source of the scrap that makes this larger piece of art so beautiful.

SINGERS & SONGWRITERS

QUIANA PARLER

Quiana Parler has been a singer since well before she could drive. She started in church, where her limber, inexhaustible voice quickly led to paying gigs, some during school hours, and while in college she had a brief run on *American Idol*. Now Parler fronts the acclaimed Gullah-influenced band Ranky Tanky, whose music illuminates a culture developed among the enslaved and their descendants long unheralded outside pockets of the Lowcountry. The music she and the Charleston, South Carolina, band create is spiritual, playful, heartbreaking, wise—a celebration, Parler explains, not just of life but also "of death," grief and joy intertwining with the will to keep moving forward even when your feet are mired in mud.

What was your childhood in Harleyville, South Carolina, like?

I've been singing professionally since I was about ten years old. I was in *Annie*, the only little black girl. *American Idol* happened when I was twenty-two. After that, I went on the road. I've never had a full-time job other than singing. My dad was a singer. He was in a funk band and they recorded an album, and my mom and dad would sing at weddings around town, so it's been in me from when I was little. I know nothing else but music.

Was it difficult performing so young?

I missed my prom. I left my own high school graduation party to go to work. I had to get to a show. I missed the senior trip. I missed so many things, but I don't feel like I really missed *out*. Music was a way of life for me, something I've been committed to from childhood.

When did you first realize that your voice would take you places?

I guess my first paycheck. I grew up singing in church. Where I'm from, I'm a country girl. There wasn't a club or a bar—music was in the church, you know? That was my only outlet to hear music. That, and my aunt would order thirty records for a penny, remember that? She would order me a bunch of tapes and I would listen to them over and over. And that's all I knew.

Do you ever hear a song on the radio, or hear someone sing, and feel it reverberate through you?

Well, definitely my parents. I think I sound like my mother when I sing. But also Whitney Houston, the "Greatest Love of All" album. That really changed me. And Sarah Vaughan in the jazz world. Those two artists changed my whole way of thinking about music.

How so?

Whitney was different. The big notes, the big voice—she was so versatile. She didn't sound like you could just put her in one box. She's who I aspired to be. I wanted to have that big sound. And as far as Sarah, her deep rich tone and the way she would interpret a song. My love of jazz came through Sarah Vaughan.

How does it feel to be familiarizing a new generation with Gullah music and culture through Ranky Tanky?

There are so many people who don't have a clue what it is. On the first album we didn't veer too far away from the interpretations of the elders when they did it first. When I approach these songs, I try to stay as honest and pure as possible so it won't be disrespectful to them. All of [the songs] have a special meaning to me because it's from my ancestors and what we went through as slaves. It's about our struggle. The songs take me to a place sometimes that I don't want to go. My job is to perform, but with this band it's been the hardest for me emotionally. You can feel and understand what the elders went through back in the day. I mean, normally, I'm strong when I sing onstage, believe me. But these songs take me somewhere else.

What has kept you in the South?

I want to raise my twelve-year-old son with and around family. I was thinking of moving to L.A. But when I

found out I was having him, everything changed. And it was a blessing. I still have the same friends from school. I love home. I really love my home state. I'm proud of Charleston.

If you could sing only one song for the rest of your life, what would it be?

There's a song we do now called "Freedom," coincidentally, that's powerful, and considering where we are right now in the world, it means a lot. "Break these walls / Break these chains / Trouble won't last always / When only love remains."

What does a successful career look like for you?

It would be nice to get some Grammys on my shelves. But that's about it. Where I'm at professionally is where my dad wanted to be. He gave up his career for his family. I think I'm carrying on the legacy of what he was trying to create. I think that's why I go so hard. I would love to retire and not have to worry about anything and to be known as a legend. There's a difference between being famous and being remembered as a legend.

"My mother says the reward for hard work is hard work. And that's the truth. It's satisfying to finish something and feel like it's the best you can do."

—*Alison Krauss*, bluegrass musician, on why she doesn't keep her record-breaking twenty-seven Grammys in her Nashville home

"I was just singing about what was going on. I guess people just weren't ready for it. 'The Pill' didn't hurt the record. It helped it sell more! The disc jockeys would tell me it wasn't good, but they weren't used to hearing a woman talk like that. Well, they found out with me! I didn't sing anything that was wrong. I just told the truth."

—*Loretta Lynn*, singer-songwriter and Kentucky native, on her controversial songs about topics such as birth control

MAHALIA JACKSON

The singer whose gospel changed the world

BY JESSICA B. HARRIS

Precious Lord, take my hand!"
Those words flowing from the hi-fi signaled that my mother was celebrating her roots as a Baptist minister's daughter. Her quavering soprano sang along. The voice on the record, though, was a contralto—as dense and rich as molten chocolate, vibrating with feeling as Mahalia Jackson belted out the gospel classic written by the Reverend Thomas A. Dorsey. Those early childhood memories were my first introduction to "the Queen of Gospel," but her melodies would mark many moments:

Mahalia was there when I saw my first three-hankie movie, *Imitation of Life*—a 1959 drama that took on race and discrimination—and I'm sure I used a fourth and a fifth at the funeral scene of one of the main characters, Annie, when Mahalia, as a soloist in the church choir, wailed, "Soon we'll be done with the trouble of the world."

Mahalia was there at the March on Washington in 1963, when she roused the crowd at the Lincoln Memorial with the hymn "How I Got Over." Afterward, as Dr. Martin Luther King Jr. addressed the marchers, she exhorted him: "Tell them about the dream, Martin!" Inspired, he launched into his "I Have a Dream" speech—words that defined the hopes and aspirations of my generation.

Mahalia was there at King's funeral, after his assassination in 1968, singing farewell to the man who had been her ally and her comrade in the civil rights movement. Her selection: the same "Precious Lord, Take My Hand" that always so moved my mother.

Mahalia and I shared something else: She was from New Orleans, my adopted hometown—a city better known for its sinners than its saints. She was born there as Mahala Jackson in the Uptown Carrollton neighborhood, and her first musical influences were secular—she listened to and imitated blues shouters Bessie Smith, Ma Rainey, and Mamie Smith—but she began her public career singing in the choir of Mount Moriah Baptist Church. After moving to Chicago during the Great Migration, she toured with one of the early gospel groups.

Her career skyrocketed in 1929, when she met the composer Dorsey, now known as the father of gospel music; he became her mentor, and for fourteen years, she toured with him, interpreting his gospel compositions in ways that cemented them as contemporary classics. Her full-bodied contralto and expressive, joy-filled stage presence made her a crowd favorite. Often encouraged to cross over into secular music, she was adamant about singing only religious pieces. "Blues are the songs of despair," she would say, "but gospel songs are the songs of hope."

Two failed marriages and health problems marked a personal life that did not mirror the fulfillment of her professional career, but she continued, a beacon of rectitude. When she died of a heart attack and complications from diabetes in January 1972, her mentee Aretha Franklin closed her funeral ceremonies singing "Precious Lord, Take My Hand." Mahalia Jackson is buried in Providence Memorial Park in Metairie, a suburb of New Orleans, her home. The woman Harry Belafonte referred to as the "single most powerful black woman in the United States" left behind a legacy of activism and a repertoire of songs that she'd interpreted so gloriously for the world.

GINA CHAVEZ

I t wasn't until Gina Chavez had to belt out "Amazing Grace" in front of her classmates during middle school choir tryouts that it began to dawn on her. "I'd always loved to sing, but that was when I realized, *Oh, I'm relatively good at this*," says the Austin, Texas, native. The bilingual singer-songwriter has since earned numerous accolades and a fervent international following. Chavez, who is of Mexican and Swiss-German descent and writes and sings in both English and Spanish, has served as a cultural ambassador with the U.S. State Department, traveling to communities around the globe to share her Latin folk-pop hits—as well as her messages of inclusion and connection. "We're all so siloed in our own echo chambers that we're not talking to each other anymore," she says. "It's hard to find a way to connect with people who may not see things the way we do, but it's still possible."

How did your work with the State Department come about?

They have a program called American Music Abroad, which presents American music, in all its forms, to communities around the world. We put together a trio out of my six-piece band and got accepted the first year we applied. We went to five countries in a month—Guatemala, Venezuela, Dominican Republic, Mexico, and Argentina. Now we get invites from embassies or other cultural exchange organizations that want us to come play. We went to Uzbekistan and Kazakhstan and it went really well, so then Kurdistan was like, "We'd love to have you." So it was, "Okay! Back to the 'Stans!"

What a wild time to be a cultural ambassador.

I don't know that I've ever considered myself an overly patriotic person, but I definitely have a greater understanding and awe of freedom and what we have in the States. Even being a Latina lesbian in Texas, I have so much more freedom because of the time that I live in, because of everyone who has come before me to fight for the rights that I do have. We truly have a chance to be ourselves.

Your album Lightbeam *was deeply personal in that regard, in that you were open about your relationship with your wife, Jodi Granado.*

It took us a while to get to a point of "Can we talk about this?" and then to writing songs that aren't just amorphous love songs without pronouns in them. Jodi and I have been together for twelve years, and we're still so in love. Sometimes we both look at each other like, *How did I get away with it?* I have a wife! In Texas! How cool is that?

Do you have a favorite lyric you've written?

There's one in my song "Heaven Knows" that says, "Heaven knows our souls, our story / the shape of your heart when you hold me / wouldn't tear us apart or disown me." We don't know who somebody else is called to be, but heaven knows. Part of my faith journey was coming to grips with being in love with a woman. At first, I thought I needed to be "fixed." I was so confused because I was like, *God, this is the most amazing thing I've ever experienced, but it's wrong?* And it took a long time for me to unknow what I thought I knew. That's what that line is about. Heaven knows the kind of love we have for each other, and if you don't get it, that's your conversation with God, not mine.

What does being a Southern woman mean to you?

I'd definitely consider myself a Texan before I would consider myself a Southern woman, but that's just my Texas pride talking. Honestly, when I think about being Southern, I think of all the ways that I don't identify with that word. I think of white women in the Bible Belt with big hair and sweet Southern accents. I see the stereotypes I've swallowed. That's what's so interesting about being a practicing Catholic and a lesbian. Most people look at you like, *How?* It's about realizing that it's possible to be all the things that you are called to be. We're all multidimensional. We don't have to fit in a box, but we try so hard. And we fit other people into boxes, and that's where the stereotypes come in with words like *Southern* and *pride*. There's a part of me that wants to reclaim the word *Southern*.

How would you reclaim it?

The South is so open in a lot of ways. There's open land, open sky, open roads. Why can't it also mean open-minded? Why can't it mean open for everyone? Texas is right on the border with Mexico. How can we not embrace the fact that we're all immigrants? I would love it if "Southern" meant sharing and opportunity for everyone. I do love that so many people equate being Southern with hospitality. Somebody the other day was telling me they had come to Texas and they were weirded out by how nice everyone was. I like that. Let's freak people out because we're so nice.

AMANDA SHIRES

A fiddle player, singer, and songwriter, Amanda Shires got her first taste of life on the road with the Texas Playboys, a Western swing band, when she was fifteen. "I learned the importance of not making excuses—just doing the best you can and learning from your mistakes," she says. Shires evolved into a bandleader herself, touring solo in between raising a daughter, Mercy, with her husband, fellow Nashville musician Jason Isbell; earning a master's in creative writing from Sewanee; recording music; and playing with Maren Morris, Brandi Carlile, and Natalie Hemby in their supergroup, the Highwomen. Her 2018 release, *To the Sunset*, paired poetic observations about fear and hardship with messages of growth and determination.

You're a bandleader, but you played for others for many years. What have both sides taught you?

Starting out as a side-person, I learned a lot about how to work for other people—how to work within different personality types and group dynamics. A lot rides on a leader being generous, both with their time and their respect. In that way, it's just like any other job. It was hardest to transition into being a leader when I found myself with musicians who wouldn't try. I had to learn how to move on from people—even people whom I'd grown close to.

How did you deal with that?

I wasn't conditioned to present issues in the way men are raised to—shortly stating exactly what you want, being direct, and trying not to associate business with another person's feelings. As women, we're raised to be nurturing, and caring. Not that men aren't, but women are conditioned to present ourselves in a certain way.

I see that changing. I try to be conscious and not let my own daughter worry about how she presents basic problems or celebrations. I ask myself, *How would Jason say this to a band?* Or, *How would Billy Joe*

Shaver have told me this? Aside from that, I try to be true to myself and try to be a good human being. Then whatever else happens is really not my fault.

You keep a journal. How did that start?

I've done it since Billy Joe Shaver, whose band I once toured with, thought my songs were worth something. He said, "You should keep writing and move to Nashville and be a songwriter." At first I thought it was a polite way to fire me. I was like, "No, Billy Joe! I love my job. I absolutely *don't* want to do that." Then just a couple of years later, there I am, packing up my U-Haul and driving the sixteen hours from Lubbock, Texas, to Nashville to pursue my dreams of being a waitress.

You are inspired by your mother, too—you wrote about her in a song on To the Sunset.

Having me young, having my sister young—it took her a long time to find the right husband. She's my role model, and she's made the tough decisions to move on and start over. But she wouldn't take away those relationships, because she wouldn't have us. The sun sets on some dark days and some bright days. You can celebrate the losses and the wins. And then, toast to the sunsets we haven't had yet.

What surprised you the most about motherhood when it became your turn?

I was never going to have a child, before Mercy. During the pregnancy and touring, I had a lot of doubts about how I was going to be able to bring somebody into the world and still keep my identity—keep writing, keep playing music. I had doubts about how to even *be* a mom. I had a lot of fear, as a lot of people do with their first child.

Then she was born. I realized all of the clichés are true. It really is life changing. You see things in a different way, because even your own shadow becomes something fascinating. And as far as the work goes, *of course* you can still do your job. You make little mistakes as you go along, but you start figuring stuff out. In the end, you're still a woman in the music business, no matter how you spin it—whether you have kids or not.

What do you mean by that?

The music business is really a patriarchy. There are only a couple of spots available for women to fill, so there's more competition than there needs to be. In country music especially, you have to be sold or presented as somebody who's available—as a person who makes people think, *Oh, that could be my girlfriend. That could be my girl next door.* For me, art isn't competitive. I can see things are changing, and hopefully it will get better. We're not solely objectified—there are exceptions, of course—but that's how the majority of women's music has been sold for a long time.

Rewind to when you first started out: What advice would you give yourself?

Don't expect people to reciprocate all the time, on anything you're giving. Try to be a better listener, because I wasn't a very good listener early on. And always pack a swimsuit—you never know when you're gonna need it. You never know! Could be a creek, could be a Slip 'N Slide.

On Being Southern
BY MARSHALL CHAPMAN

I grew up in the 1950s and 1960s in Spartanburg, South Carolina. So the only Southern women I knew were either society ladies like my mother, all of them white, or the black women who worked for our family and other families like ours. Spartanburg didn't have much of a middle class back then. You either owned the mills or worked in them. Oh, there were doctors, lawyers, store owners, and whatnot, but the main economy of Spartanburg revolved around textile mills.

My family owned Inman Mills, which at one point employed close to two thousand workers. The summer I was seventeen, my father had me work in the mill, after I'd announced I didn't think college was necessary. I imagine he put me there to give me a sneak preview of life on minimum wage. If so, it worked. That fall I enrolled at Vanderbilt University in Nashville.

But that summer I worked in the mill, there was a woman named Grace Stone who had worked there for as long as anyone could remember. Grace was everything my mother disdained. For starters, she dyed her hair blond and smoked cigarettes. I had noticed Grace watching me as I sat at my post at this machine that tested sliver (ropes of cotton) for any defects before it was spun into thread. Since I was the president's daughter, I never left my post. After several days, Grace had seen enough. She introduced herself and invited me for a cigarette break.

"Honey, you're taking this work thing way too serious," she said as she offered me a Marlboro.

Grace could've been forty and she could've been seventy. It was hard to tell. Her face was lined with wrinkles from years working in the mill, but she had an easy laugh, and I loved her smoky, lived-in voice. She worked hard. And she played hard, too. Whenever she got any vacation time, she and her friend Myrtle would take off for Las Vegas, which was Grace's favorite place in the world. My seventeen-year-old brain could only imagine what went on once they got there.

Then there was my mother, who, at six feet tall, was drop-dead gorgeous and smart as a whip. Mother was raised to be a proper Southern lady, but there was so much more to her than that. She loved politics. She was the first woman appointed to the State Election Commission, by Governor Bob McNair, in 1968, and Governor Jim Edwards later appointed her for a second term. In 1979, she became the first woman elected to the South Carolina State Development Board. When Edwards was elected governor in 1974, Mother reluctantly agreed to chair his inaugural ball. A few days before the inauguration, while in Columbia working on the final event details, she was approached by three state law enforcement agents.

"Ah, Mrs. Chapman, we need to discuss something."

"Yes?" said Mama without looking up.

"Ah, ma'am, we need to know if there's an evacuation policy in place in case we have a bomb threat."

Still not looking up, Mama replied, "We're not having a bomb threat."

I always sensed that Mother resented having to play the role of Mrs. James A. Chapman Jr. And to say she was outspoken would be an understatement. When my father was once approached about running for governor, he declined, saying, "I'd have to divorce Martha first." That's because Martha Cloud Chapman could make Martha Mitchell look shy and retiring.

Mother was a mover and shaker who got things

done. Which means she was always on the go. I once told her I had no memory of her from when I was a young child. The only people I remembered were the black women who worked for us, including Cora Jeter, who was my family's cook in Spartanburg. Like Mother, Cora was six feet tall, but whereas Mother was slim and willowy, Cora was built like a linebacker and strong as an ox.

One time, when my parents were out for the evening, my older sister, Mary, caught the kitchen on fire while trying to cook french fries. Cora was upstairs with me and my younger sister and brother. Whenever Cora babysat for us, she'd tell us the wildest stories you ever heard. Like the one about the tree frog that attacked her while she was picking cotton down in Union County. Anyway, when Cora heard Mary's cries and smelled the smoke, she grabbed my younger brother and sister, and, with one under each arm, she somehow managed to lift me up, then carry the three of us down the stairs and out the front door.

Then there was the time my father was awakened in the middle of the night by the ringing of the telephone. It was Cora.

"Mr. Chapman, you better get down here quick. Rob's 'bout to kill me!"

By the time Daddy pulled up in front of Cora's house, it wasn't Cora that was dead. It was Rob. Cora had broken a glass pitcher over his head and worked him over pretty good. There was never a trial, and no mention of this was ever in the newspaper. Daddy took Cora to the white hospital to get her head stitched up and then brought her home to our house, where she fixed and served us breakfast as usual.

Grace Stone, Mama, and Cora Jeter epitomize the Southern women I grew up around. And despite their class and racial differences, they had much in common. They were smarter than most of the men around them. They were strong (just ask Rob), generous of spirit, and fun-loving. They were all great storytellers. And for better or worse, they were larger than life.

Marshall Chapman is a lauded singer-songwriter whose works have been recorded by the likes of Emmylou Harris and Jimmy Buffett.

AMY RAY & EMILY SALIERS

Amy Ray and Emily Saliers met as grade schoolers in Decatur, Georgia, two curious girls searching for meaning and magic through music. In 1985, while in college at Emory University, they formed their band, the Indigo Girls, and proceeded to reinvent and recast Americana folk and rock from a female perspective, with cerebral lyrics and deep, soulful questions that reverberated in the hearts of listeners and made the pair a worldwide phenomenon. Throughout all the success and recognition, Ray and Saliers chose to remain in their home state, raising their own families amid the same magnolias and sticky heat.

How did your friendship form?

Emily Saliers: We both will probably answer this the same way. Amy was a year younger than I was in school and you don't really, like, hang out with the different age groups, ya know? But I was definitely aware that she was the other girl in elementary school who played guitar.

Amy Ray: I remember seeing Emily play, and then when we got into high school, we were both in chorus together, right, Emily?

ES: Yeah, and our families lived relatively close together ...

AR: And then there was a talent show and we decided we would try to do a song together. We got together in the basement of my house and we would learn cover songs and play them in our English classroom for our teacher Mr. Lloyd.

ES: Mr. Lloyd was the catalyst for us learning songs with the goal of performance. We were also writing songs by that point. We really wanted to infiltrate our set list with original material from very, very early on. And then it just became our favorite thing in the world to do. To get together and learn music and play.

Was there a moment when you each realized there was something really special about your collaboration?

ES: When we started to arrange our songs together. Amy had more of a rock style. She had a lower voice and I have a higher voice, and I was more of a picker. So immediately we just covered different ground together. It was much more interesting than us both doing the same thing. It was really satisfying on many levels.

AR: I remember when we first started playing together it was an emotional epiphany for me, like, *This is what I want to be doing.* I sang in the church choir, but I didn't really know how to do anything beyond just my little church parts that my choir director taught me. With Emily, she could pretty much sing harmony to anything. It was like, *Wow, this is a different experience.* I'd been trying to be in these rock bands with different guys in my church and it never seemed to work out.

Why not?

AR: They just were completely inflexible. And I remember I showed up for practice one day and they had fired me. They came to the door and said, "You're not in the band anymore." Because I couldn't sing Led Zeppelin the right way or something. With Emily, she was someone willing to really work with me on what I could do.

ES: Amy and I became really, really close friends at the same time that we were writing songs. We got our fake IDs, started playing at local bars. The goal was always to get the next best gig, whatever that was.

AR: A lot of our style we came upon because I didn't know what I was doing at first. Back then, I couldn't play the same chord fingerings that Emily could because I wasn't as advanced. So I would learn a simpler version. I learned the harmony parts as if they were melodies, and I would do countermelodies because it was easier. We had our handicaps. And that was also a great thing, because I was working with someone who didn't see it as a drawback. It was like, "Oh we'll just work around that."

Do you classify yourselves as Southern musicians?

AR: I do.

ES: We are Southern musicians because we're from the South. I mean, Amy is fourth generation. But I never thought about us as characterized in the way that you might, say, Lynyrd Skynyrd, even though our songs have all kinds of South in them, particularly Amy's songs.

AR: The Indigo Girls don't have that "Southern music" identification musically, but I think lyrically and philosophically we are *of the South*. And that influenced everything from our business model to how we approach activism. When we were growing up in Atlanta, the Southern music scene had a different vibe than a lot of other regions because you helped each other out. It's a community, you share gigs, it's a slower pace. Politically, we're in the birthplace of the civil rights movement, which has a spiritual base and a spiritual heart, which we could easily relate to and be part of and be educated by. And I think we could relate to it because we both had spiritual foundations.

How important is spirituality to both of you and your work?

ES: At this point, there's no life for me without my faith. I have a song called "Come a Long Way" that is a thank-you for the spiritual help that's gotten me through the worst of my struggles. I grew up Methodist, my mom was Presbyterian, my dad is a theologian. We'd go to church, then come home and eat something special, like a roast chicken, and sit around and talk about what we'd absorbed that day. We were allowed to ask questions, so I was able to see the beauty in spiritual life and faith. But then in the same breath, I know so many people who were wounded by organized religion. Both those things play in my mind when I write songs and think about the human struggle.

AR: Faith is one of the things that link me and Emily. My granddad had been a Methodist preacher in Florida. He raised money to build churches in the South. I went to Friday night youth group, Sunday Bible school, Sunday service, Wednesday choir practice, from six years old on. Our church was conservative. And I had to find my way through that. I had one youth minister who I could talk to about any questions I had. He saw me struggle with my sexuality. He saw me struggle with alcohol and drugs. I could go to him and it was a safe place for me. So even though church could be oppressive and taught me self-hate, it also set me free in a lot of ways.

That's a very Southern experience—the contradictions knotted together in our institutions.

AR: Yes. It's still my construct in that Joseph Campbell way, the way I make sense of the world even though I know it's myth, you know? Jesus is still the thing I can relate to. I write a gospel song and Jesus is in the middle of it. I wouldn't be anything without my spirituality, but at the same time I know there are a lot of things that are problematic about my attachment to it. The church we grew up in, the Methodist church, it's still homophobic. It's a slow-to-change thing.

You've both stayed in Georgia, where you grew up. Why?

ES: If we wanted to, I suppose Amy and I could've lived anywhere. But there's so much about this place, the important dialogue that happens between African Americans and whites and Hispanics. Atlanta is hugely multicultural. The South also has a pace that's more suited to me. It's like what Amy described, when we were coming up, everybody wanted everybody else to do well. And then there's the beauty of the South, little things like boiled peanuts and peach trees—the quiet, quiet beauty of the South resonates with me. It's just home through and through. I cannot think of any other place in the country or the world that I would live if I could snap my fingers and be there.

AR: I'm on the same page as Emily about all that. Not to say we haven't felt the weight of sexism and homophobia. For me, it's about family legacy and history and how much I love this place, and of course I want my daughter to love it, too. It's important to raise her here because this is where I have my roots. I want her to understand where people are coming from.

ES: Yeah, I think I also want . . . Sorry, Ame, were you done with that thought?

AR: Yeah, go ahead.

ES: Okay, what Amy's describing—the South is a perfect place to rear a kid, to grow up among these dichotomies. My daughter Cleo's being reared in an environment that talks all the time about what's going on in this country and celebrating differences. We're learning about being a human being in the South and the history that we struggle with. To me, philosophically that's what life is all about—holding the sorrow with the joy and seeing their equal weight and importance.

What do you love the most about the other?

ES: Awww.

AR: Well, there are so many things. I love what she does musically. I love Emily's ability to constantly evolve. Her willingness to look at herself and the context of the world and analyze how she can effect change or make a difference. She's rooted in a conviction that has to do with the greater mystery of life. She's always doing the work. That's invaluable and makes it possible to do what we do as a partnership.

ES: This question makes me feel emotional because I want to tell you twenty million things, you know? But

I could almost have a bumper sticker on my car that says, *What Would Amy Do?* Because one of the things I love most about Amy is the depth of her integrity. I don't know if I've ever met anybody else with that rootedness and conviction. When you say someone's "a good person," Amy through and through is a *good person.* I always feel like I'm about five years behind her in what she's learned about life. We are so different from each other. But Amy is at the center of everything for me.

AR: Wow.

ES: It's true, man. I'm just telling my truth.

The hardest-working woman in country music

BY JULIA REED

When Tammy Wynette's mother died in 1991, it was during a fan club cookout at the Nashville house she shared with fifth husband George Richey. The fans were lining up for hot dogs, Leeza Gibbons was setting up for an *Entertainment Tonight* interview, and an unconscious "MeeMaw" was hooked up to a respirator in a room off the kitchen. At the very moment Leeza was "introduced" to MeeMaw, the woman breathed her last and Wynette fell apart, mascara streaming down her face. Gibbons offered to greet the fans in her place, but the star wouldn't hear of it. She pulled herself together and went out to hug, kiss, and pose for countless photos. Finally, after MeeMaw had been wheeled away, Wynette got on her bus and went straight to Canada for a single show.

"You tell Tammy two hundred people want to see her in Branson [Missouri] and boom, she's on the bus," her former publicist Susan Nadler told me at the time. Wynette was of the generation of country entertainers who never stopped touring until the end—her last performance was less than a month before her death on April 6, 1998, from a blood clot in her lungs. "It was always 'There but for the grace of God, I might still be picking cotton,'" Nadler recalled. Wynette kept a crystal bowl full of the stuff in her living room as a reminder.

Virginia Wynette Pugh was born in Itawamba County, Mississippi, in 1942. Her father, a farmer and musician, died when she was nine months old, and she was raised by her grandparents in a house with no plumbing. Growing up, she picked cotton, okra, and beans but also taught herself to play her father's guitar. She left her first husband, Euple Byrd, when she was twenty-two, after five years of living in a cabin with no stove, refrigerator, or running water. When she moved to Nashville in 1966 with their three children, Byrd told her to "Dream on, baby, dream on."

It didn't take long. Producer Billy Sherrill needed a singer for "Apartment No. 9" and decided to take a chance on the unpolished Wynette as soon as he heard her voice. It was, he said, "husky and soulful and tearful and dynamic . . . and she lived it. She lived every tear everybody ever heard her sing." He dubbed her the "First Lady of Country Music," and together they produced five number-one hits in 1968 and 1969 alone, including "Singing My Song" and "Stand By Your Man," both of which she cowrote. Of the latter, she said she'd spent twenty minutes writing it and more than twenty years defending its lyrics.

Altogether Wynette sold more than 30 million albums and had thirty-nine top ten hits between 1967 and 1988, many of which were duets with third husband George Jones. Theirs was a tempestuous union, marked by Jones's penchant for whiskey and cocaine, but she graciously took half the blame for the marriage's demise, attributing it to "his nippin' and my naggin.'" But then she was always gracious. When Hillary Clinton appeared on *60 Minutes* with then candidate Bill to defend him against allegations that he'd cheated with Gennifer Flowers, Clinton said, "I'm not sitting here, some little woman standing by my man like Tammy Wynette." The irate singer shot back: "With all that is in me I resent your caustic remark. . . . I believe you have offended every true country music fan and every person who has 'made it on their own' with no one to take them to a White House." When Clinton apologized, Wynette agreed to perform at a fund-raiser. She also rejoined Jones for one last album of duets in 1995 and is buried near him in Nashville.

"When I got pregnant, I had several peers of mine, women, who said to me, 'Now that you're pregnant, you're probably gonna give up the music thing, right?' No one ever asks that of men. I'm sure that men who travel miss their children equally, no doubt about it. But it's insane, the double standard. 'Wild Women,' on the [*All American Made*] record, that's totally what it talks about. Men can go out and do this, but for some reason it's so edgy when a woman does it. And I'm still struggling with this. Emmylou Harris probably missed a birthday here and there—she had kids. I'm sure Loretta Lynn missed some birthdays. And it's so hard because I feel so much guilt about it anyway, but I've got to put food on the table."

—*Margo Price*, singer-songwriter, on working in Nashville as a woman

RHIANNON GIDDENS

T hough Rhiannon Giddens was immersed in music for most of her life, playing with Joe Thompson, one of the last Tar Heel fiddle players carrying on the black string band tradition, proved most formative. "It's hard to imagine I'd be the same musician today without having that experience," Giddens says of the times she and other members of the Carolina Chocolate Drops would gather at Thompson's house to jam, or bring the now-deceased musician onstage at a show. In the decade-plus after that first meeting, Giddens, a native of Greensboro, North Carolina, has garnered praise and a prestigious MacArthur Fellowship for her careful musical study of the past. In Giddens's hands, centuries-old artifacts, such as the 1800s slave advertisement that prompted the track "At the Purchaser's Option" on her 2017 album *Freedom Highway*, provide context to address contemporary issues. "Things that are coming to the surface in this country now may be four hundred years in the making," she says. "And as difficult as some things have been in the last couple of years, there are a lot of people whose eyes have been opened."

How did your family and your roots affect the path you took with music?

My early years were in a rural area around Greensboro called McLeansville. When I turned eight, I moved to Greensboro, but I still spent most of my weekends out in the countryside with my grandparents. Starting my life in the country definitely had an impact—I came back to that life through my music. Both my grandmother's and my mother's taste in music shaped what I heard and the soundtrack of my childhood. My grandmother was into jazz, and blues, kind of R&B from back then, but she also watched [Tom] T. Hall and loved Roy Clark's banjo playing. She was really of her time and place. My mom was really eclectic—it could be black gospel one minute and Andrés Segovia the next.

What was the biggest struggle you faced early on in your career?

The most important obstacle I had to overcome was my own fear of failure—the realization that I was the only one driving this car, that I was the only one in control here. I took a workshop about how to be a professional musician, and that was my key takeaway: It's your career, and *you* have to make it happen. To do that, you have to face down that whole *I could have been a contender* thing—if you don't ever try, you *could have* been the best singer in the world. You'll never know, so you'll

never know if you weren't either. People take comfort from that in an odd way. They live in that *I could have been*. After a few years, it's an empty thing. You just have to decide, *I'm going to find out whether I make it or not, and I'm going to do everything that I can.* That was my big turning point. The fear of failure is important to recognize, and then to ignore, because if you fail, then you've learned a hell of a lot. If you're going big enough to fail, you're really going for it.

You wrote the score for the ballet adaptation of Caroline Randall Williams's book Lucy Negro, Redux and are working on a historical musical based on a coup and massacre that took place in Wilmington in 1898. What inspired you to take those leaps?

I believe that if an opportunity comes, you take it. The older I get, the more I learn how to listen to an opportunity and listen to myself and listen to the environment around me and what I'm being led to do. I do believe that we are led to the experiences that we're uniquely created for. But I don't believe in blind faith. I believe in instinct and faith that is backed up with a lot of experience—calculated risks, you could say. I don't ever want to bite off more than I can chew, but I also don't want to be afraid of it so much that I don't take an opportunity that will stretch me in ways that might be uncomfortable at times.

What's the best piece of advice you've been given?

My mom said to me a long time ago, "Don't do anything for money, property, power, or prestige, because you end up with nothing in the end." And I totally believe that. Of course I have to work, but you know, you can't do anything solely for the money—it never turns out well. It may seem like it turns out well on the surface, but then when you get to the end, what do you have? Nothing. Money is nothing.

You've spoken before about your music having a mission statement. What is it, and how does it factor into the choices you make with your art?

I want to tell stories that haven't been told or haven't been told enough. If I didn't have that mission, I probably wouldn't be in music. Uncovering American stories or world stories that can be helped along with the aid of a well-crafted song—working with the ballet, for example, and telling a story that means a lot in this day and age—as long as I have that, I'm good. I'm good with the crazy travel and the expenses and the late nights and the early mornings. I'm good with all of that stuff if I feel like we're telling a story that's making an impact.

BEYONCÉ KNOWLES-CARTER

(1981–PRESENT)

The musical prodigy turned powerhouse who lifts up others

The year is 1990, and Tina Knowles's Houston hair salon, Headliners, is bustling. In the center of the room stands a young girl facing a row of inattentive women under dryers. Unprompted, Beyoncé Knowles begins to sing. Her audience's ears perk up past their hair rollers, Beyoncé relates in her autobiographical documentary, *Life Is but a Dream*. She's only a few notes in, but the women are all thinking the same thing: Beyoncé was born to perform.

Tina and her then husband, Mathew, a Xerox salesman, and their two daughters, Beyoncé and Solange, lived in Houston's Third Ward, where Mathew encouraged his daughters' talents. Despite her shy nature, Beyoncé pushed herself to perfect her sound and her image. In 1990, she began fronting an all-girls group, Girls Tyme, at talent shows, wearing handmade outfits sewn by her mother.

In the late 1990s, Girls Tyme evolved into the popular pop-R&B trio Destiny's Child, which rose to the top of the Billboard charts with songs such as "Say My Name" and "Survivor." By the time the group disbanded in 2006, Beyoncé was already making history as a solo artist. With the release of her solo debut album, *Dangerously in Love*, in 2003, Beyoncé became the first female artist to top both the singles and albums charts simultaneously in the United States and the United Kingdom. Over the course of her solo career—with hit singles such as "Crazy in Love," "Irreplaceable," "Single Ladies (Put a Ring on It)," and "Formation"—Beyoncé became the first artist in

history to have all six of her solo albums consecutively top the Billboard charts.

Beyoncé is now one of the best-selling artists of all time. And as an outspoken feminist and advocate for minorities, she has also become one of the most recognized and influential people in the world. Her 2016 visual album, *Lemonade*, catalogued Beyoncé's personal feminist evolution, and featured imagery exploring and celebrating black Southern womanhood, including Tina's Creole roots in Louisiana.

The mononymous multihyphenate also uses her power to empower others: She supports movements such as Black Lives Matter and #MeToo, and her philanthropy includes scholarships to students at historically black colleges and universities. When she made history as the first black female recording artist to be featured on the cover of *Vogue*'s September issue, in 2018, she called on the magazine to hire Tyler Mitchell to shoot the cover image, making him the first black photographer to do so for *Vogue*. And even when there have been hardships—family strife, a miscarriage, infidelity—Beyoncé has used those experiences to inspire art and to inspire others.

"Imagine if someone hadn't given a chance to the brilliant women who came before me: Josephine Baker, Nina Simone, Eartha Kitt, Aretha Franklin, Tina Turner, Diana Ross, Whitney Houston, and the list goes on," Beyoncé wrote in that *Vogue* issue. "They opened the doors for me, and I pray that I'm doing all I can to open doors for the next generation of talents."

Candi Staton
My Sewing Notions

Over the last five decades, Candi Staton, dubbed the "First Lady of Southern Soul," has charted hits across the soul, R&B, disco, and gospel genres, including 1976's number-one song "Young Hearts Run Free."

When we were very young, I watched my mother sew all of our clothes. We didn't have a lot of money. My dad was a coal miner in the wintertime, and he was a farmer in the summertime, and he was a weekend alcoholic. So he spent a lot of the money he made on himself, which left the family destitute. My mother had a sewing machine—not an electric machine, the kind that you have to work with your foot.

She would go to the general store, in a little country town called Hanceville, Alabama. She would get flour that you make biscuits out of, and it came in the most beautiful floral sacks. She would buy two sacks, and she'd make me tops and little skirts to match, and that's what we wore. I would watch her and imitate what she did. When I was big enough for my feet to reach the pedal on the machine, she taught me how to sew on it, and I would make little skirts and doll clothes.

When I was thirteen, my sister, Maggie, and I went on the road with a group called the Jewell Gospel Trio. We were singing for a school called the Jewell Academy [in Nashville], and we were singing for our tuition. We met people like Sam Cooke and Aretha Franklin and the Staple Singers, Mahalia Jackson. The other singers were getting paid for their work, but since we were so country, my mother didn't know a thing in the world about music.

We had very few clothes to choose from, so my sister and I would use the little money we did get at the store to buy material. I learned how to make little gathered skirts, and put a little band around 'em. It didn't look any different than anybody else's because my mother taught me how to do patterns. Years later I even made my daughter her graduation dress—she looked just as pretty as anybody else.

"The South was like our home. Our records were hot there first, before they were hot in the North, and we were traveling down South to sing when I was still in school. My father let us know that everyone might not love us or be friendly. And we knew what to expect anyway because he would often send the two youngest of us to stay with our grandmother in Mound Bayou, Mississippi. We sang in black churches, and then in black schools and auditoriums when the churches got too small. We didn't start any trouble— though I did inadvertently integrate a washateria one time. The black side was full, so I just went over on the white side. There were two ladies sitting there, and they didn't say anything to me and I didn't say anything to them. I just put in my fifteen cents and started washing my clothes. And once the black women saw I was washing my clothes, they all started coming in, too."

—Mavis Staples, legendary songstress, on performing
in the South during the civil rights era

DOLLY PARTON

An inspiring country queen

BY ALLISON GLOCK

I married my husband because he loves Dolly Parton. (That wasn't the only reason, but I'd be lying if I said it wasn't up there with "incredibly smart" and "kind to children.") Dolly is a litmus test. People who love Dolly tend to understand that life is a huge mess of contradiction and struggle but that is no reason not to have a great time while you're here. Dolly is nothing if not pure inspiration. Sprung from Tennessee mountain dirt, one of a dozen children living ankle by cheek in a single-room cabin, Dolly rose to become the most important female songwriter in the world. She is also an uncommonly generous philanthropist, an actress, an award-winning film producer, a pop culture icon, a canny businesswoman, a gifted musician, and most famously, a singer, blessed with an idiosyncratic soprano so twangy-sweet it brings grown men (see above) to their knees.

Unlike other country music legends, Dolly has never gotten tangled up with drugs, or fallen drunk out of a limo, or married a no-good man who treated her like a needy cur, or posed topless. Dolly doesn't play tragic. She smiles! She laughs! And by laughing loudly and often, she—amazingly, magically, in her saucer-plate sequins and vaudevillian makeup—embodies dignity. Also, good sense.

Back when she was just starting out, Elvis himself asked to record her song "I Will Always Love You." Catch was, he wanted half the rights. Dolly turned him down. That ballsy decision ended up earning her millions of dollars years later. Not to mention admission into a club of what surely must contain very few members: women who said no to Elvis Presley.

Dolly has always said no to the right things. (With the exception of *Rhinestone*.) No, I won't sell my songs. No, I won't tone down my look, or my ambition, or my intelligence. As a result, her list of accomplishments is as massive as her proudly enhanced assets, but what makes it unique is less length than breadth. What other woman has garnered a *Ms.* magazine Woman of the Year Award, a Kennedy Center Honor, forty-five Grammy nominations (eight wins), a Good Housekeeping Seal of Approval (the first ever awarded to a *person*), and a recurring role on *Hannah Montana*? Dolly reaches the high and low, feels Jesus *and* gravity, and through it all radiates humility and graciousness. She is the anti-Madonna. And the antidote to the reflexive cynicism and weariness of our world.

"Dolly is an angel," my husband says, only half joking. Okay, not joking at all. I see her more as a role model. WWDD? Well, work harder than a lumberjack, for one. And do it in high heels and a push-up bra with a grin on her face. Dolly bleeds optimism, which is not the same as naivete. As she sings in a song, "I'm just a backwoods Barbie, too much makeup, too much hair. Don't be fooled by thinking that the goods are not all there."

When she is given grief (or death threats) from folks who, say, can't reconcile her Christian faith with her inclusive personal politics, Dolly punctures their bigotry without rancor. "God and I have a great relationship," she explains with a wink, "but we both see other people."

Which is the true genius of Dolly. Brains big as hers, used only for the power of good.

With more than sixty indelible years in show business, Dolly has integrity and bone-dry honesty that remain as unassailable as her wigs. "If I have one more face-lift, I'll have a beard," she jokes.

She has lived her life on her terms; killed the whole country with kindness; showed women the green, golden ground between doormat and tiger lady. Dolly is a walking self-help book, an animate example of the classy way to get it done. It all starts, she says, with owning your crazy. WWDD?

"Find out who you are," she advises. "And do it on purpose."

HOLLY WILLIAMS

I love telling stories," says Holly Williams—they can be found in her music, three albums' worth of Americana ballads that cover love, loss, and family history (she's granddaughter and daughter to Hank Williams and Hank Jr.); on display at her shops, White's Mercantile and H. Audrey; and under construction all over the Tennessee countryside, where Williams rents out historic homes she has renovated to travelers with an eye for Southern architecture. But Williams's stories don't revolve around the material stuff—they're about people. "What it means to be Southern is that you try to treat your neighbor right," she says.

How did where you grew up shape who you are today?

I was born in Cullman, Alabama. We moved up here to Nashville when I was two years old, in 1983. I lived a very quote-unquote "normal" life. People assume so often that because I'm Hank Williams Jr.'s daughter that I was at Garth Brooks's house for lunch or at all these awards shows and concerts. It was the total opposite. My dad always said, "I'm not Bocephus, I'm Daddy." He was on tour a great deal, but when we were with him, we were hunting, we were fishing, we were on his farm. We were very sheltered. We grew up in a very small community of friends and family—same church every Sunday. We got to have a very stable childhood.

Hank Sr. died when my dad was three, and his wife Audrey, that's my grandmother, she died in 1975, before I was born. So the family we were around were my mom's parents, Warren and June White. They lived in Mer Rouge, Louisiana. We spent every Christmas, Thanksgiving, Halloween, summer vacation, July Fourth, everything with them. Papaw would give me a dollar per bag for pecans I would pick in the huge front yard. At the cemetery, I can trace back all the way to five grandfathers—our whole family was born and died within a mile of there. It's my favorite place in the world, and it gave me a real love for small towns, a real love for the country and just for a slower pace.

When did you start writing songs?

I always loved lyrics, always loved telling stories, but didn't ever really think I was going to be a singer. I didn't pick up a guitar until I was seventeen. But that was always there; music is in my blood. When I started playing guitar and piano, it felt very natural to me. I spent about four years playing every bar I could—anywhere people could hear me. Eventually, I got signed. I did two albums with two major labels, and yet the one that was most successful by far was *The Highway*, which I ended up putting out on my own. It was the most successful record, and it was the most exhausting, the scariest. Taking out a loan to get the album going, driving the Suburban, like, *all* over America, all the time, with different band members. It was all very, very DIY, but eventually, I was able to build the career that I wanted to build.

You wrote a song about your mother on your album Here with Me. What's the most important thing you've learned from her?

She is my best friend, and she's the most amazing woman—had two young kids and a husband on the road all the time, and took that job and dealt with it with such grace. She focused on teaching my sister and me that kindness is everything, and love is every-thing, and acceptance is everything—whether you're running a business, whether you're at school, whatever you're doing. Everyone called her Perma-smile, just a Southern belle from Louisiana, so joyous and smiling all the time. The first time I went to New York City, I thought everyone smiled at each other like that. I was nineteen, getting on the subway, saying, "Hi, how are you?" to everyone, smiling so big. People looked at me like I was crazy. But my mom taught me that you need to show people you're happy to meet them. You need to be kind to people, and you need to have proper Southern manners. Hopefully, that's helped me in business. As stressful situations come up, running stores and houses, everything in the world is in how you treat people.

You have two daughters and a son with your husband and fellow musician Chris Coleman. Is there anything about the way your mother raised you that you try to keep in mind as you raise your own children?

She was very present, and she was always there for me. For me, it's so important to give them that sense that if they need Mom, she's there. I never want my kids to look back and be like, *Mom and Dad were always on their phones. They were always working. They were always busy.* I just want them to be able to have a childhood. I feel like because all of us are so busy these days, that's getting taken away from a lot of kids, as parents and people are overstressed and over-worked.

I'm still trying to find the same balance that everyone is looking for these days. We've got these sand timers at our store, so I'll flip one over and sit with my computer, and it's kind of like exercising—I do a sprint. I become a crazy person, and I drink my tea, and I do thirty minutes of rapid-fire work. Then I stop and say, *Okay. Breathe. Take the kids out to the backyard and play.*

LUCINDA WILLIAMS

The Americana star turns troubles to triumphs

BY BETH ANN FENNELLY

I'm nobody to her. That's hard to believe, when she's scored my South; her guitar frets are the train tracks I've hoboed along. She's mapped my region more accurately than Siri: West Memphis, Jackson, Greenville, Pineola, Slidell. Nacogdoches? Never been there, but I can't hear the word in any register but hers, the twangy, elongated *a*, an insistence on the homely syllables, her voice a silk shirt being ripped from a rusty nail.

I'm nobody to her, and that's perplexing, given our intimacy. Lucinda Williams has bought me shots of tequila and held my hair back when I puked approximately zero times. But, listening to Lucinda, I'm not alone. And I'm not alone in feeling not alone, listening to Lucinda. The three-time Grammy winner has used her fourteen albums to chase down her demons and lasso them with ropes of riffs for our commiseration. Along the way, she's morphed from early straight-up country to an idiosyncratic Americana that borrows blues, soul, funk, or rock, as needed. The constant is her devotion to truth telling, hers and our own, and a ragged vulnerability that must exact a price.

"Singer-Songwriter-Saint" is printed above her woodblock portrait on a letterpress poster that hangs over my desk, and "Raised on Poke Salad and Poetry." The poetry I can vouch for; her father was Miller Williams, with whom I studied poetry in grad school at the University of Arkansas, though by the mid-nineties, Lucinda was long gone, first to L.A., then Nashville. Her formal education ended a good bit earlier than my own—she never graduated from high school—but her father guided her through the Southern greats, even driving her to meet Flannery O'Connor when she was

five. Until he died in 2015, Lucinda sent her lyrics to her father for his edits, and they sometimes performed together. In her 2014 double album, *Down Where the Spirit Meets the Bone*, she recorded a song adapted from one of his poems.

"Raised on poetry," yes—but poke salad? Maybe that was a flourish of the poster designer. But a certain kind of Southerner—the hardscrabble kind—practiced foraging long before the Brooklyn hipster hobbyists. Pokeweed blooms early in these parts. Picked young and cooked long with onions and vinegar, it makes a nutritious supper, with the added bonus, according to the old folks, of deworming.

It seems Lucinda's family experienced some hardscrabble times, moving frequently among strapped Southern cities. Her 1998 masterpiece, *Car Wheels on a Gravel Road*, describes these days of slamming screen doors and raised voices; in the title song we meet a "child in the back seat, 'bout four, five years / looking out the window / little bit a dirt mixed with tears / car wheels on a gravel road."

Perhaps it's that child, grown up, whom we encounter "in a yellow El Camino, listening to Howlin' Wolf" with a man about to do her wrong. Indeed, Lucinda has perfected the breakup song. Her tonal range comes in handy: What's your flavor of heartache? There's the spare, plaintive "denial" stage: "All the way to Jackson," she assures herself, "I don't think I'll miss you much; / Once I get to Lafayette / I'm not gonna mind one bit," the cities and assertions stacking up like badly folded maps. We have the mournful, resigned ballad from 2001's *Essence*: "I envy the wind / that whispers in your ear / that howls through the winter…" And the pissed-off, acerbic

"Those Three Days" from 2003's *World without Tears*, detailing an affair in which promises were made, then broken. "Did you 'love me forever,'" she snarls, hitting her *r*'s, little fishhooks, "just for those three days? / For those *three days*." Such a perverse pleasure, listening to her heartbreak songs while heartbroken—pressing "Play" is like pressing a bruise.

One more thing about pokeweed. Straight from the ground, it's toxic. To make poke salad, you wash the leaves three times before cooking. And maybe there's a metaphor there. With seeming ease—but really decades of discipline and devotion—she's taken her poisons and applied fire, rendering them, and therefore our own, delicious.

WRITERS
& READERS

NATASHA TRETHEWEY

When Natasha Trethewey first eyed her Evanston, Illinois, house, with its two big verandas, neoclassical columns, and a fleur-de-lis window in the center, she thought of her childhood in New Orleans. "This is where I was meant to be," Trethewey says of the home, which she and her husband moved into when she joined the English department at Northwestern University in 2017 after fifteen years teaching at Emory University, in Atlanta. "I felt like I brought my ancestors with me." Since her 2000 debut, *Domestic Work,* the Mississippi-born Trethewey has written five additional collections of poetry, including 2006's *Native Guard,* for which she earned the Pulitzer Prize. Along the way, she's secured just about every fellowship and honor to be had—including two terms as the nineteenth poet laureate of the United States.

In 2017, your Illinois house burned—you used the word **displaced** *to describe how you felt, a word attached to those who lost their homes in Hurricane Katrina, which you wrote about in a 2010 nonfiction work.*

We were displaced, though we are certainly comfortable in ways people who are struggling through natural disasters are not. It did make me think a lot about the role personal geographies play in our lives. When I wrote the poem "Theories of Time and Space," I was thinking about the places we have been at some point in our lives that are familiar with places we've grown up. In particular, when we move away from them and go back to them for the first time, they seem so transformed, yet even if they haven't, they seem that way because we are the ones who have changed.

The funny thing about that poem is even though I was thinking figuratively about how we change, I turned the book [*Native Guard*] in to my publisher in March 2005, and by the time the book came out, that poem had become literal because Hurricane Katrina just devastated my hometown. And did change Mississippi in ways that I could not have imagined.

You've dealt with other tragedies, too—how did writing help you cope with your mother's death after your stepfather murdered her in 1985?

I firmly believe that in order to survive a trauma, you have to be able to tell a story about it. The biggest story I tell about devastation is the story of my mother's death. My becoming a writer in the aftermath of that [helped me] to contend with the deepest wound that I have. It gives it meaning, in the meaningfulness and purpose of my own life. Otherwise, it's just senseless, and how could I live with that if there wasn't something meaningful to be made of it?

And so, in telling the stories, in the narrative, in what I try to do in my own work, is an act of not only survival, but I would go so far as to say an act of thriving. I've not merely survived my mother's death; I would argue that in spite of it, because of it, I thrived.

How did you get to that point?

Right after her death, I tried to write a poem about it, but I wasn't writing poetry at that point. The decision to write a poem when I was nineteen was more about what we often think poetry offers us that other forms of expression may not. I turn to poetry in the way Lisel Mueller talks about in her poem "When I Am Asked." At the end of the poem she says, "I . . . placed my grief / in the mouth of language, / the only thing that would grieve with me." When I sat down to write my poem about the day my mother died, I was thinking about how maybe poetry seems like the only kind of sacred heightened language that might grieve with us.

Your poem "Pilgrimage" features the line "I can see her / listening to shells explode, writing herself." That feels like a nod to your mom.

That's absolutely right. I think for a lot of readers, or a lot of people who hear my story, they often land on the

easiest interpretation of how I've come to be a writer. I'm a daughter of a writer—my father was a poet—and therefore I am a poet. But that's actually not quite right. Yes, I've had a poet in my family, but I'm not a poet solely because of my father. I think the primary reason I'm a poet is because of my mother. I think other people miss her role in my life, and how important she is to why and how I do what I do.

Your father pushed you to be a writer because he knew you had something important to say.

I think my father was very aware of what it meant for me to be both black and biracial in the Deep South at that particular time. That it meant I would have a different and necessary perspective on the world, on the place that I was growing up, and on the history of not just that place, but the United States. We are seeing the rise of more visible forms of white supremacy; I've always been concerned with these kinds of deeply ingrained and unexamined notions of racial difference that are the bedrock of white supremacy that even "good white people" carry inside them. And the way that it was often manifested in my childhood was people saying to me if I did anything well, "Oh, that's your white side."

Who were those people?

White people would say that. Or they would say, "Well, you aren't like the rest of them." And I would say, "Who's the rest of them? My mother? My grandmother?" It was as if they were trying to say that the fact that I had white blood somehow made me better, made me distinguished from the rest of my people, and that made me so angry. I wanted to always be seen as exactly like my people, representative of the myriad varieties of my people. Not somehow special or extraordinary, because if I'm special and extraordinary, then it diminishes everyone else. It diminishes my mother and her humanity and my grandmother and everyone else in that community that I came up through.

Who were you thinking about when you wrote the poem "Domestic Work, 1937"?

That poem was about my grandmother. She worked as a domestic in Mississippi in the thirties. She told me about the different jobs she held in her life. But I also saw her as the woman in the poem cleaning her own house. There was something so wonderful about the difference of the work she had to do outside the home, but that she still could take such pleasure in the care of her own home and her own family.

In your poem "Articulation," you describe a painting of Saint Gertrude, and the piece also seems to become a tribute to your mother.

[Saint Gertrude's] calling was to be a religious writer. She had a vision of the sacred heart of Christ, and that's what called her to devotion, and to devote her life to writing religious text. Obviously, I'm making a connection to her, her call to devotion, and to the kinds of writing that I do. The poem ends, "How could I not, bathed in the light / of her wound, find my calling there?" My calling is to answer my mother's life with mine. That is my highest devotion. Christ gave his life for us, and the faithful are supposed to be devoted. That's how I feel about my mother.

In addition to being a poet, you are stylish. In 2015, while you were doing a reading at the Museum of Modern Art, your Christian Louboutin heels stood out.

I love that, because I feel like we ought to be many things and that they shouldn't necessarily fit into some mold that people expect. Before I went off to graduate school, my stepmother told me to get rid of my accent. She thought if you have a Southern accent and were a cheerleader, people were going to think you were stupid. So for years, I never told people that I was a cheerleader. I finally began to say it. I liked being able to put the fact that I was head cheerleader at the University of Georgia next to Pulitzer Prize winner. How many times do you have that? And I'm going to wear some red-soled shoes, too!

Dorothea Benton Frank
My Mother's Fruitcake Pan

Dorothea Benton Frank is the New York Times *best-selling author of twenty books, including* Sullivan's Island *and* Same Beach, Next Year. *She divides her time between New Jersey and the South Carolina Lowcountry.*

My mother was the worst cook—the *worst.* If the Department of Health in Charleston, South Carolina, could have, they would have repossessed her stove. But her fruitcake was *out of this world.*

It always started around September or October; somebody would bring my mother twenty-five pounds of pecans in a burlap sack, and we'd sit around after supper and start cracking them. There was one big bowl for ones that came out whole, and another for broken pieces. It took a month to crack all the pecans; then they would be assigned to things my mother made at the holidays—nut cake, rum balls. But fruitcake was the big deal.

My stepfather worked at the navy yard; he had this thing he used to cut a pattern for the inside of my mother's fruitcake pan, and then he would lay the pattern on top of brown bags and cut out the pattern pieces to fit inside the pan, and then they would grease them on both sides, put the batter together, and it would cook. You never smelled anything so fabulous in your life. Heaven smells like my mother's fruitcake. It was moist, very flavorful. She would have the exact amount of cherries versus pineapple versus the nuts versus the brown sugar—she probably soaked it in booze; I soak mine in applejack brandy.

When I go to reach for that pan, my heart clenches. The memories come back in a flood. I tell the kids the same story every year. They're like, *Here comes the fruitcake story!* This fruitcake was as important as any present that was ever underneath the tree. Because it was the whole process of the family sitting down to do something together.

FLANNERY O'CONNOR

The chronicler of the wild and weird South

BY MEG DONAHUE

I first came across Flannery O'Connor in the library of the All Saints Catholic Church in Dunwoody, Georgia, in the 1990s. I don't mean I came across *her*. (If I did, considering she died of lupus in 1964, this would be a far different story.) But it was there that I first picked up the Georgia writer and fellow Catholic's *Complete Stories*.

I was skipping CCD (which is like Protestant Sunday school, but with 100 percent more rosaries) when I spotted O'Connor's best-known work, a collection of her short stories that was published after her death. The cover, with its multicolored peacock, stood out in joyful relief to the leather-bound and neglected books of Saint Augustine's confessions, the lives of the saints, and the various ruminations of men on the infinite.

The stories in the book struck me like the peacock on the cover: strange and out of place. There were no euphemisms in her book. No "best effort" nod to characters and no prize for second place. There were only strange people in heightened situations coming to grips with the lies they tell themselves. Her story "A Good Man Is Hard to Find," centered on a selfish and fearful grandmother whose road trip with her family ends in horrific violence, shook me to my seventeen-year-old core. If this level of self-knowledge and self-sacrifice is what God demands of us, then how could any reader take comfort in that?

O'Connor herself had a hard time selling her ideas to her publisher. While working on her first novel, *Wise Blood*, the publisher wrote her a letter complaining that in her early drafts, "he sensed a kind of aloneness in the book, as if she were writing out of her own experience," but he did admire her as a "straight shooter." O'Connor wrote to her agent, Elizabeth McKee, that the letter was ". . . addressed to a slightly dim-witted Campfire Girl, and I cannot look forward with composure to a lifetime of others like them." O'Connor stuck to those straight-shooting guns of hers in the end and *Wise Blood* was published in 1952, with a subsequent film shot in 1979 by the director John Huston in Macon, Georgia, in a home now belonging to one of my friends.

Since that time in the All Saints library all those years ago, I've moved to Macon myself and have a fuller understanding of O'Connor's work. I live about forty minutes down the road from Andalusia, her home in Milledgeville where she raised her beloved peafowl, and have, on a lazy Saturday or two, put down my laundry and gone to visit the former dairy farm. I've seen her ground-floor bedroom (due to her severe lupus, she could only walk with crutches, and a bedroom on the second floor was out of the question), her typewriter, and the barn where her story "Good Country People" was set.

I've seen that the characters she writes about, the slightly mad people of a faded South, still exist even today and that, if anything, she was downplaying their quirkiness. In my growing age and years of therapy, I've also learned that she was right in her demand of personal honesty. That there can be no growth or grounded compassion until we accept who we are and that the sins and strangeness we see in others are a dim reflection of what we see in ourselves.

Through Flannery, I've realized that the beautiful world holds darkness, but the only darkness that is truly to be feared is the darkness that keeps us separated from one another and from ourselves: the darkness of misunderstanding and self-deceit.

MOLLY IVINS

(1944–2007)

The spunky columnist who translated Texas to the world

For any journalist, a gig with the *New York Times* would seem a career pinnacle. Not so much for Molly Ivins, the Texas columnist whose acid-tongued commentary attracted editors in NYC only to, well, throw them for a loop. Things came to a head when Ivins covered a poultry slaughter, adding to the lexicon of agricultural journalism the term "gang pluck." The phrase never saw print, but its coinage led to Ivins's homeward return to Texas— "home being where you understand the sumbitches," she wrote.

Ivins, who chronicled scandals in Austin, contretemps in Lubbock, and the rise of the Bush dynasty, became synonymous with the Lone Star State. Technically, though, she was a transplant, born in California in 1944. But she grew up in the tony Houston neighborhood of River Oaks, a privileged world she did not fit into. Six feet tall and towering over Texas debs, she described herself variously as a "St. Bernard among greyhounds," a "Clydesdale among Thoroughbreds," and a "goat" among "sheep," who would slip away from high school dances to read a book in the bathroom. She shared a friend circle with future president George W. Bush. But it was more than social awkwardness that set her apart from her teen peers. "All Southern liberals come from the same starting point— race," she wrote. "Once you figure out they are lying to you about race, you start to question everything."

A master's degree from the Columbia University Graduate School of Journalism followed her graduation from Smith College and a stint at the Institute of Political Studies in Paris. (A biography notes she was "trilingual" and spoke "private-school French, erudite Smith College English, and ribald Texan.") After gigs

in Houston and Minneapolis, she served as coeditor of the *Texas Observer* in the early 1970s, honing her trademark folksy barbs and earning the attention of the *Times*. When Texas called her back, she jumped to the *Dallas Times Herald*, and then the *Fort Worth Star-Telegram*, and was nationally syndicated.

She spent the rest of her life covering Texas, contributing to titles ranging from *Mother Jones* and *Ms.* to the *Atlantic* and *Esquire*. "In my youth, I aspired to be a great journalist," she wrote in the introduction to her best-selling collection *Molly Ivins Can't Say That, Can She?* "George Orwell, Albert Camus, and I.F. Stone were my heroes. Great writers and intellectuals who helped illuminate their times. But look, God gave those guys fascism, communism, colonialism, and McCarthyism to struggle against. All I got was Lubbock. It's not my fault." The role suited her. *Texas Monthly* described her as "the nation's favorite professional Texan," and she came to be regarded not just as one of the state's best journalists but one of the best period, anywhere—a voice people still yearn to hear today.

Ivins died in 2007 after enduring breast cancer, which she wrote about with typical candor in *Time*: "First they mutilate you; then they poison you; then they burn you. I have been on blind dates better than that."

While Ivins's career led her to cover international figures, her emphasis was always on bringing the political process home to the average person. "Politics is not about *those people* in Washington or *those people* at the state capitol," she wrote. "Politics is about us— you, me and the guy next to us. *We* run this country, *we* own this country, and *we* have a responsibility to hire the right people to drive our bus for a while."

LEE SMITH

She'll tell you with a wink to refer to her as Lee Smith, OaD. (The "OaD" stands for "old as dirt.") But it was as a little girl that Smith first began scribbling stories in the coal-mining town of Grundy, Virginia, and by her twenties she had already gained a reputation for writing about Appalachian lives in rich detail. With thirteen novels, four story collections, and a memoir, *Dimestore*, Smith has become an essential voice in the Southern literary canon, winning accolades that include the Robert Penn Warren Award for Fiction and the Southern Book Critics Circle Award. The seventy-something still writes every day, although now she does it from an antebellum outbuilding ten feet from the house she shares with her husband in Hillsborough, North Carolina. "There's nothing equal to that feeling when you're writing and it's really working," she says.

Writing is an art, but publishing is commerce. How do you reconcile them?

I may have less trouble with that than some writers, simply because I'm a merchant's daughter. I grew up working in my father's dime store. The truth is, I like to sell books. I like to work a room. Writing is very lonely. There you are, shut away for hours, days, months, years. When it's time to go around to bookstores and give readings, I'm ready.

How often does it hit you just how many people have read your books?

It doesn't, really. I live in a little town where if you throw a rock, you hit a writer, so it's not a big deal. Hillsborough has always been kind of a leafy, dreamy town that's a haven for writers and artists and outlaws.

What about when you travel?

Sometimes I sit down on a plane next to somebody who's reading one of my books. The first thing I ask is if they like it. If they do, then I say who I am.

And if they don't?

Then I don't say a thing!

Do you want to express different things in your writing now than you did earlier in your career?

Totally. I write fiction the way other people write in their journals. Fiction has always been how I try to make sense of my own life. I am not my characters, but often they are going through things I've been through. I can read over an old story and remember exactly who I was then, where I was, and what I was dealing with when I wrote it.

How does that feel?

It brings everything back. My stories now are really different from the earlier ones. When we first start writing, we're writing the great dramas of our childhoods, our young adulthoods. We're going for intensity. At my age now, I'm more interested in the long haul than the epiphany.

Storytelling is personal, but it plays a larger role in society.

Oh, storytelling is crucial to the future of our country. We cannot cover up history. We cannot cover up past lives. We have to understand who we are and why, which means we have to find out who we were, where we came from, how we lived, and what we believed, before we can understand what's happening now. I'm delighted to see the recent emphasis on oral history in schools and on the radio and in documentary films. I think it's sort of the art form of our time.

What would ten-year-old Lee think of your life now?

She'd be amazed! When I was ten, we'd run up in the mountains all day long, swinging on grapevines and running wild until we heard the big bell calling us down for supper. Ten-year-old Lee wouldn't believe all the activities for kids we have today.

I bet she'd be proud of grown-up Lee.

I don't know. I write a lot for girls and women, particularly girls and women from the mountains, from the South, ones who don't have enough power in their own lives—whether because they're children or they're poor. I hope ten-year-old Lee would be proud, but who knows? She might just want to be on her cell phone.

What advice would you give young Lee if you could go back?

"Slow down." As a young woman, I was drunk on literature and on fire with novels and poetry and writing. I'd write all night long. Now I would say, "Slow down, honey. Read. Just because you like to write doesn't mean you've got something to say. Learn about history and psychology and science and everything else in this big world. Don't fall in love all the time. Don't get married so fast. Life is going to be long."

Would you have listened?

I wouldn't have listened at all.

ADA LIMÓN

Though Ada Limón spent her childhood in Sonoma, California, the South and its influences have never been far from the Kentucky poet and National Book Critics Circle Award winner's heart.

I may not be from Kentucky, but I'm a transplant and a defender of this place. There are so many writers born and raised here, and I feel like I've been invited to the party. There's a breath here. People take their time. You can talk to your neighbor for an hour.

I had lived in New York and California, and I moved to Kentucky because my then boyfriend and now husband is in the horse industry. I joke that I followed booze across the United States—I moved from wine to bourbon. The day I landed here, it was like Lexington was showing off. Everything was blooming—dogwoods, cherry trees.

I was working on a novel, but then I found myself writing poems with Kentucky as the background. I would never have written *The Carrying*, my 2018 book of poetry, without living here. I have space now, and I have time. Green is the most creative color to me, and this is among the greenest places I've lived. It's done something to my brain.

My grandfather on my father's side was from Mexico. When I visited him as a child, I remember he had a picture of Lydia Mendoza, who sang on the border of Texas and Mexico. She would dress in giant hoop skirts and play her music, surrounded by workers. She belonged to the people. I thought she was the ultimate performer. And then I saw *Coal Miner's Daughter*. That was my first knowledge of Kentucky, and as a kid, I loved Loretta Lynn in the same way. I loved the way these women connected with people from all walks of life.

ZORA NEALE HURSTON
A literary beacon of the black South

BY LATRIA GRAHAM

"Ships at a distance have every man's wish on board. For some they come in with the tide. For others they sail forever on the horizon, never out of sight, never landing until the Watcher turns his eyes away in resignation, his dreams mocked to death by Time. That is the life of men."

I encountered the opening lines of Zora Neale Hurston's novel *Their Eyes Were Watching God* during my junior year of college. That short passage was one of the few things I read in the gilded tower of academia that I knew in my bones to be true. It was the first book I'd opened in all of my years of schooling that sounded like home. It wasn't just the language, but the philosophy—the Southern reasoning I had heard from the women at my grandma's house who used to sit on the porch shelling peas, enjoying late summer breezes and one another's company.

I had to know: Who was this woman?

Folklorist, novelist, and anthropologist Zora Neale Hurston was always half in shadow. Even when writing about herself, she was always troubling the line between myth and reality.

Though she was born in Notasulga, Alabama, in 1891, Hurston considered herself the daughter of the all-black town of Eatonville, Florida, where she was raised, blossoming among the citrus groves and vegetable rows. As a child sitting underneath a chinaberry tree, she dreamed of what it would be like to walk to the edge of the world and tried to recruit a friend to go there with her. Zora craved adventure, and she refused to give in to the respectability politics and expectations that came with her race and gender.

After Zora's mother died, she left Eatonville. Eventually her father stopped paying her tuition and she bounced around, taking jobs to survive. She was a manicurist. She was a maid. She did not let those duties inhibit her self-perception.

She became a master of seeking out opportunity instead of waiting for it to come to her. Very early on she embraced the notion of reinvention, or revision. In order to get the education she desired, she shaved a decade off her age, eventually enrolling at Barnard, where she was the sole black student at the university, making a name for herself in the field of anthropology.

She understood, though, that the work she needed to do was back home. Captivated by the layered brilliance and beauty of rural Southern black life, she set out to capture it. Armed with a camera, a pen, and a chrome-plated pistol, she made it her mission to use her delicate ear to transform the verbal art into a written one, for preservation.

Zora was the preacher's child, telling the truth as she saw it from a different type of pulpit. Instead of focusing on the mayor, she trained her lens on the citizens gathered in front of the general store. In her work the washerwoman holds as much power as the preacher and just might tell more truths. She recorded songs, sayings, and turns of phrase from turpentine camps, the weather-stained skin of the laborers gleaming under the unrelenting sun. She was Old Florida's thaumaturge, adding lyricism to the written word in an effort to describe how language lives and is performed by the body, as the speaker tells the story.

And so she traveled the South in a car she named

Sassy Susie, writing about a world that has all but vanished. She gave us shotgun weddings and clapboard houses. Purple hyacinths and palm trees and pecan groves. This fieldwork in the American South and the Caribbean would become the bedrock of her fiction.

"God was grumbling his thunder and playing the zig-zag lightning thru his fingers" is the first line of *Jonah's Gourd Vine*, published in 1934. The semiautobiographical novel about post-emancipation Southern migration and multigenerational African American communities was her first book of fiction. Most of her work went against the tide of racially tinged anger that was coming out of the Harlem Renaissance. Instead of writing sophisticated novels of manners in urban settings or pandering to white patrons eager for exotic representations of blackness, she portrayed her characters as they were: driven, resourceful, multifaceted people at war with the past and who they could become. That meant writing about sex, work, money, and joy. It meant doing some of her work in dialect, even if that resulted in the manuscript never being published during her lifetime. *Barracoon*, the story of the last victim of the transcontinental slave trade, was only released in 2018.

Intense, colorful, inimitable, and uncompromising, Hurston authored works that include four novels, an autobiography, short fiction, even a play written with Langston Hughes. The story of her difficult life and her extraordinary legacy were almost lost to history after she died in 1960, buried in an unmarked grave with few material possessions to her name. Her work went out of print, and she almost faded into obscurity. Then Alice Walker wrote Zora a new ending by bringing her back to the fore in the article "In Search of Zora Neale Hurston," published by *Ms.* magazine in 1975. The literary afterlife has since been kind. Her books are back in print; her works are in our schools.

Zora's vessel is no longer on the horizon, but Time did not ravage it. Her ship has become a star, a bright white gleam that helps us black women writers find our place in the world. We form a sentinel on the shore, keeping watch as our ships, with wishes on board, weather wind and rolling seas. We celebrate the ones that land safely, and we pray for the others still out on the horizon, refusing to turn away.

LAURA LIPPMAN

Laura Lippman, a former Baltimore Sun *reporter, is the* New York Times *best-selling author of the award-winning Tess Monaghan series, which features a female heroine and detective in Baltimore; she splits her time between that city and New Orleans.*

I was born in Atlanta and grew up in Baltimore, but my cousins were very adamant, as are my grandparents, that I am a Yankee. I've always been defined by what I was *not*—not a Southerner, and when I went to college at Northwestern, outside of Chicago, they didn't think Baltimore was in the East. So I was supposedly not a Southerner and not an Easterner. But the more I looked at my family, the more Southern I realized I was, and I was happy about that. I have two Uncle Bubbas. *Two.* I call my mother's parents Big Momma and Big Daddy, and called my father's parents Sweetheart and Lulu. My father had an aunt known as Lil Sister, even though she wasn't. It went on and on.

There are a lot of steel magnolias in my family. My grandmother was the oldest of three girls, and when her father died, she was forced to learn to drive—at the age of ten—so she could drive her mother. I'm very comfortable with the stereotype of strong Southern women who are capable. I've got the steel part down.

When I'm in New Orleans, where we keep a house in addition to our place in Baltimore, people can call me "baby" and "sugar" and I don't get spitting mad the way I would somewhere else. There's a dark side to the South, too, I know. Years ago

I asked my mother, a librarian, to write on a piece of paper how many slaves our family had. She pulled up a census from the 1800s, then wrote, "40." I kept that piece of paper in my day planner because I wanted to think about it every day.

I feel like a lot of things fell into place when I understood that I was a Southerner, just as Southern as my cousins. I write books based in Baltimore. I'm still a little hesitant to write about the South. I feel like the South is waiting for me, as a topic.

CARLA HAYDEN

(1952–PRESENT)

The book lover bringing the Library of Congress into the twenty-first century

On April 28, 2015, before heading to work, Carla Hayden checked in with her mother. This was not unusual; the two have condos in the same Baltimore building. But the circumstances were hardly ordinary. As CEO of the city's Enoch Pratt Free Library, Hayden had made the decision to keep open all of its branches, including one in the "epicenter" of the violent protests that followed the death of Freddie Gray, who had been taken into police custody earlier that month.

Hayden's mother, Colleen, a retired social worker, who was then age eighty-three, remained unruffled. "Make sure you have coffee, and take water for the people," she advised, adding, "Don't forget the cups and the napkins."

As National Guard troops surrounded the library and TV cameras rolled, Hayden and her staff went about their business. "If we close, we're sending a signal that we're afraid or that we aren't going to be available when times are tough," Hayden told *American Libraries* magazine later that week, giving an interview as troops patrolled outside. "We should be open especially when times are tough."

More than a decade earlier, Hayden had defended libraries as sanctuaries in a less literal, though no less vital, sense. As president of the American Library Association, she spearheaded protests against a Patriot Act provision that would have allowed government access to library patron records. That fight to protect privacy led to skirmishes with then attorney general John Ashcroft and earned Hayden accolades as a *Ms.* magazine Woman of the Year. "Libraries are a cornerstone of democracy—where information is free and equally available to everyone. People tend to take that for granted," Hayden told *Ms.* "They don't realize what is at stake when that is put at risk."

In 2016, after being nominated by President Obama, Hayden was confirmed as head of the Library of Congress, making her the first female and the first black chief librarian in the history of the largest library in the world. But almost equally significant is that her thirteen white male predecessors included only one other *actual* librarian. She succeeded a Reagan nominee known for brilliant scholarship on Russia and woeful efforts to digitize the LOC collections. She, on the other hand, possesses skills needed to bring the sprawling historical collection into the technical present, and her duties also include appointing the U.S. poet laureate and overseeing copyright. Plus, she's on Twitter (@LibnofCongress) posting about everything from the legacy of Stan Lee to the thrill of browsing Rosa Parks's papers. And she commutes to her job in D.C. from Baltimore, earning her praise as the "most loyal Baltimorean" from the *Baltimore Sun*. "Who cares if she wasn't born here?" the newspaper noted of the "faithful daughter of her adopted city."

Hayden, who was born in Tallahassee, Florida, in 1952, and lived in New York City, moved to Chicago following her parents' divorce. There, she earned her master's and doctorate degrees in library science at the University of Chicago. While a graduate student, she began working at the Chicago Public Library, eventually serving as a children's librarian, and then later as chief librarian and deputy commissioner before being tapped as CEO of the Baltimore libraries in 1993. And over the years she has often cited one of her own early experiences as a library patron: repeatedly checking out *Bright April*, a children's book depicting an African American Brownie scout.

TAYARI JONES

Tayari Jones—the author of the critically acclaimed 2018 novel *An American Marriage*, which Oprah Winfrey snapped up for her book club, as well as for a film adaptation—spotted Alice Walker, the Georgia-born writer of *The Color Purple*, across the lobby of the InterContinental Buckhead Atlanta hotel while attending a National Book Club Conference. She sat for a minute, wondering if she should walk over and introduce herself, eventually deciding she should. "I know who you are," Walker responded. "I love your book." A product of southwest Atlanta, a predominantly black area, Jones says her introduction as a child to books and black authors such as Walker was simultaneous, and she's worked to add to the common narratives about the Southern black experience in four novels. "It is wrong to define black life in terms of suffering," she says.

In 2018, you accepted a position at Emory University, allowing you to return to Atlanta after years teaching at Rutgers University–Newark. What made you decide to return?

You know, I just want to be back home. One, my parents are getting older. My daddy is eighty-two, so I wanted to be closer to them. And also, I'm just from Atlanta. Like, that's who I am, and I felt like I was a Southern writer in exile in New York.

And it wasn't until you left the South that you experienced racism.

People in the North, they have this weird dichotomy where they say, "Oh, in the South, the racism is overt, and in the North, the racism is hidden." And I don't know where this narrative came from. Then people argue back and forth asking what type of racism they prefer. Do they prefer in-your-face racism or subtle racism? I'm like, I don't like racism in any form. But people just assume that because we're from the South that we just grew up having people throw things at us and calling us out of our name. But that just has not been my experience.

In your work, you interrogate class and privilege within race.

Whenever there's racial segregation, then you're going to get a lot of diversity within that segregated group. When you say [to a black person], "Do you know anyone from a different class background?" [they're] like, "Yeah, I call them my cousins." I think that we as black people, and as black writers, have a very nuanced understanding of class because we have intimacy with people from different class backgrounds. And I think probably more so even in the South because of the ways that we live together across class.

You've talked about ownership of the word **American,** *and you've wondered if the title* **An American Marriage** *made it seem like a story about a white couple in Connecticut. How do you feel about the word* **Southern?**

I have a lot of friends who are white Southern writers, and they sometimes feel pigeonholed. They don't want to be called Southern. They want to be American. But I felt like I was banging on the door to be called a Southern writer because I'm black and because I'm "urban." That is not what people think about when they think about Southern writers. They think it's rural by tradition; they think it's a white tradition. Also they expect historical writing. They expect the Civil War to keep coming up. And so I wanted to be called a Southern writer. When I got elected into the Fellowship of Southern Writers, I was very proud to be in that fellowship. People don't think of Alice Walker as a Southern writer. She's totally a Southern writer. And so that was important to me. And, you know, it's funny, I had less trouble owning *Southern* than owning *American.* I do not have a fraught relationship with the South. I've been reading a lot about black Southerners writing about loving a home that doesn't love you. I do not feel that way. Maybe it's because I'm from Atlanta. I feel like I love Atlanta [and] Atlanta loves me back.

It was also here that you built strong relationships with other successful women, including while getting your degree at Spelman College.

I met my mentor, [the novelist, playwright, and poet] Pearl Cleage, at Spelman. I was seventeen years old and she took me up under her wing, and I have been there ever since. There's an exhibit at Emory about friendships between black women writers, and they have some of my letters to her on display. I was a little shocked, but I have been writing letters to her for thirty years, and I've always turned to her when I've had a problem. I'm so grateful for being grounded in that tradition.

NIKKY FINNEY

The poet who exercises audacity

BY LATRIA GRAHAM

Nikky Finney cut me open once. I was sitting in a dark room staring at a video of her on my computer screen when she began to carve into me expertly with her poetry.

Her voice crisp, words pointed and intentional, she was reading "Black Orion," a poem about her great-uncle, Frederick J. Davenport, who received an F on a paper he wrote in the 1950s that predicted man would walk on the moon. She puts us in his "pine tree galaxy" to help us understand the extraordinary interior life of someone known simply as a farmer.

This is her signature—her ability to use evocative imagery to explore history, womanhood, ancestry, and racial justice. Intensely intimate and specific but ultimately universal, her poetry binds the personal and the political, and she draws from her family's history by the sea in South Carolina for her subject matter. The desire to dismantle the power structure of brutality that has gnawed at the people she knows permeates her work.

In "Cotton Tea," she talks about an old folk remedy used by slaves to induce abortions.

In "Making Foots," she uses an ordinary appendage to express the black man's anguish at forced labor, his discomfit while marching during the civil rights movement, and his yearning to be free enough to just "put his feet up."

In "Easy-Bake," young women are wedged between the conventions of the oven and the bullets from a school shooter's gun. Finney published "Easy-Bake"

fifteen years ago, before the epidemic, before the chronic rash of mass shootings that stream across our TV screens.

Finney, it seems, like the great-uncle before her, is an oracle. We have yet to fully understand the depth and gravitas of the gift she has given us.

Her writings are an exercise in audacity. She is America's conscience, speaking gently about all the things we wish we could bury, prodding at memories that express themselves in the tightness of our bodies.

In a video simply titled "Nikky Finney on Pencils," she eulogizes the goods of the Blackfeet Indian Pencil Company. "They don't make them anymore," Finney says to the camera. "So I have to write carefully." In 2011, her fifth collection of poetry, *Head Off & Split*, won the National Book Award. Her acceptance speech, which included the penal codes and a list of punishments for teaching enslaved people to read, now lives in the National Museum of African American History & Culture.

The University of South Carolina professor's labor gives a name to our vulnerabilities so that we may offer them up and receive grace in their place. She treats her own ancestors' truth as a matter of craft, sowing, tending, and harvesting her version of Carolina Gold. Her poetry is scripture, a tangible written reverence for a region and a tradition that have all but fallen away, but that made the South what it is. Read it. Remember. Recite it out loud.

JESMYN WARD

(1977–PRESENT)

The leader of the new Southern canon of essential books

The characters that populate Jesmyn Ward's stories are the types of people often disregarded in popular literature, and in life: African American twin brothers coming into adulthood in the summer after high school—one finding a low-wage job, the other resorting to selling drugs; a pregnant teen trying to save her family as a hurricane barrels toward their home; a little boy, his drug-addicted mother, and all the ghosts they carry on a road trip to pick up the child's father from a notorious Mississippi prison. But by framing her stories around the disregarded, the two-time National Book Award winner and MacArthur "genius" grant recipient has become a voice of the modern South and one of the twenty-first century's great American novelists.

Written in lyrical prose, each of Ward's novels takes place in Bois Sauvage, a fictional town on the Mississippi Gulf Coast based on her hometown of DeLisle, where she was raised and where she now lives with her husband and two young children. Growing up, Ward was bullied, both by black classmates at the public school she attended until middle school, and white classmates at the private school she attended later, paid for by a wealthy family for whom her mother cleaned houses. So she buried herself in books, particularly about spunky girls—though none of the protagonists looked like her. When Ward left DeLisle to go to Stanford for a bachelor's degree in English, and then a master's in media studies and communication, she was the first in her family to attend college.

She planned on entering a "practical" occupation—law, or perhaps something in health care. But when her nineteen-year-old brother, Joshua, was killed in a hit-and-run by a drunk driver in 2000, the course of Ward's life changed entirely. Writing, she deemed, would give her life the most meaning.

In 2005, Ward graduated from Michigan's MFA program. Four months later, she was home in DeLisle when Hurricane Katrina struck. Her grandmother's living room, where they'd been waiting out the storm, filled with water quickly, so she and her family evacuated toward a church, but were instead forced to take shelter in their truck in a field full of tractors because of the deluge. When the white family that owned the land came to check on the tractors during the storm, they refused to let Ward's family come inside for refuge. They survived, but the community was devastated.

It took a while, after the storm, for Ward to be able to write again—she felt the experience had "silenced" her. Her first novel, *Where the Line Bleeds,* was published in 2008. She then began writing *Salvage the Bones,* a reflection on Katrina that would win the National Book Award, as would her 2017 novel, *Sing, Unburied, Sing.* And while all her fiction gathers inspiration from her life and surroundings, the most forthright are her nonfiction works: her 2013 memoir, *Men We Reaped,* which examines the deaths of five young men in her community over five years, and *The Fire This Time,* a 2016 anthology of essays and poems on race. In every work, Ward speaks for those who have for so long been overlooked beneath the cloud of poverty, addiction, desolation, and history. But through all the pain roiling through Bois Sauvage—and DeLisle—Ward maintains that there is always family, and there is always hope.

DALIYAH ARANA

To the amazement of her parents, Haleema and Miguel, Daliyah Marie Arana began sounding out words at age two and read her first book before her third birthday. When Daliyah finished her thousandth book at age four, Haleema wrote to the Library of Congress in Washington, D.C., asking if her daughter could shadow Carla Hayden, the first woman and first African American to lead the nation's library. Hayden agreed, and in January 2017 photos of the pair strolling the marble halls—Daliyah neatly dressed in a pink frock, pink glasses, and a pink hair bow—went viral. By the second grade, the Gainesville, Georgia, resident had ticked up her book total to an estimated 2,700 and could read some college-level texts. She still gets a kick out of kid lit, though—her favorite book is Mo Willems's *The Pigeon Finds a Hot Dog!*

Where do you think you get your love of reading?

From my mom. Although she started reading at a normal age, like seven. She does insurance for her job: auto, life, and . . . I forgot the last one. When she gets stressed out, she starts to read.

What was it like to go to the Library of Congress?

The best thing was all the books! I think they have over ten million—that's a lot more than we have at our library at home. I knew that it was the biggest library in the whole world, but I thought it was going to be smaller. I don't even know how many workers they have. I was like, "Whoa, I didn't know there was a library like this."

You spent the day with the Librarian of Congress, Carla Hayden. What do you think the best part of her job is?

Probably reading books to children. There's this area with beanbags, so the children can read. They have an area like that at our library [in Gainesville], too. The worst part would be organizing all the books! I'd be, "No thank you. Not today."

Some kids say they don't really like reading. What do you say to them?

Well, if you don't like reading, then you don't get any education in your mind. Learning new things is what makes reading fun . . . plus learning big words that you don't already know. I usually tell my mom if I don't know a word, and then she helps me sound it out.

Are there any women or girls from history that you like to read about?

Ruby Bridges. She was the first black woman child to go to a white school. That took a lot of courage. Ruby Bridges wrote a book about her life, so she's a writer, too. And Rosa Parks . . . how she refused to give up her seat. She showed perseverance.

What about women who inspire you?

Oh, the president's wife—the First Lady. I think she wrote a book about a hundred or two hundred years ago about her life. She was George Washington's wife, and she was also a famous writer, back in the eighteenth century. Also my mom, because she taught me how to read.

In 2017, you recited a famous speech, "I Have a Dream," for Martin Luther King Jr. Day. What did you think of that speech?

It was inspiring . . . but there was a part I couldn't read, because it was not appropriate for children under age five. But, other than that, I think it was pretty good.

Do you have an idea of what you want to do when you grow up?

Oh yes, I want to be a paleontologist. Do you know what that is?

Someone who studies—

Dinosaurs! They dig them out, but you have to be careful and patient, because they might break. I like all the dinosaurs, and it sounds really fun digging up their bones. Do you know how much money you get for one *T. rex*? One million dollars! That's a paycheck!

"I can remember my mother telling me that when she was going through hard times, she couldn't have made it if it weren't for her female friends. I wrote *Fried Green Tomatoes* based on stories I had heard from her and my great-aunt, who ran the café in Irondale, Alabama. She was so funny. She was a scream. And everybody adored her. And her sister, my grandmother, was very funny. That's the thing I love about the South: Everybody is a character. We love to talk, and the weather is conducive to sitting around on porches and talking."

—**Fannie Flagg,** best-selling author and Birmingham, Alabama, native, pictured here at center with the cast of the 1991 film based on her book *Fried Green Tomatoes at the Whistle Stop Cafe*

EUDORA WELTY

Her words captured the South's cadence

BY FRANCES MAYES

Read Eudora Welty. Start with the short stories. They're sharp, funny, and deeply humane. I especially love her novel *The Optimist's Daughter*, a meditation on memory and place, Southern style. Read every word she produced—the experience will bring you to the taproot of the region.

Welty wrote in Jackson, Mississippi. After her education in the North and the Midwest, she returned to 1119 Pinehurst Street, where she spent her time gardening, participating in the intense social life of a Southern city, reviewing books, roaming the countryside photographing people. And writing from the heart of a place. She knew that *where* something happens *is* what happens. Her ear was fine-tuned to the local idiom. I love coming upon a phrase like "I swan!" "I can just hear that," we say as we read.

Southerners can small talk each other to death without a trace of boredom crossing anyone's face. Welty captures cadence, the lulling storyteller voice, loops of lyric, then brings them up short with sharp declarative sentences—she used the tone of conversation without succumbing to talking, talking, talking.

Here's what most of us never admit: Southerners

are the most private people on the globe. Within tight interconnections of family, the real caring for each other, the incessant stories, the visiting, Welty is onto the truth that all these rituals offer an elaborate continuity for solitary figures.

You can tour her Tudor Revival house and garden. When I visited, the word that came to mind was *plain*. Her desk and typewriter stand along the window wall of a bedroom. The house is colorless but full of books. Books everywhere, even stacked on the sofa. Walking through, I recognized: This was liberation.

Years ago, I happened to stand behind Eudora Welty in line at an airport shop. She was buying mints. Elderly and hunched, she counted out the change. As she turned, I said, "Miss Welty, I just have to say how much I admire your work."

She snapped her purse and put her hand on my arm. "Well, thank you. You are just so sweet to say so."

Her Southern grace abides in all her work.

Of the monumental twentieth-century writers—note that I do not limit my claim to Southern writers—she had the biggest heart.

DOROTHY ALLISON

Dorothy Allison calls herself "trashy" with a chuckle, but she stops laughing when asked what Southern women have in common: "Oh, God. We can survive what seems unsurvivable." Though she now calls Guerneville, California, home, it was Greenville, South Carolina, where Allison survived the childhood she later drew upon to write her debut novel, *Bastard Out of Carolina*. Depicting the brutal physical abuse and emotional suffering of a young girl, the book was named a National Book Award finalist even as it was banned in countless schools across America. While it rose to the status of a classic, Allison followed *Bastard* with works that include another best-selling novel, a memoir, and a collection of feminist essays.

Why did you begin telling stories?

My mama worked. My aunts worked. I was probably ten or eleven, and I was left with the care of my dumb cousins, some of whom were older than me. To keep them from killing each other, I'd tell them scary stories. If I got their mouths to drop open, they'd stop hitting each other for a few minutes.

When you started writing, did your family know?

My mother did. She adored country western and gospel music. That can lead to a lot of really bad poetry in an adolescent girl. But every time I'd write a poem, she collected it. That helps a lot when you're a little baby writer, having someone who adores everything that you utter or write.

Have you always written with an audience in mind?

Of course. When I began, my audience was my mother and sisters. But at the same time, there was this overwhelming sense that the world did not understand or approve of us, and that became an audience. You can write against that. You can write to say to that audience, "You don't know who we are." That's one of the great beginnings for any story: "You don't know what it was like. Let me tell you." That audience doesn't have to be approving and friendly. It can be very adversarial, and that's strong.

So you're trying to show people what they got wrong?

To tell you the truth, what I'm reaching for is *glory*.

What do you mean?

Glory is language on the page that doesn't just resonate but evokes an immediate, emotionally tinged response in the listener or the reader. Glory does not require approval. Glory is like the angels take over and you're flying.

You've been a guest professor at several colleges and universities. What's the biggest obstacle you try to help students overcome?

They've been conditioned—especially young Southern writers—to write in a voice that is not their own. I try to get them to take a breath and let that go. By that I mean you have to allow yourself to use a voice that is unique and your own, that is not what you've read before. There is a certain impulse in all writers to want to please. You have to give up wanting to please.

That's hard to do when you're young.

When I was young, the majority of books that I could find were all written in the Northeast, and they were written by middle- or upper-class people. That did not say anything about the world that I inhabited, and in fact when they mentioned the world that I inhabited, it was always with great contempt.

And that motivated you?

What I wanted was to have us—which is to say the people I loved and feared and was also in an embattled relationship with—I wanted us to at least be real. To make us real meant to write in a language that could not only speak beautifully about the people I love but also make the reader uncomfortable.

Do you ever feel completely comfortable and accepted, or do you always feel a little different?

Both things are true. I always say I'm a visitor from another planet! I take a certain joy and power out of being that survivor growing up poor, that embattled female, that lesbian feminist, that Southern accent. It's a kind of reverse authority. The resistance to contempt really is very powerful.

You wrote once that Bastard Out of Carolina **"disturbed the peace." Is that part of the purpose of literature and music?**

Yes. That never changes. And let's be clear about what the peace is. The peace is a kind of silence about the very issues that writers exist to call attention to. It's so easy to disturb the peace. All you really have to do is tell the truth, and it will disturb and upset people. In the kind of writing I love, the language is encouraging and comforting while the content is profoundly disturbing.

That's an effective combination.

It's one of the things I love about a lot of Southern literature. We do it better than anyone. We can make you laugh and cry at the same time, which is my favorite thing. I work hard to do a kind of seduction in which you read sections that are very funny and charming, and then, two paragraphs later, it ain't charming. It ain't funny. It's horrible. And to have both of those things happen at the same time, that's life.

MARGOT LEE SHETTERLY

The Charlottesville, Virginia, author Margot Lee Shetterly wrote the book Hidden Figures, *which highlights the black female mathematicians who helped NASA win the space race in the 1960s, after discovering that one of her favorite childhood Sunday school teachers at First Baptist Church in Hampton, Virginia, was a retired NASA mathematician—no small feat in midcentury America.*

During the space race, the astronauts were the most visible, and below them were the guys in white shirts with skinny ties—mission control. But then you had all these people behind the scenes. In the same way that we rely on our electronics today, the astronauts and mission control relied on women who they literally called "computers." At the bottom of the pyramid, the women did the numbers.

Many of the women were from the South. With so many black colleges throughout the South, Langley was a natural next step for top black talent. Many of the engineers were from New York and the Midwest, and it created an unusual work environment—a federal office that had to adhere to federal laws for hiring but still had the influence of Jim Crow locally. The African American women were called the West Area Computers, and there was a "colored" section sign in the cafeteria. It chafed because they were hired for their professional acumen. They're doing excellent work and yet they have segregation in their faces.

There wasn't an expectation that they would come out from the shadows, particularly in the early days. But some of the older generation, like Mary Jackson, fought to get included in important decisions. Many younger women followed their lead and said, "I want to be the one out front giving the research report and presenting at conferences." The women built alliances across race and age and worked to support each other's careers.

When I sat in their living rooms and interviewed these women, they were very matter-of-fact about their stories. They would say, "Listen, I was just doing my job." There wasn't this sense of self-awareness that they were doing amazing work.

I hope people remember that the civil rights and women's rights movements, as well as the space program itself, came out of a fundamental optimism. We were shooting for our best selves and shooting literally beyond the earth. We ultimately saw the triumph of imagination over fear—which included the ability to imagine putting a human on the moon and imagining that a black woman might be able to help him get there even in a time of Jim Crow segregation. It took a lot of imagination and curiosity to drive forward higher ideals, and that's what these women represent. Theirs is a story about the triumph of curiosity over fear.

TASTEMAKERS & TRENDSETTERS

LELA ROSE

Since launching her first collection out of her apartment in the nineties, the Dallas native Lela Rose has built a fashion empire that now includes couture, ready-to-wear, resort, and bridal collections that have charmed boldface fans, from fellow Texans Jenna and Barbara Bush to Catherine, Duchess of Cambridge. That means the designer, wife, and mother of two rarely has a minute when she's not parenting, preparing for a show, or thinking a season ahead. But in those rare moments of peace, Rose doesn't rest—she celebrates, entertaining her friends and family with the same whimsy she brings to her clothing.

Where did you get your creative drive?

My mother. She still influences me all the time. She should have started a million businesses. She was an amazing cook, and I loved being with her in the kitchen. She wasn't making regular recipes. She was always teaching herself things and learning something new. We were the kids in the car-pool line eating soufflés! Everything she did was always creative and interesting.

She also taught you about traditions—and bending tradition.

Yes. She loved to entertain, but there was always something a little irreverent about it, and you always knew you were going to have a good time. I love to stick a thumb in tradition just enough to make it fun, and I learned that from her.

You're an entertainer yourself.

My kids always ask me, "Who's coming over tonight, Mom?" It gives me energy to have people over. I'm cooking all the time, and I need people to come over to help me eat all this food! I can't help but stop in the green market on my way home from work. I really love this part of my life so much. It doesn't have to be stressful. People just like to be invited over.

What does having a career in fashion mean to you?

Sometimes I've been like, *I'm a dress designer—shouldn't I be doing something better?* But one of my main jobs is to make women look and feel beautiful. Is it heart surgery? No. But you are at your best and most productive self when you feel good. That's a big contribution.

What is your definition of great personal style?

Confidence in what you're wearing and not trends. I love people who have married themselves to one color—maybe their whole life has been buttercup yellow.

Why do you think Southerners love color so much?

Maybe it's so hot you can't wear black! I don't wear black. I never will. My world is in citrine and pink and coral.

You are friends with other Southern women in the design world, including the Florida native Celerie Kemble.

Celerie and I have always been close, and all of my friends are supportive. Everyone wants to help each other. I launched a new part of our business based on the idea of women helping women. We handpicked female stylists across the country to host trunk shows in different communities.

Your husband is also a Texan, and you and your family return often to your home state. Beyond their Southern roots, what else do you want to instill in your children?

That being a nice person and caring about other people are important. To say hello, and thank people, because every person *is* a person. The other thing I'd really love to teach them is the importance of being an entrepreneur. I think I've bugged my son too much about it already, though!

Is there one particular piece of advice that's helped you in your career?

Fashion is an extremely difficult business. It's a grind, but I adore it, so it makes the constant battle worthwhile. One of the attributes that I've always had is persistence. I just keep going and keep going. I'm never going to give in or give up.

PEGGY MARTIN

A Louisiana gardening maven, Peggy Martin is the namesake of the Peggy Martin rose, the cuttings of which proliferated around the South after Martin's plant withstood 150-mile-per-hour winds, submersion in twenty feet of salt water for more than two weeks, and scorching heat to survive Hurricane Katrina.

My grandmother had long rows of roses along the entrance to her place in the country. It was called Shangri-La, in St. Tammany Parish, Louisiana, a gorgeous place along a creek with sandy banks, a beautiful home, and a big garden. I just followed her around and watched everything she did, saw how she kept her coffee grounds and crushed up her eggshells and put those around her roses. My mother was a career woman and never did garden, but I watched and learned from my grandma. I had the gene in me.

I joined the New Orleans Old Garden Rose Society in the 1990s, and a whole new world opened up to me. I had always loved to garden, but now it was like a treasure chest full of jewels. I learned about every kind of rose and collected them from all over. Before Katrina, at my home along the Mississippi River in Plaquemines Parish, I had twelve acres and 450 antique roses.

One day, I was at my hairdresser's, and we always joked that she accidentally killed every plant I gave her. But that day she wanted me to see something she had growing and blooming on her fence in her backyard. It was a rose, a solid mass of blooms that took my breath away. It was part of a rose her mother-in-law had grown in the Garden District in New Orleans. She gave me cuttings right then and there. I planted that rose along my tractor shed, and it just took over. That rose never had a name, and I asked people from all over if they could identify it. It's just an old rose that has grown for a long, long time in Louisiana.

When Katrina was coming, my husband and I left. Our area filled up like a bathtub. My parents, who lived next to us, wouldn't evacuate. They drowned. I was like a zombie—I don't even remember months of time. When I finally made it back to our property, it looked like a nuclear bomb had detonated. Black sticks and ash, trees with no leaves, branches snapped in half. I walked past my parents' house and our garden and house to see if anything was salvageable. I happened to glance toward where my shed was, and there was this little green growth. Forest green. It was the only green thing left in the whole entire garden. I thought, *My God, how did this rose survive when everything else is totally destroyed?* I felt in my heart that

my mother and father knew how devastated I was going to be, and they asked God to leave me something, anything. It was that old garden rose.

I brought the rose back to where we had evacuated in Gonzales, Louisiana, and it kept growing in a pot. But I was in such a state of shock, losing my parents like that. I swore I would never have another garden. People in the rose society found out where I was and started bringing me roses. Nurseries gave me roses. So many people were giving me roses, and saying, "Peggy, you need to grow roses again." And they were right. Every time I got roses, I got a truckload of soil and just planted and planted. I know my roses like they're people—I know them by their names.

The rose that lived through Katrina became the Peggy Martin rose. Now it's growing across the big wrought-iron fence at our entrance. Fifteen feet across and entirely Peggy Martin rose. The pink blossoms are so thick, they hang down like clusters of grapes. Some people call it a climber rose, but it's really a rambler, graceful and elegant.

CRISTINA LYNCH

Cristina Lynch launched Mi Golondrina, her line of embroidered dresses, skirts, blouses, bedding, and table linens, from her hometown of Dallas in 2013, but the textiles celebrate the sewing traditions of her family's native Mexico, thread by colorful thread. The floral motifs take months to create by hand by the Mexican artisans with whom Lynch collaborates, with pieces often traveling from one village known for one type of embroidery to the next. In the end, the blooms come to life in stripes and sun-drenched hues, turning her breezy cottons into beautiful billboards for the Latin American art form.

What sparked the idea for Mi Golondrina?

I knew I wanted to start a brand that celebrated Mexican culture as early as high school. But it wasn't until college that I realized how much I loved fashion. Working in sales for Oscar de la Renta in New York motivated me to think outside the box. I saw how many techniques they were using in their clothing, and I told my family about my idea for a company that would show off Mexico's culture, and they said, "Do it right away or someone else will." So I moved home. And I read every single book my mom had on the arts in Mexico.

And then you traveled to Mexico with your mom, who was born there.

Yes. My mom also had her own clothing line, and has an incredible aesthetic, from houses to dresses. She just makes everything gorgeous. I wanted to continue that. I learned that the product I was thinking about and reading about went so much deeper than what I knew. It ignited a passion. The first trip was to Oaxaca. We went to the markets and met with female artisans from all over. We came back with five full suitcases of things we saw and loved: embroidered dresses and tablecloths and pillow covers and strips of embroidery. I am attracted to very feminine details and loved the bright colors. Maybe it was the happiness in them that I was attracted to. In New York I didn't wear bright colors.

What was it about that form of sewing that spoke to you?

The history. In Oaxaca we work with four hundred artisans representing five communities, [who use] their traditional designs. We are also working with two communities in Chiapas. Some of the communities, like San Antonino Castillo Velasco, have been known for certain types of embroideries for two hundred years. One community does hand crocheting, another does embroidery, and yet another, smocking. The women we work with favor *pensamientos*, or pansies in English, as their flower of choice. The word means "thought" in Spanish.

The look feels both incredibly old and current at once.

We are coming along in an age of fast fashion, and cool machines are being invented all the time, and that's great. But with all of that, I think people crave slow processes and things being hand done, too. It feels very real, very human.

Where did the name Mi Golondrina come from?

My maternal grandfather's cattle ranch was in Northern Mexico. I grew up in a family of entrepreneurs, and it grew to be one of the biggest in the country. When my mother was little, she noticed there were little swallows everywhere. We loved the idea of these tiny birds flying through Mexico to new communities. Mi Golondrina means "my swallow" in Spanish.

What has being back in the South meant to you?

I loved Texas growing up, and I think that's because of the women here. They are so supportive and strong and just *doers*. I feel like I've met so many women here who say, "Let's try this." Texas and the South breed women who are excited to *get going*.

Why is what you do personally and culturally important to you?

A lot of the women we work with still speak Mayan languages. To learn it and understand it and be open to what they are doing—there is nothing more beautiful. I was just in Portugal looking at embroideries that were nearly identical to the Chiapas pieces we create in Mexico. I went to Venice and saw lacework that was similar to that of the artisans we work with in Aguascalientes. I wish I could see the voyages that brought these cultures and art forms together. They connect all of us.

KATHARINE GRAHAM

The newspaper maven with savoir faire

BY HASKELL HARRIS

Before reading Katharine Graham's memoir, *Personal History*, I already felt simpatico with the late publisher of the *Washington Post* and CEO of the Washington Post Company—I had grown up around a daily newspaper in small-town Virginia, and my grandfather and my father had spent their lives in the business. I understood the idea that for print people, holidays are just words on calendars because the news never stops.

What I didn't know was that Graham, born Katharine Meyer in 1917, had survived a high-pressure childhood in one of the most influential families in America (her father, the übersuccessful financier Eugene Meyer, had purchased the *Post* in 1933); the loss of a baby as a young newlywed; the heartbreaking infidelity of her husband, then the *Post*'s publisher; and his subsequent suicide by shotgun while she was in the same house. And after all that, she not only stepped in, with great trepidation, to lead the *Post*, but then proceeded to make history, becoming the first female board member of the Associated Press and the American Newspaper Publishers Association. We can thank Graham for helping hold our political system accountable and making real news matter (pan to Richard Nixon boarding that helicopter in disgrace). And *I* have Graham to thank for teaching me what true grit, tenacity, and grace are all about.

When I'm asked about my dream dinner party guest list, she is the only invitation I'd care to send. Mostly because she often dreaded dinner parties, as I sometimes do, and I admire that she routinely entertained some of the most powerful people in the world at her home anyway. She could work a room in spite of her introverted nature—she knew how to turn it on and draw people out. She was the best kind of host because she listened more than she talked. And while some might balk at associating her with style—in her memoir, she muses that Truman Capote made her the guest of honor at his fabled Black and White Ball because she was less glamorous, more of a "Cinderella," than his other friends—to me, her lack of pretense defines a uniquely Southern strain of grace and hospitality. I'm not saying every stylish Southerner has it. I'm saying the best ones do.

As a longtime style editor in the South, I've interacted with plenty of so-called tastemakers and icons. One woman known for her inimitable manners chewed through a ham sandwich during a phone interview with me and then demanded (through bites of an extremely tough baguette) that the story we were discussing make the cover. Another Southern designer held in high esteem rolled up a rug he disliked and pitched it in my direction in disgust on a photo shoot. Luckily (and hilariously) it was heavy and landed with a thud right next to him, not on me.

Those experiences, and those people, who lacked humility but possessed "style," are the opposite of Graham. She ran what would become one of the most influential newspapers in the country, defending and empowering her staffers to achieve Pulitzer-winning work (a prize she herself won for *Personal History*). And at home, she made titans of industry and movers and shakers and members of all political parties welcome over drinks and dinner. Most important, she kept going in the face of extraordinary fear. That's an elegance to aspire to.

"The biggest gifts my parents gave me were manners and sociability. They cared about people and making them feel at home. This was something that was instilled in us. When people come over, they shouldn't be intimidated by the house or the room or anything in it."

—*Bunny Williams*, the celebrated interior designer
from Virginia, on Southern hospitality

SARA BLAKELY

(1971–PRESENT)

The entrepreneur shaping women's lives in more ways than one

Great ideas are like a perfect pair of pants—they don't fit a single set of criteria. You know the right pants when you find them, though, and the shape they take has everything to do with the person who picks them up. As it turns out, it was a not-so-perfect pair that led the Clearwater, Florida, native Sara Blakely to *her* brilliant idea: Spanx, her shapewear empire, all started with an unworn pair of white pants hanging in the closet. Blakely, who was then a door-to-door fax machine salesperson, couldn't put them on without some kind of faux pas—her underwear would show through, or the pants would hug the wrong places. So she snipped the feet off a pair of pantyhose, tried them on under the problem pants, and looked in the mirror at her billion-dollar idea.

Taking the idea to market proved to be slightly more complicated than taking scissors to a pair of tights. Blakely, who had by then moved to Atlanta, was dismissed by every manufacturer she met with, not only by those who wouldn't hear her out, but also by businessmen—and they were mostly men—who simply didn't understand the product. When she finally persuaded a North Carolina mill to give her a chance, it came only after the owner sought counsel from his daughters over dinner. Fortunately, sales came far more naturally when Blakely was speaking directly with women about her miracle product, dubbed Spanx. Much might be made of deals being made on the golf course, but Blakely's big break came in the ladies' room—during a meeting with Neiman Marcus, she asked the buyer to join her in the restroom to see the difference Spanx made for herself. It was unconventional, but one glimpse at the before-and-after magic of the simple idea landed Spanx a spot in seven stores around the country.

When Spanx hit the shelves, the work was just beginning. Relentless, Blakely would camp out all day in department stores, explaining the product to shoppers. She sent friends in different cities to buy out the stock, creating buzz and demand. Samples of her product were mailed to anyone she thought might really understand it, striking gold when Oprah Winfrey, the recipient of one such package, placed Spanx on her annual list of "favorite things" in 2000. Blakely's willingness to gamble against conventional wisdom paid off in other ways, too. Why couldn't the same product sold at Neiman Marcus and Saks be sold on home shopping networks, like QVC? Six minutes into the company's first appearance on the network, eight thousand pairs of Spanx sold—an exponentially larger haul than any single day on the rack.

Spanx grew from an idea to a brand to an entire industry, complete with plenty of copycats. Today the Atlanta company remains self-funded, and Blakely, who owns 100 percent of it, is a billionaire. But as her own influence continues to grow, she's determined to give others a leg up, too—her nonprofit, the Spanx by Sara Blakely Foundation, offers scholarships, education, and entrepreneurial coaching for young women around the world. With more diverse boardrooms, maybe the next generation of investors won't need to run home to ask their wives or their daughters to weigh in on an idea for the female demographic—they'll be able to just look in the mirror.

MIMI McMAKIN
& CELERIE KEMBLE

Comfortable rooms with soul and style are the hallmark of Kemble Interiors, the much-lauded design firm founded by the fourth-generation Palm Beach native Mimi McMakin in 1982. Personality rather than perfection is the goal, an ethos that was ingrained early in Celerie Kemble, McMakin's daughter, who spent much of her Florida childhood trailing after her mother through antique stores and construction sites. That relaxed approach, combined with high-profile partnerships with the likes of J.Crew, Benjamin Moore, Schumacher, Henredon, and Arteriors; headline-grabbing projects such as the Dominican Republic–based Playa Grande Beach Club; a healthy dose of flawless taste; and dogged determination, has made their Kemble Interiors a design-world darling.

Not all mothers and daughters could work together.

Celerie Kemble: Well, we've never stood in front of a client and done what we would do at home, which is argue till one of us has won, either through passive-aggressiveness or obstinance.

Mimi McMakin: There's a great respect between us. I will call her and ask, "Is this as dull as dishwater?" And Celerie will look at it and be very honest.

CK: We have such a shorthand. There's a lot of "Remember that thing that I didn't like then? Well, why is that coming up to me now?" And somehow, we'll both be able to be say, "Oh, yeah. Okay. Okay. Bye." And we may not have used a noun or a verb.

Mimi, you worked for the legendary Palm Beach interior designer Polly Jessup while Celerie was growing up. Celerie, how did your mother's career choice ultimately influence yours?

CK: When I look back at my childhood and Mom being a designer, I learned because she included me in things. She was a working mom, so I was often brought into the office. For a little kid, a real design studio is an awe-inspiring place—bigger, better than any art room. As I got older and we traveled, we always went to see beautiful houses—to be brought along as a child to these spaces piqued my interest and set my taste level early.

MM: I remember bringing you because I just assumed that you would come with me. It wasn't as though I was trying to teach you anything at all. I giggle about this now—but Celerie told me numerous times that interior design would be the last profession she would ever choose.

CK: Well, I did have to spend many weekends waiting for you to get off the phone because you had a client who was calling with a design emergency.

MM: Perhaps I just said I had a client on the phone.

CK: Actually, Mom, in terms of a trade, I think the biggest influence on me being a designer was living in our house. It's what you brought home in terms of creativity, resourcefulness, and absolute devotion to making our unusual home an epically beautiful place.

Mimi, it sounds like you encouraged creativity early.

MM: Yes. I used to hand Celerie and her sister something to color. And I'd say, "You don't have to color in the lines, and if you would like to cover the elephant in stars, I think that's a brilliant idea." One of my favorite activities was taking them out into the garden at night. We lived in an old church, so we'd come out barefoot with flashlights. Because we lived in Florida, we had these wonderful fragrant flowers. And in order to get them interested in the garden, we would have what I called "scent wars." They would go out at night when the flowers were in bloom, and they'd have to choose which of the "ladies" that evening had the most divine perfume. It was magical.

Celerie, you're based in New York City now, but Palm Beach is important to you both—personally and professionally.

MM: We love this land. We are irreverent about it. Everyone thinks it's such an elegant town. Well, there's a whole other side of scuffed knees and lemonade stands. We treasure it, because there are very few little towns that are as beautiful and well maintained but still have a sweetness—you know, walking out on the beach with your children or going fishing with bacon.

CK: Everything under the dock wants to eat bacon.

MM: Bacon is the best bait ever.

CK: When I think of Palm Beach and its influence on me, it is how I wish my children lived. And if it influenced my career, it's that I think there is something whimsical, escapist about Palm Beach. In the early 1900s, people were like, "What the hell. We're going to that new resort, that new crazy place where there are bugs and birds and big tropical weird flowers." There was a wildness. It set the stage for people saying, "Our homes here are for fun and for playfulness." That irreverence and the desire to let pretty lead as opposed to proper, that's in my DNA.

MM: Comfort. Add the word *comfort* in there, too.

CK: Of course. So, what I hope to bring to our profession is pretty things that are fun and comfortable, but also make statements of character and soul.

LIZ LAMBERT

How did a one-time New York City prosecutor become the country's hottest boutique hotelier? It's a query Liz Lambert has heard before. But even she isn't completely sure how the metamorphosis happened. Looking back, though, perhaps it shouldn't be a surprise that the independent West Texas native with a creative writing degree (with a concentration in poetry) would be enough of a dreamer and a doer to transform a seedy motel in South Austin into the hippest hotel in town. Today that once run-down stretch of highway, South Congress Avenue, is a booming beacon of arts and culture—and so is Bunkhouse Group, the hospitality company Lambert founded in 2006.

Of the nine Bunkhouse Group properties, seven are located in Texas—in Austin, San Antonio, and Marfa. Do you have a favorite locale?

It's a real toss-up between Marfa and Austin. Austin is very near and dear to my heart. As Texas became more and more conservative over the years, it seemed like Austin was still this not-so-secret gift for people like me who were creative and gay and genuinely loved Texas to the very root of their being. But my love for West Texas may be even deeper.

You grew up in the West Texas ranch country—near Odessa.

West Texas is high desert and big, wide-open spaces and a the-road-goes-on-forever kind of place. And I think that sensibility, that sense of openness, gets rooted into your DNA and knit into your worldview. When you grow up on a ranch, which I didn't but a lot of my family did, you depend upon your neighbor more. No matter how different you may be, there's nobody else out there, so you'd better get along with whoever's closest. That's a real lesson—that you can be really different from someone else and still be interde-pendent. And I think that's a nice thing in the world, especially today.

You were the first openly gay Manhattan DA before coming back to Austin to work for the state attorney general. How did you end up in hotels?

Had I known then that I was going to end up where I am now, I don't know that I could have made the journey. I thought I was going to do one hotel, which was the Hotel San José [in Austin]. I had no idea that South Congress would become as popular as it is, or that my career would continue into hotels. I just stumbled across the San José Motel. I would go to the Continental Club all the time, which was across the street from the motel, which was only twenty-four rooms, and honestly didn't seem open. I thought: I can create this nice little place where musicians who are coming through town can stay for something like seventy-five dollars a night.

But it took you a while to take the plunge into the hospitality business.

Yeah, even though I thought about the San José a lot, I didn't do anything about it until a friend of mine, who was HIV positive, died. It was one of those moments that jolt you out of everyday life. I decided to go find out whether [this dream] was even possible at all. It was complete serendipity that the San José's owners were about to put it up for sale the next week. And I was like, "No, don't do that. Hold on. Let me see what I can do."

You've said how important it is for each Bunkhouse property to create community, but also to root itself within the broader society that surrounds it. How do you create that organically?

We talk a lot about authenticity these days. And there is no shortcut to authenticity. It's something that you have to spend time, money, and heart and soul to develop. It's about making connections and being curious about people and what's happening in a place.

I think another one of the reasons that the places we design don't feel contrived, and feel as if they have been there a long time, is that we try to look around and figure out what a space wants to be. With the Saint Cecilia [in Austin], we responded first and foremost to the Victorian mansion that was there and the language it evoked. When we did El Cosmico [in Marfa], we went to the local feed store to find out what we could build out of, that was in abundance in West Texas—oil field pipe, corrugated tin, those kinds of things. We tried to use what was natural.

How do you keep your creative spark lit?

I travel. Whether you're going just down the block or overseas, it's good to go and look at other design. Whenever I'm really stumped, and I can't figure out what something should be, or which way a project is going to go, it's super helpful for me to visit places that I admire. Short of that, magazines. I mean, I read books and magazines all the time. I know everybody does it, but it's the quickest way to travel.

What do you think is the secret to a really successful hotel?

A great bed. Nice linens. A hospitable staff. Good food and a great bar. But also, I think one of the best things a hotel can do is adjust your perspective—take you out of everyday life.

JANIE BRYANT

A native of Cleveland, Tennessee, the Emmy Award–winning costume designer Janie Bryant has garnered praise for her distinctive work on such hit TV series as Deadwood *and* Mad Men.

My maternal grandmother, Etoile Lillard Chesnutt, or, as we called her, Gran Gran, had impeccable taste and loved clothes and fashion. She designed and made clothes for herself and also for my mother. My mother, Dorothea Chesnutt Bryant, influenced me as well. She and my father threw many parties and always dressed to a tee while hosting. When I was growing up, my mother made clothes for my sister and me. The three of us would often be in matching or coordinating outfits for holiday parties.

From a very early age, I was playing dress up and pretending to be different characters. I was drawing ballerinas, and obsessed with the female form and fashion from the age of six. I was making Barbie clothes from my mother's scraps of materials, her decorating swatch books, and socks that my father brought home. My father owned Bryant Yarns, and we always had the latest in socks and tights. They made great pieces of Barbie knitwear!

The movies were my inspiration. My mother would take us to see old movies at the Tivoli Theatre in Chattanooga. *Wuthering Heights* and *On the Town,* for example. At home I would watch *Gone with the Wind, The Wizard of Oz, Guys and Dolls,* and many more.

[When I design for a Hollywood project,] it's a combination of designing and building costumes from scratch, buying vintage, sometimes redesigning vintage pieces, and doing rentals from the amazing costume shops in Los Angeles. I have used some of my mother's dresses—one that was made by my grandmother—and I used my grandmother's aprons for [*Mad Men*'s] Betty Draper. My grandmother made aprons to match every outfit that she wore.

MARY CELESTE BEALL

Mary Celeste Beall will warn you that she has a propensity for rambling. "I tend to go on and on," says the proprietor of the beloved luxury resort Blackberry Farm and its sprawling addition, Blackberry Mountain, both nestled in the foothills of the Great Smoky Mountains in Walland, Tennessee. Some common themes: her five children; her late husband, Sam, who died in a ski accident in 2016; her passion for cooking and entertaining; and her love of the natural world. Mary Celeste and Sam, who met in Mobile, Alabama, took over Blackberry from Sam's parents in 2002, turning the quaint country inn into a dream destination that attracts the best chefs and musicians in the world. After Sam died, Beall took his place at the helm, continuing to advance their vision. "Grace. Grit. Patience. Respect. Dignity," Beall says. "There's no real formula for how your life will turn out, but if you focus on these things, everything will be fine in the end."

Who inspired you as a child?

I grew up in Mobile, the youngest of four children. My mom grew up on the same street I grew up on, and my grandparents lived up the street from us. My grandmother is somebody I really admire. She lived to a hundred and a half—we always count that half for her!

What was she like?

She was graceful and independent and very well read. Her father had died at a young age, and her mother had taken her and her sister to live in Europe when she was a young girl. She was well traveled and took French classes and was an artist. My grandfather was a federal magistrate and very stern and just very serious. She really balanced that out, raising four children with this positive spirit. She could throw a lively party and had the greatest handwriting. It makes me emotional talking about her because she was such a light to all of us. She was always trying new things. I love that she was always knitting, sewing, making crème brûlée . . . one time when she was in her early eighties, we walked in to see her with a blowtorch in her hands. We were like, *Grandma!*

She sounds like a woman ahead of her time.

She was—and such a great example to me. She was Phi Beta Kappa and so smart and worldly and exposed everyone to the arts, but also took pride in her role as a mother and a wife. I think making a warm and hospitable home, and taking care of other people in the community, are so important and aren't celebrated as much as they should be. And they are things my grandmother did so naturally. I don't really have the luxury of pouring 100 percent of my time into my children right now, which can be hard. But I'm so thankful for what I have and love, love, love Blackberry so much.

What is juggling those responsibilities like for you?

I need to take care of myself, my family, and Blackberry as a business. Anytime I can combine two of those into one activity, it's a win to me. The beauty of Blackberry is that it's a family business and the children see what I do and understand it—it's not like I disappear to a tire factory every day. We live on the property, and I try to involve the kids when I can. If I'm hosting a dinner and it's a school night, I might bring the kids a little early so they can experience some of the food before bedtime, or talk to a guest chef, or go for a bike ride, or experience some music. They see the community we've built here and can really benefit from that. Some of our greatest friends—our village of people who care about us—we've met through Blackberry.

How do you think the role of Southern women is changing?

Southern women have historically been really focused on their family, focused on their husbands, and tend to put themselves last. Sam used to really encourage me to take care of myself and be the best version of myself. It's hard not to feel guilty. I should be doing something

in the house or in the community. What I've learned so much over the last few years is that I need to put my cape on first.

What do you think about when you wake up every morning and look out over the Smokies?

I've always been inspired by nature. When we designed our house, Sam and I positioned our bedroom so we get beautiful light. I woke up this morning to fog, and now it's a sunny gorgeous day. I love hearing the chickens and sheep as I start the day. I just feel like every day is a new day, and you never know what it's going to hold, which unfortunately I learned in a terribly hard way. But I now try to spin that into a positive. I try to acknowledge all of the things I need to accomplish but also try to be aware of being present and allowing the day to unfold. Soak up the twists and turns.

What do you think the next generation of Southern women needs to know?

That it's important to be gracious and respect our heritage, but it's also okay to be strong and direct and share their opinions. Take risks! Stand up for what you believe in. I think there's a way to be direct in a gentle way—that was the way my grandmother was. You can deliver a powerful message without being angry or full of hate. It's a challenge to deliver a strong message without sacrificing your dignity, but it can be done. It just takes some thought, and a smile.

CHARLOTTE MOSS

(1951–PRESENT)

The designer whose distinctive feminine style belies a steely work ethic

It's been almost forty years since anyone had the gall to question designer Charlotte Moss's aesthetic judgment.

The Richmond native, who was born in 1951, wasn't yet a designer at that time in the eighties, at least in the professional sense. Five years after marrying her boyfriend from Virginia Commonwealth University, Moss was divorced and living alone in New York City. She took a secretarial job at an investment firm and worked her way up to the executive ranks. In those days of fax machines and dot matrix printers, a vice president had paper aplenty to keep organized, so Moss set a woven basket on her desk.

"Too fluffy," her boss ruled. Wall Street was a place for black plastic and polished wood, not materials with texture and personality. Moss gave up her offbeat in-box, and not too long thereafter, she gave up her seat, too.

In 1985, following an antiques-buying spree through England that was financed by her last bonus check, Moss launched an interior design business. Charlotte Moss, the firm, quickly became known for its eclectic and feminine style, demonstrated in dining rooms in the Hamptons and bedrooms along Fifth Avenue. And Charlotte Moss, the woman, gained a reputation for the vision, decisiveness, and bravery that helped her cut short a lucrative banking career.

Philanthropic boards are drawn to Moss because she gets things done: She's a trustee for nonprofits, including Monticello's Thomas Jefferson Foundation and the Bone Marrow Foundation. Yet she's not inclined to broadcast how much she does, since boasting strikes Moss as unseemly.

"She has the business shrewdness of a Wall Street person but has managed to preserve the perfect manners of a Southern belle," the antique dealer R. Louis Bofferding told *W* magazine in 2008, explaining a success that can be measured in books (ten, including *Garden Inspirations* and *Charlotte Moss Entertains*), projects (such as lines of furniture and jewelry), and speaking engagements around the world.

Etiquette aside, Moss also doesn't have time to waste on showing off. Despite what New Yorkers might think, she's in fact not a Southern belle, but the daughter of an army colonel who believed in the value of hard work. "I have very little tolerance for people who are lazy," she has said. "If you're going to stand out, you've got to do something, and it's called work."

The payoffs for all that work? Garden strolls; hours with good books; and leisurely dinners with friends: Moss remembers her grandmother, who sold china at a department store, hosting family buffets on Sundays to celebrate the end of the week. "We work hard all day long, so if you can't have fun, where the hell are we going with this? Life is short," Moss once told the *Houston Chronicle*.

Pausing to appreciate pleasure is one of the few rules that Moss strives to uphold. She doesn't believe in putting off parties until interior decorating is done, turning down opportunities to entertain because the silver isn't polished, or getting hung up on which napkins pair with what dish. "Just send the invitations," she advises.

BARRIE BENSON

The work of the Charlotte, North Carolina–based interior designer Barrie Benson has appeared in such magazines as Architectural Digest, House Beautiful, *and* Elle Decor, *as well as* Garden & Gun.

My mom went to Duke in the late fifties. Back then women were not allowed to have cars, but men were. So she took a car from her family's farm and let all of the girls on East Campus borrow it until some girl ratted her out and she got kicked out for a semester. She's proud of it! She inherently knew it was wrong that men were allowed the privilege and women were not. She had an incredibly strong moral code, but she knew when to step out and step up. And that's how I approach my design and raising my children. Instead of doing what you "should" do, I want to turn it to the left.

I also owe that idea to going to Camp Merrie-Woode [in Western North Carolina]. There is something in the Kool-Aid there that teaches women to be strong. Some of my most successful female friends went there. Our glass ceiling was mastering class-four rapids. It was constant confirmation that you can do things you never thought you could.

Still, it's not easy doing things you never thought you could do. I feel tremendous guilt for being a working mother sometimes. A few years ago my daughter, Kay, was a little down and out that I missed watching her compete in one of her equestrian events. And I thought it was time to let it all go and stay at home and be a horse mom. But when I told Kay about my decision, she said, "I love what you do! What about the girls who work for you? What about Martin, who makes furniture? What will they do? Can you just come *sometimes*? I don't want you to be a horse mom!" At the age of eleven she was so perceptive and proud. Even though I'm still stumbling and tripping my way along, it's making a huge difference to her.

CINDY CHAPMAN

A Southern mother sows a love of horticulture

BY GRAY CHAPMAN

I grew up playing in a Middle Georgia backyard dense with squat fig trees and vines laden with scuppernongs, climbing roses, and beds of pansies, all carefully propagated by my mother, Cindy. But when I ventured north to Atlanta as a young adult and began tending to my own scraps of landscape, I came to realize an important distinction: Like so many Southern women, her flair for the horticultural arts isn't merely a hobby—it's her love language.

After one warm Saturday spent day drinking, a friend and I were reconstituting ourselves on my porch when, woozily, she looked askance at a bird feeder perched atop the steps. "Was that . . . here before?" It had not been. We took a blurry inventory of our surroundings, also noting a new potted plant and a pair of turquoise pillows propped on my creaking porch swing. The scraggly rosebush enveloping my mailbox had also been freshly manicured, its canes studded with lime-green flesh.

"Well, I was *in* the area," my mom glibly explained on the phone later, "and I had my pruning shears in my car, so . . ." While the first half is almost certainly untrue, I can easily imagine the latter: Cindy cruising down Peachtree, a small arsenal of gardening implements rattling in the trunk of her sedan. After all, a good guerrilla gardener is never caught unawares.

My spade-brandishing mom was raised by green thumbs: Her father, Jimmy, was nicknamed "Jack the Ripper" because of his penchant for stress weeding his Mobile backyard after clocking out at the neighborhood pharmacy. My grandmother Claire still tends to her enormous decades-old staghorn fern, which resembles something one might see undulating in a Jacques Cousteau frame. And Cindy knows her boxwood the way some people know Bible verses. For me, this gene has only half bloomed: I have a modest bed of vegetables, which I keep a whisper away from death. Last summer, I tried trimming the azalea in our front yard and wound up giving it a mullet.

Yet, Cindy's faith in my latent gardening skills hasn't wavered. Our first Christmas as newlyweds, she gave my husband, Dane, and me a potted camellia. By next year's holiday parties, she said, we could float its blooms in a bowl of water. Dane and I traveled to the Grand Canyon the next day, leaving the unattended shrub to wither on our dining room floor. Suddenly it was spring, and Cindy was on the phone, casually inquiring about the plant's health. I stuttered a clumsy lie.

After I hung up, we raced to the nursery and threw ourselves at the mercy of a sales associate, who looked up her order history and identified the cultivar (Yuletide, appropriately). We put it in the dirt as soon as we got home.

The con worked, insofar as it convinced my mother I could handle floriculture. That fall, when we gathered at an Italian restaurant for my thirtieth birthday, she lugged a cumbersome gift bag up on the white tablecloth and watched with glee as I unwrapped it: thirty-nine daffodil bulbs. And a shovel.

We would plant them together, my mom announced. Instead, she was called to Florida to help my grandmother through a bout of illness that wouldn't ease up. We rescheduled our bulb-planting session, and canceled; we made new plans, and canceled those, too. While she stayed at my grandma's, the bulbs remained in their box, growing more desiccated by the day. When my mom finally returned to Atlanta, she assessed their onion-like husks and shrugged, quietly disappointed—in the box of duds, and maybe a little in me.

Women who garden are often described with soft, feminine words: She nurtures. She tends. She likes pretty flowers floating in crystal bowls of water. But to grow things is less about an instinct to nourish, and more a question of grit and unflinching optimism. It is, like mothering, to look mortality straight in the eye and brazenly accept its dare, season after season.

Blithely unattuned to the calendars of daffodils, I went ahead and planted the damn things anyway. It was late February: far too late, the man at the nursery scolded. Six weeks later, thirty-some sturdy green stems had poked through the mulch, and soon yielded a few tightly furled yellow buds. This unlikely triumph was, much to my surprise, intoxicating. I texted a photo to my mom, less out of a sense of duty than out of genuine excitement and pride. "How wonderful!!!" she wrote back, her enthusiasm bubbling out of my phone.

"And," she continued—ever hopeful—"this bodes well for next year's blooms!"

ELAINE GRIFFIN

The interior designer Elaine Griffin grew up in Brunswick, Georgia, a slip of Lowcountry mainland that borders Jekyll and St. Simons islands. She left the sleepy coastal town at the age of eighteen, heading first for Yale University, then Paris, then New York, where she developed her eye for interiors under the tutelage of the legendary architect Peter Marino before founding her own firm in Harlem in 1999. After publishing her book, *Design Rules: The Insider's Guide to Becoming Your Own Decorator*, the in-demand Griffin now lives back in her home state, splitting her design time between the South and the Big Apple.

Your mother taught middle school math, but she had a creative streak. How did she influence your work?

My mother is half Cuban, a legendary beauty and a fashionista. She still has a size two waist! My favorite part of creating beautiful rooms for clients is choosing fabrics, and that all comes from my mother because she is a couture seamstress. I also inherited my sense of color from her. She hates beige and loves sherbet colors. To this day, I can't do a room without yellow—her favorite. Orange is always a primary accent color for me, too.

Your father also looms large in your memory.

He was the first physician of color to operate at what was then the Glynn-Brunswick Memorial Hospital, and he was the doctor who would accept a bushel of crops when patients couldn't afford to pay, and if you didn't have crops, that didn't matter. We were both morning people, and some of my favorite moments as a little girl were when I would wake up before dawn and hang out with him as he got ready for surgery, just the two of us. I would sip some of his coffee out of the saucer with a spoon. He taught me to see people as human beings that deserve your best, no matter where they are on the social spectrum. And he also taught me everything I know about hard work, and that when you have the inner confidence that you've been given the skills to do a job well, then you don't have to scream that "you can, you can, you can!" because your work speaks for itself, and that's what earns the respect of others.

When did you know you wanted to be a designer?

After Yale, I became a fashion publicist and moved to Paris. During that time I got into a huge fight with a *Vogue* editor, and she was in the wrong, but I sent her flowers because that's what you do. That night I called my mother—Southern girls always call their mama when it gets hot in the kitchen. And she said, "Dahlin', why don't you find a hobby that you like and make it your job?" You never know if it's the right time to do anything until you take the first step, and if it's meant to be, the universe will aid you in taking the second and the third and the fourth.

What is your design philosophy?

I want your house to look like you. The one rule I never break is that rooms should look like the people who live in them—an authentic mix of where you've been, where you are, and where you are going.

You spent two decades away from Georgia. What made you come home?

If you are born and raised in the South to Southern parents, you are a forever Southerner, no matter where else in the world you may live or whether you retain your accent or not. One day in 2015, I received a call from a neighbor at home who saw my mother looking dazed in a parking lot. I packed my bags, and after two weeks I realized that my mother was a better actress than Bette Davis. She had been giving an award-winning performance, but her dementia was far more progressed than anyone knew.

Was it strange to be back?

It took me six weeks to adjust to the fact that I couldn't leave the house in sweats with no makeup.

BUNNY MELLON

(1910–2014)

The garden designer who knew pretty didn't have to mean perfect

Bunny Mellon's life was far from flawless. Her father, a Gillette executive who made a fortune persuading Americans they stood to become social pariahs if they didn't swish Listerine, spurned her pleas to go to college. Her brother died in a plane crash; her daughter was hit by a truck; she had two rocky marriages; and she was investigated by the Federal Bureau of Investigation at the age of 101 for unwittingly funding Democratic candidate for president John Edwards's attempt to hide his pregnant mistress.

From the outside, though, it appeared as though Mellon, who was born in 1910, had it made. By adulthood, she had seven homes arrayed along an Atlantic triangle that stretched from Cape Cod to Antigua to Paris, including Oak Spring Farm, the Virginia estate where Mellon immersed herself in nature—a pastime she had adored since she was a girl, playing among the buttercups and apple trees. One of the horses raised on the farm in Upperville, Sea Hero, won the Kentucky Derby. And her jewelry collection was so vast that a maid once discovered a million-dollar necklace lodged beneath a living room cushion: Mellon hadn't noticed it was missing.

Mellon knew what the appearance of perfection required but found balm in the beauty that can arise in its absence: She even instructed a groundskeeper who'd painstakingly picked up every fallen apple in her orchard to return the fruit to where he'd found it. "Nothing should stand out," Mellon in 1969 told the *New York Times*, voicing her life and landscape philosophy, which still informs topiary displays and dining room centerpieces across the South.

"When you go away, you should remember only the peace."

It was Mellon's exacting eye and reverence for serenity that prompted President John F. Kennedy to invite her to redesign the White House Rose Garden, then dominated by blocky privet hedges chosen by Edith Wilson. Mellon didn't have any formal training, but even as a little girl in Virginia, she'd insisted on having a garden plot to tend. Though her father decreed that she wouldn't attend college, Mellon embarked on a lifelong course of self-education, collecting a library's worth of horticulture books.

Kennedy adored the garden. Two days after the Cuban Missile Crisis ended, he sent Mellon a letter saying, "I need not tell you that your garden has been our brightest spot in the somber surroundings of the last few days." When Kennedy was assassinated, Mellon arranged his funeral flowers; she later landscaped the Kennedys' home in Martha's Vineyard and the John F. Kennedy Presidential Library.

When Mellon died in 2014 at the age of 103, it was during Lent, when flower displays are forbidden. But Trinity Episcopal Church in Upperville, which Bunny and her husband Paul Mellon built in 1960, permitted two bouquets for the service. Even after death, her contributions continue: She left her Oak Spring Garden Library in Virginia and its 16,000-plus artifacts, rare books, manuscripts, and artworks relating to horticulture, decorative arts, and more to be available to those who would wish to study and carry on her love of natural beauty.

Mary Ella Gabler
My Grandma's Quilt

In 1973, Mary Ella Gabler founded her Dallas-based luxury linen line, Peacock Alley, a company whose distribution stretches from Canada to South America.

I was always surrounded by textiles and watched first-hand the work that went into making beautiful pieces of art. The love of textiles was in my blood.

There's one quilt that's particularly special to me because my grandma made it, probably in the 1940s. She made many quilts, but I love the simplicity of this green-and-white one. It's a very soft green, and I can just picture her sewing it and looking at the pattern. Her name was Ella, and I'm named after her and my other grandmother. This quilt was on my mother's bed. It's similar to a Mennonite quilt with very detailed work. I love the fact that it's a quilt that works in almost every room I put it in. Right now, it's in my bedroom at the farm in Texas.

I love a simple environment, whether it's in the country or in Fort Worth, or whether someone lives in the North or the South. I think the simplicity of beautiful bedding and a peaceful, comforting environment is so important. I've always been a traditionalist. Comfortable beauty was always important to me and my family. The South has a very welcoming way of embracing those traditions.

LAURA VINROOT POOLE

When Laura Vinroot Poole opened Capitol in her hometown of Charlotte, North Carolina, in 1997, few boutiques in the South carried such a carefully edited range of styles, from evening wear to everyday, from designers the world over. She's since opened three more spots, Poole Shop and the menswear-focused Tabor, in Charlotte, and a Capitol outpost in Los Angeles, the success of all hinging on Poole's warm and pretense-free service, a Southern-inflected point of view, and an appreciation for the stories behind the pieces—where some might see a froth of chiffon skirting a floor, she sees the artistry of the dozens of hands that sewed it into life.

What sparked your curiosity about style?

I felt like I didn't always fit in, because I was more curious. I noticed details. I noticed paintings in other people's homes. I noticed the way someone held a cigarette at a cocktail party. I noticed my babysitter's blue suede clogs. I found glamour in everything.

After you finished art school at the University of North Carolina, what led you back to your hometown?

My dad was the mayor of Charlotte in the seventies, and they were really building a world-class city. The art museum, the ballet, the opera, the football team, having I. M. Pei compete to design the Bank of America building. I heard about it all the time at the dinner table, and I knew if I was going to come back, there was a real opportunity—my mother and her friends went shopping twice a year in New York and Atlanta and made trips to Charleston to buy shoes at Bob Ellis, but that was it.

At the time, Capitol carried designers never available before in Charlotte—what gave you the confidence to build something new?

Maybe it was the hubris of being a twenty-four-year-old! I've always felt confident because my self-worth comes from a place that is unwavering and is not about fashion but relationships. I have spectacular parents that pushed character and kindness over achievement, and that has served me well. And I really, truly *knew* my client. Always. People underestimate the South and think we're unsophisticated. I never did. People here travel a ton. They know. They see things. I just left the shop a minute ago and one of my mom's friends was shopping. They buy Gucci. They buy Saint Laurent. I buy in a way that is respectful of the people who live here, and I try to interpret collections through Southern eyes. And when designers come here from all over the world to visit with clients at Capitol, they've never met people so interested in their stories.

Your mother influenced you in other ways, too.

I was raised by a beautiful mother who is whip smart and would never want to be identified as anything but an intellectual. But one of the most enduring lessons I learned from her was about beauty. Every afternoon, in anticipation of my father's return from work, I watched her reapply her lipstick, Love That Pink by Revlon. I never commented on it or discussed it with her, but I took note. When I grew up and Lululemon hijacked women's wardrobes everywhere, it reminded me of my mother's quiet dignity and that small moment of "getting herself together," as she called it. Hence, I may not reapply my lip gloss on time, but you will never find me making supper in exercise clothes.

You are on the road for weeks out of each year buying for the shop. How do you fight fatigue and stay inspired?

During the recession in 2008, we almost went out of business. I recognized very clearly that I loved what I do, and it could go away in a minute. Now every trip I take, I add a few days to either side of it to enjoy myself. Most recently I went to Bergamo, outside of Milan. I need that palate cleanser. I have to see something that's not clothes. I need to look at churches and just be on the subway, observing.

What was the key to surviving the recession?

We looked at the landscape, especially the new competition that developed with e-commerce, and identified three things that made us special: an incredibly beautiful space to shop, exemplary customer service, and our edit. We focused on those three things and marketed around them and made them our mantra, every day. We also trimmed budgets, tightened up buying practices, and worked carefully to be prudent. I probably didn't sleep for a good four to five years, but those years taught me more than I could have ever learned in any business school, and I'm grateful for them. They showed me how tough I really am.

You also invest time in the female members of your staff.

I've always supported the right of women to have a career and a family. And even in 2019, there's not a lot of support for that. All of my staff go through leadership training and development training. We work with our leadership coach on an ongoing basis, as a group and individually. She has also helped to transition our working mothers to come back to work happily and as free of guilt as possible. A full-time job, taking care of your child or children, tending to your relationship with your partner, time with friends, exercising—it's too much! Ask for help, outsource what you can, and talk to your partner about sharing in all of the responsibilities. Most important, you have to start with self-care. If you are tired, beaten down, unfulfilled, or not finding joy, the people around you are suffering. We also believe in harmony versus balance. We tend to silo the concepts of work and life, which puts them in opposition to one another. Working to harmonize them can make the transition back so much easier and happier.

You and your husband have a daughter, Fifi, who is in her early teens. What advice do you give her?

Remember where you are from. Find meaningful work and people you love. Above all else.

Acknowledgments

This book would be nothing without the extraordinary Southern women who contributed to it, both the subjects and the writers. To them, I say thank you, for their generosity of time and spirit, and for trusting us with their stories. You'll find the contributors' bios in the following pages, and I hope you'll read them, for one last shot of inspiration. I was honored to work with each and every one of them.

I have long dreamed of editing a book, and so I am most grateful to *Garden & Gun*'s editor in chief, David DiBenedetto, for giving me the opportunity to do just that.

Also here at *G&G*, almost every female member of the editorial team played a part. The spectacular images you've seen throughout are due to the creativity and execution of photography and visuals director Maggie Brett Kennedy, nimbly assisted by photo editor Margaret Houston and art production assistant Jacqueline Stofsick. Art director Julia Knetzer made certain the *G&G* aesthetic infused every page and shepherded the work of Lara Tomlin and Joel Kimmel, who drew the portrait illustrations throughout.

I'm grateful to copy chief Donna Levine for bringing her keen eye to the pages, ensuring every word sang and every fact rang true. Style director Haskell Harris, senior editor CJ Lotz, editorial assistant Caroline Sanders, digital director Kim Alexander, and digital editor Dacey Orr Sivewright all contributed entries and ideas, and editorial intern Abigail Tierney ably assisted in fact-checking.

G&G contributing editor Allison Glock built on the ideas in her original "Southern Women" essay, which ran in *G&G*'s August/September 2011 issue, to write the beautiful foreword, and she brought her peerless ability to get people to share their hearts and minds to many of the book's interviews.

Karen Rinaldi, the publisher at Harper Wave, and Julie Will, the editorial director, shared—and sharpened, step by step—our vision for this book. Leah Carlson-Stanisic wove the design together to striking effect, and Milan Bozic created the beautiful cover with a print by Marika Kandelaki of Moonshake Studio.

We are so thankful to our literary agent, Amy Hughes of Dunow, Carlson & Lerner, for advocating for this book from the beginning.

At *G&G*, we are lucky to have a remarkable woman at the helm: Rebecca Wesson Darwin, our cofounder and CEO. She and the other co-owners, Pierre Manigault and J. Edward Bell III, are the greatest champions of the *G&G* brand and of the journalism we do.

My husband, Justin, has supported me every day of our marriage—he is my biggest fan, and I his. My dad, Lee, brother, Patrick, sister-in-law, Sarah, nephews Anthony and William, and in-laws Pat and Bill Heckert bring me joy. And these Southern women forged me: My mother, René, the first female manager at her hospital pharmacy, showed me what it looked like to break the glass ceiling. Her mother, Grandbunn Eloise, taught me that rolling tires for a living is no reason not to have fabulously hot pink nails—and how to get up with gumption when life knocks you down. Grandma Mary Alice stoked my love of reading with her favorite books: *Alice's Adventures in Wonderland*, *Little Women*, and *Heidi*. And my best girlfriends, the Godivas—you have my heart. And I've got your backs.

—*Amanda Heckert*
Deputy editor, *Garden & Gun*

Contributors

Amanda Dalla Villa Adams is a writer, historian, curator, and educator based in Richmond. She is a contributing art critic to *Style Weekly* and has written for *Artforum*, *Burnaway*, *Hyperallergic*, and *Sculpture*. A mother to three kids under the age of five, she has toted her children to countless museums, galleries, interviews, and art events. If you believe that art can change the world, why not start with a young audience?

Kim Alexander is the digital director at *Garden & Gun* and lives in Folly Beach, South Carolina, with her husband and twin daughters, Josie and Bree.

Brooke Baldwin hosts *CNN Newsroom with Brooke Baldwin* and *American Woman* on CNN. She lives in New York City but credits her Atlanta upbringing for her manners and vernacular. Listen closely, and you'll hear her slip in a "y'all" or "yes ma'am" on live TV just to remind viewers where she's from—and to make her mother proud.

Mary Logan Bikoff is an editor at *Atlanta* magazine and *Atlanta Magazine's HOME*. She covers lifestyle topics from design to travel, but she loves writing long-form profiles most of all—particularly about women who provoke and inspire. She learned early from her vivacious maternal grandmother that a Southern woman could be both as tough as nails and as lovely as a camellia.

Jordan Breal is a writer and editor based in Austin, Texas, whose roots run deep in the Deep South. While her family hails from Biloxi, Mississippi, she's a native Texan best known for chronicling the people and places of the Lone Star State for *Texas Monthly*, the *New York Times*, and Wildsam Field Guides. Still, she much prefers shrimp po'boys to barbecue.

Katie Bridges is a writer and editor who when asked where she's from, will say "Arkansas," even though she's recently put down roots in Phoenix and previously called Washington, D.C., home. A former editor at *Arkansas Life* and *Washingtonian* magazines, she usually writes about art, architecture, and travel, and is ecstatic that her home turf of Northwest Arkansas is now a hotbed of all three.

Rebecca Burns lives in Athens, Georgia, and is the publisher of the student media organization the *Red & Black* and teaches at the University of Georgia. After two decades in Atlanta, including seven years as editor in chief of *Atlanta* magazine, she's embraced college town life, trading a downtown loft next to a freight yard for a ranch house with deer in the front yard and rabbits in the back.

Parker Butler is a former editorial intern for *Garden & Gun*. Born and raised in Mobile, Alabama, she graduated from Washington and Lee University with a degree in journalism and a minor in creative writing. Her work has been featured on *TheKnot.com* and in *Mobile Bay* magazine, and her hobbies include eating boiled peanuts and shopping in her mother's closet.

Gray Chapman is a freelance journalist who writes primarily about culture, food, and spirits (liquid, not haunted). She lives in Atlanta with her husband, Dane; their two dogs; and a rash of precisely thirty-nine daffodils in the front yard. Everything she knows about keeping camellias alive, eating oysters, and making a decent Ramos gin fizz she learned from her mother, Cindy.

Marshall Chapman is a semiretired badass. Based in Nashville, the singer-songwriter-author-actor enjoys cooking, playing Ping-Pong, and picking up trash around her neighborhood. Her former husband, Chris, swears she's a multihyphenated American treasure.

Bronwen Dickey is a contributing editor at the *Oxford American* and the author of *Pit Bull: The Battle over an American Icon*. In 2017, she was a finalist for the National Magazine Award in feature writing. She lives in North Carolina.

Meg Donahue is a freelance writer who was born in Boston but has spent her life in the South. Currently based in Macon, Georgia, she believes that if she were a character in *Game of Thrones*, her house sigil would be a chicken-fried Maine lobster. Which, yum.

Candice Dyer is a writer based in northern Georgia. She has published a book about the musicians of Middle Georgia—including Little Richard, Otis Redding, and the Allman Brothers—called *Street Singers, Soul Shakers, and Rebels with a Cause: Music of Macon*. She likes to say that her beat is the offbeat.

Helen Ellis is a New Yorker who clings to her Alabama accent like mayonnaise to white bread. She is the author of *Southern Lady Code* and hosts a podcast by the same name.

Osayi Endolyn is a writer who explores food, culture, and identity. Her work has appeared in *Eater*, the *Washington Post*, the *Wall Street Journal*, the *Oxford American*, and the *Splendid Table*, among others. *Southern Living* named her one of "30 Women Moving Southern Food Forward." She received a 2018 James Beard Award for her column in *Gravy*. Her favorite Southern women are Ruth Rushen, her grandmother from Mississippi, and Josephine Rushen and Louella Kirkum, her great-aunts from Louisiana.

Jenny Everett is a Charleston, South Carolina–based journalist covering food, health, fitness, and parenting. She writes the What's in Season column for *Garden & Gun* and is a cofounder of Lil Bit Lit, a company that publishes art-forward books for children.

Beth Ann Fennelly is the poet laureate of Mississippi and the author of six books. Her favorite Southern woman is her mother-in-law, Betty Franklin, who never once seemed to indicate that her grandsons should wear smocked shirts.

Allison Glock has been a magazine journalist and author for twenty-plus years. Her writing has appeared in the *New York Times*, the *New York Times Magazine*, *Esquire*, *Rolling Stone*, *Men's Journal*, *Marie Claire*, *GQ*, the *New Yorker*, and many other publications. Her poetry has appeared in the *New Yorker* and the *Portland Review*. She is currently a senior staff writer for *ESPN the Magazine* and *espnW*. She has written seven books, including the acclaimed young adult novel series *Changers*, and received the Whiting Award for her book *Beauty before Comfort*, a memoir of her grandmother's life in West Virginia and a *New York Times* Notable Book of the Year. She also writes for television.

Latria Graham is a writer and fifth-generation farmer living in Spartanburg, South Carolina. Her work has appeared in *Outside*, the *Guardian*, *espnW*, the *New York Times*, and a number of other local and national outlets. You can usually find her traveling the back roads of the Deep South, watching the sky for woodsmoke, hoping it leads her to the local barbecue joint.

Haskell Harris is the style director at *Garden & Gun*. The Virginia native's favorite things include Farrow & Ball paint, real Cokes, Fornasetti, authentic human beings, and cussing. In her downtime in Charleston, South Carolina, you'll most likely find her decoupaging anything that sits still too long or otherwise living up to her nickname, Task-ell.

Jessica B. Harris is a Yankee raised in the preserved-amber South of the Great Migration. She is learning to savor her retirement, and splits her time between New Orleans, Martha's Vineyard, and New York. Her favorite Southern women were her grandmothers and her mother, who was also a Yankee, but the most Southern woman you'd ever meet otherwise.

Amanda Heckert is a deputy editor at *Garden & Gun* and the editor of *Southern Women*. A native of the proud peach town of Inman, South Carolina, and a graduate of the University of South Carolina, she previously served as the editor in chief of *Indianapolis Monthly* and as senior editor at *Atlanta* magazine. She now lives in Charleston with her husband, Justin, and dog, Cooper.

Vivian Howard is a cook, author, and challenge seeker from Deep Run, North Carolina. She is best known for her dramatic portrayal of herself on the PBS series *A Chef's Life*, and her current obsessions are true-crime podcasts and Korean skin-care products.

Elizabeth Hutchison Hicklin is a contributing editor for *Garden & Gun* who lives in Nashville. A native of Charleston, South Carolina, and a graduate of Clemson University, she contributed to *The Southerner's Handbook* and *S Is for Southern*. She also produces the magazine's annual Made in the South Awards.

Ashley M. Jones received an MFA in poetry from Florida International University. Her debut poetry collection, *Magic City Gospel*, was published by Hub City Press in January 2017 and won the silver medal in poetry at the 2017 Independent Publishers Book Awards. Jones received a 2015 Rona Jaffe Foundation Writer's Award and a 2015 B-Metro Magazine Fusion Award. Her second collection, *dark // thing*, released in February 2019, won the 2018 Lena-Miles Wever Todd Prize for Poetry from Pleiades Press. She currently lives in Birmingham, Alabama, where she is second vice president of the Alabama Writers' Conclave, founding director of the Magic City Poetry Festival, and a faculty member in the creative writing department of the Alabama School of Fine Arts.

CJ Lotz is senior editor at *Garden & Gun* in Charleston, South Carolina, where she covers travel, books, gardens, and some of the quirkiest bits of Southern history, such as key lime pie, socialites, and outsider artists. She grew up in rural Missouri, spent her summers in North Carolina and Florida, and comes from a long line of outdoorswomen, including all four of her great-grandmothers (whom she knew personally and who lived into their nineties): Millie, Emma, Nina, and Opal.

Lydia Mansel is a writer and editor based in Charleston, South Carolina. Born in Greensboro, North Carolina, and raised in Bedford, Virginia, she previously worked as the social media editor of *Garden & Gun*. She attributes her attachment to the South— particularly Southern food—to the strongest woman (and best cook) she knows, her mother, Lisa Mansel.

Jennifer Rainey Marquez is a writer based in Atlanta, where she is raising two Southern women of her own. She directs research communications at Georgia State University and was previously an editor at *Atlanta*, *Parade*, and *O, The Oprah Magazine*.

Frances Mayes's book of travel narratives, *See You in the Piazza: New Places to Discover in Italy*, was released in March 2019, at the same time her novel *Women in Sunlight* came out in paperback. She lives in Hillsborough, North Carolina, and in Cortona, Italy.

Jessica Mischner is a writer, editor, and content strategist for Ballyhoo + Co, the agency she cofounded in 2017. From 2009 to 2015, she served as a contributing editor and then senior editor for *Garden & Gun*, where she produced stories on food, drinks, arts, entertainment, travel, and more. Her work has also appeared in the *Wall Street Journal*, *Domino*, *Food & Wine*, *Gourmet*, *Elle Decor*, and *Travel + Leisure*, among other publications.

Tara Nieuwesteeg is a writer and editor based in Dallas, where she's the nightlife columnist for *D Magazine*. She's also a certified master naturalist dedicated to extolling the virtues of Texas native plants. Wine-cup flowers are her favorite.

Mary Laura Philpott is a writer based in Nashville—the city where she was born but did not grow up, and to which she returned as an adult. She is the author of the books *I Miss You When I Blink* and *Penguins with People Problems*, as well as a firm believer that fried shrimp is one of the major food groups.

Queen Quet is a published author, computer scientist, lecturer, mathematician, historian, columnist, preservationist, environmental justice advocate, environmentalist, film consultant, and "the Art-ivist." She is the founder of the Gullah/Geechee Sea Island Coalition, which is the premier advocacy organization for the continuation of Gullah Geechee culture. She was homegrown on historic St. Helena Island, South Carolina, in the Gullah/Geechee Nation. Queen Quet was selected, elected, and enstooled by her people to be the first Queen Mother, "head pun de bodee," and official spokesperson for the Gullah/Geechee Nation. As a result, she is respectfully referred to as "Queen Quet, Chieftess and Head-of-State for the Gullah/Geechee Nation."

Hanna Raskin is food editor and chief critic at the *Post and Courier* in Charleston, South Carolina. Like generations of Southern newspaperwomen who edited food pages before her, she keeps a bottle of bourbon beneath her desk and a Jerusalem artichoke relish recipe at the ready for sentimental readers.

Julia Reed is a contributing editor for *Garden & Gun* and writes the magazine's column the High and the Low. She is the author of eight books, including *Julia Reed's South: Spirited Entertaining and High-Style Fun All Year Long*; *Queen of the Turtle Derby and Other Southern Phenomena*; *South Toward Home: Adventures and Misadventures in My Native Land*; and *Julia Reed's New Orleans: Food, Fun, Friends, and Field Trips for Letting the Good Times Roll.*

Caroline Sanders is the editorial assistant at *Garden & Gun*. Raised in Athens, Georgia, and a graduate of Washington and Lee University, she's been surrounded by amazing Southern women her entire life—none more inspiring than her mother, Beth, who's showed her what it means to be a strong, gracious woman.

Dacey Orr Sivewright is the digital editor at *Garden & Gun*, where she contributes to the magazine's website and online presence. An Atlanta native and a graduate of the University of Tennessee, she spent three years as an editor and producer at *Paste Magazine* and has contributed music and culture stories to the *Village Voice*, *Nashville Scene*, and the *Bluegrass Situation*, among other outlets.

Sonia Thompson is a writer, editor, and nineties R&B enthusiast. Her love of Southern women began with Clairee Belcher and Truvy Jones. She lives in Oxford, Mississippi, with her family.

Toni Tipton-Martin is a food and nutrition journalist, activist, and author of the highly acclaimed *The Jemima Code: Two Centuries of African American Cookbooks*. She is an adopted daughter of the South who splits her time between Texas, Maryland, and Colorado. She is known for spending ridiculously on rare black cookbooks.

Linda Vaccariello is a writer and editor in Cincinnati whose work has appeared in publications as disparate as *Reader's Digest* and *American Archaeology*. Each spring she decamps to Louisville for the Humana Festival of New American Plays, where her favorite intermission refreshment is Woodford Reserve. The magical elixir seems to make good theater even better and, when necessary, eases the pain of sitting through a clunker.

Christine Van Dusen has lived in Atlanta for eighteen years, writing and editing for such publications as *Atlanta* magazine, the *Atlanta Journal-Constitution*, the *Chicago Tribune*, and *Garden & Gun*. When she's not working or spending time with her husband and two sons, she's singing in a band, teaching fitness classes, or crawling through the mud during an endurance race.

Jenisha Watts is a features and commentary editor at *espnW*. Her work has appeared in the online and print editions of *People*, *TIME* Books, and *Essence*, among other publications. Watts gracefully bows to one of her favorite Southern women: Sade Jackson, a pink-lipstick-wearing, book-reading belle.

Jewel Wicker is an entertainment and culture writer from Atlanta. She was raised in a family of outspoken Southern women, including her mother, Tawanna Brooks, aunts Alisha Sherrill and Ellen McFarland, and grandma Frances Brooks. This lineage of Atlanta-bred women continuously inspires her to tell the often overlooked stories of black Southern life.

Credits

Photographs

Melanie Acevedo: 36; Rinne Allen/courtesy of AC: 123; Brittany Ambridge: 200; Eric Ryan Anderson: 207; Cedric Angeles: vii, 47; Johnny Autry: 28; Elizabeth Bacon: 111; KC Bailey: 20; Kat Borchart/The Licensing Project: 10; Michael JN Bowles: 108; Kelli Boyd: 214; Lynne Brubaker: 4; Andrew Brusso: 96; Dan Callister: 174; Hannah Carpenter: 118; Chris Charles: 103; Robert Clark/courtesy of TSC: 114; Cybelle Codish: 40; Paul Costello: 26; Amy Dickerson: 16, 205; Chris Edwards: 22; Peter Frank Edwards: 31, 88; Everett Collection: 182; Andrea Fremiotti: 74, 126; Matt Furman: 187; Daymon Gardner: viii, 7, 34, 56; Paige Green: 184; William Hereford: 176, 190; Byron Herring: 92; John Huba: 149; Brent Humphreys: 202; Andrew Hyslop: 45; Rush Jagoe: 64; Robby Klein: 138; Andrew Kornylak: 163; Brooks Kraft: 15; Erika Larsen: 100, 116; Kate LeSueur: 128; Patricia Lyons: 228; Matt Malicote: 106; Marianna Massey: 192; David McClister: x, 133, 134, 147, 156; Sean Murphy: 78; Wynn Myers: 136; Frank Ockenfels: 142; Kate T. Parker: 180; Nigel Parry: iv, 2, 67; Jared Roberts/REDUX: 171; Linda Foard Roberts: ii; Tim Robison: 72, 73, 222; Lara Rossignol: 124; Joey Seawell: 210, 00; Peggy Sirota/Trunk Archive: 8; Julie Soefer: 59; Jack Sorokin: 50; Art Streiber: 25; Chris Strong: 153; Sully Sullivan: xiii, 60, 62, 82; Jack Thompson: 220; Jayme Thornton: 84; Stacey Van Berkel: xii, 218; William Waldron: 188, 198; Brie Williams: 160; Gately Williams: 131; Kelsey Wilson: 194; Geoff Wood: 168; Forest Woodward: xx; Susan Worsham: 98; Peter Yang: 53, 54; Ford Yates: 90, 91

Illustrations

Joel Kimmel: 13, 19, 24, 38, 49, 52, 58, 69, 77, 80, 85, 97, 105, 113, 121, 151, 152, 165, 167, 175, 179, 199, 209, 216, 217
Lara Tomlin: 9, 18, 42, 70, 76, 86, 94, 112, 120, 135, 146, 154, 158, 166, 172, 178, 183, 197, 212

Index

Index